FOUNDATIONS IN
STRATEGIC MANAGEMENT

FOUNDATIONS IN STRATEGIC MANAGEMENT

Jeffrey S. Harrison
University of Central Florida

Caron H. St. John
Clemson University

SOUTH-WESTERN College Publishing

An International Thomson Publishing Company

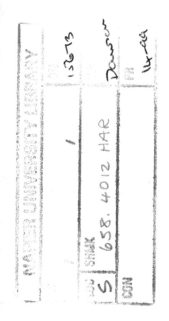

Publishing Team Director: John Szilagyi
Acquisitions Editor: John Szilagyi
Developmental Editor: Katherine Pruitt-Schenck
Production Editor: Kara ZumBahlen
Marketing Manager: Steve Scoble
Production: Bookmark Media
Text Composition: Bookmark Media
Art: Miyake Illustration and Bookmark Media
Text and Cover Design: Michael H. Stratton
Cover Photo: © Photonica

COPYRIGHT © 1998

by South-Western College Publishing
Cincinnati, Ohio

I T P®

International Thomson Publishing
South-Western College Publishing is an ITP Company. The ITP trademark is used under license.

23456789 PN 654321098

Printed in the United States of America

Library of Congress Cataloging-in-Publication Data
Harrison, Jeffrey S.
    Foundations in strategic management / Jeffrey S. Harrison, Caron H. St. John
        p. cm.
    Includes bibliographical references and index.
    ISBN 0-538-87844-4 (alk. paper)
    1. Strategic planning. I. St. John, Caron H. II. Title.
HD30.28.H3757 1998
    658.4´012--dc21

                                                                97-17197
                                                                CIP

CONTENTS

7 STRATEGIC CONTROL AND RESTRUCTURING

8 STRATEGIC CHALLENGES FOR THE TWENTY-FIRST CENTURY

CASE NOTE

PREFACE

A FOCUS ON LEARNING

Although most students of Strategic Management will not become chief executive of a major corporation in the near future, the decision-making tools you will develop during this course are relevant at all levels in an organization and in your own career planning. You will also discover that techniques such as industry analysis and organizational analysis are highly relevant in all types of organizations, including small entrepreneurial firms and nonprofit organizations. In addition, the material contained in this book will help you understand and appreciate many of the trends that are of current and future importance in the business community.

The study of strategic management will help you become better prepared to deal with important issues in a complex business environment, regardless of your position or the industry in which you work. We encourage you to apply the concepts of strategic management to your own employment and career planning decisions. Many of our students have told us that their understanding of strategic management techniques impressed recruiters and allowed them to ask perceptive questions during interviews.

A Solid Foundation in a Unique, Functional Format

Foundations in Strategic Management is a unique text that offers a concise, complete, and up-to-date treatment of the most current topics in the field. This book provides instructors and students with the opportunity to study all the important management strategies and with its succinct format, affords them the time to supplement these concepts with outside cases and readings. *Foundations* is a cost-effective alternative for those looking to create their own curriculum in Strategic Management without compromising the learning of the most current issues and trends in the field. With less than 200 pages and eight concise chapters, it is about half the size of other leading texts.

All Current Topics Are Covered

Topics of current importance are given in-depth treatment, including resource-based theory, stakeholder management, ethics and enterprise strategy, transactions cost theory, agency theory, restructuring, global competitiveness, and strategic alliances, based on current research findings. Strategic management also deals with creating a future for an organization. Thus, long range or "strategic" planning is a central topic. Other topics that will be covered in this book include environmental analysis, organizational analysis, joint ventures and strategic alliances, restructuring, mergers and acquisitions, leveraged buy-outs (LBOs), manufacturing strategy, crisis management, ethics, and stakeholder management.

Solid Organization

The organization of the book is very traditional. Chapter 1 covers the strategic management process. Chapter 2 discusses the external environment, including both the task and the broader environment. Chapter 3 treats the internal environment, internal resources, and strategic direction. Chapter 4 discusses corporate-level strategy. Chapter 5 covers business-level strategy. Chapter 6 focuses on the implementation topics of functional strategy and organizational structure. Chapter 7 treats strategic control and restructuring. Chapter 8 covers in more depth the important topic of global strategy.

Extensive Global Coverage

Global issues and examples are woven into each chapter, in addition to detailed treatment in Chapter 8. While from this description it is obvious that individual attention is given to implementation issues and global strategy, these topics are also integrated into the rest of the chapters. Many non-U.S. based firms and U.S.-based firms with international ventures are used as examples of strategic management theory. Also, many of the formulation topics include implementation tactics. This is especially true in Chapters 2 and 3, where we describe formulation activities and their implementation together.

A FOCUS ON TEACHING

Many instructors of strategic management face a significant challenge fitting all of the material they want to cover into their courses. Courses often include simulations and other exercises, readings, and comprehensive case studies, in addition to readings from a standard text. Furthermore, strategic management texts are increasing in their size and scope. Consequently, instructors may not have time to discuss all of the material from the text or, alternatively, only assign sections of it. Perhaps due to frustration, some instructors have dropped use of any published text, instead substituting with their own readings packets.

Foundations is short enough to allow readings, simulations, numerous case assignments and other exercises to be added to the course. Lower cost was not a primary driver of the project; however, it is an added benefit for students. *Foundations* covers all of the major strategic management topics, including classic and modern theory, based on contributions from the most important authors in the field. It was concisely written, intended to serve as a foundation for class discussion, supplemental readings, and case analyses.

The three theoretical foundations which most influenced this book are (1) the traditional process model, which includes a situation analysis (SWOT), formulation, implementation and control; (2) the resource-based model, with its emphasis on acquiring and managing resources to develop sustainable competitive advantages; and (3) stakeholder theory, which places the organization at the center of a network of contacts with whom the organization forms mutually beneficial relationships.

Complete Instructor's Package

This package (ISBN: 0538-878452) includes:

(1) discussion questions and answers to those questions
(2) outlines of the chapter material
(3) overhead transparency masters for tables and figures
(4) supplementary lecture materials
(5) case teaching notes (ISBN: 0538-87841x)
(6) a test bank written by the authors
(7) hands-on student exercises called strategic applications.

Note: As a case book addition to supplement the text, *Cases in Strategic Management*, 2e (ISBN: 0538-878428), a collection of cases put together by the authors, can be used in combination with *Foundations*. This set of cases comes complete with a set of full-length instructor's/case notes.

In developing this text, we would like to gratefully acknowledge the assistance of our colleagues in the field in providing insightful comments and advice on what the current needs of today's instructors are. We appreciate their involvement in this project:

Joseph E. Benson
New Mexico State University

Karen A. Froelich
North Dakota State University

Sidney L. Barton
University of Cincinnati

Roy A. Cook
Fort Lewis College

Rodley C. Pineda
Tennessee University

Douglas Polley
St. Cloud State University

Dwaine Tallent
St. Cloud State University

Ernest H. Hall
University of Southern Indiana

Walter O. Einstein
University of Massachusetts, Dartmouth

Kenneth Aupperle
University of Akron

Arthur Goldsmith
University of Massachusetts, Boston

Lavon Carter
Harding University

Benjamin Oviatt
Georgia State University

We hope you enjoy this text and find that it accommodates your individual needs. If you are looking for a more in-depth treatment of strategy, based on a stakeholder model that is increasing in importance in our field, you may want to consider our other book, *Strategic Management of Organizations and Stakeholders*, 2e (ISBN: 0538-878398).

Jeff Harrison and Caron St. John

To Our Parents

FOUNDATIONS IN STRATEGIC MANAGEMENT

1

The Strategic Management Process

The Walt Disney Company

"Can Disney Tame 42nd Street?" This headline from a recent *Fortune* article announces another of Disney's many ambitious projects. The Walt Disney Company is pouring millions of dollars into the development of one of the most crime-ridden areas in New York City—42nd Street between Times Square and Eighth Avenue in Manhattan. The area will feature a live production theater, a Disney Store, cinemas, hotels, game parlors, and restaurants. In response to criticism, Michael Eisner, Disney's chief executive officer, responded, "I think the Disney brand is going to be enhanced by being on 42nd Street. It's a magic word and a magic place."

Why not? Under Eisner's leadership, the sleeping giant that was once Disney has been transformed into a worldwide entertainment superpower. Investors are delighted. In fact, over the past ten years an investment in Disney stock returned an average 28% per year, compared to 16% for the Standard and Poor's 500 companies. Disney has major theme parks in the United States, Europe, and Asia and owns several movie production companies, which have turned out major motion picture successes such as *the Lion King, The Hunchback of Notre Dame, While You Were Sleeping,* and *Father of the Bride.* With the success of its live Broadway version of *Beauty and the Beast*, Disney plans to release a new Broadway production every year. Its television shows, such as *Home Improvement,* have also enjoyed great success. Disney merchandise is sold in a large and growing network of Disney Stores. Finally, in a move that shocked the entertainment industry, Disney acquired Capital Cities/ABC, one of the three largest broadcast networks in the United States.

Disney's successes are attributed to masterful management of the internal environment as well as the creation of a tangled web of strategic alliances with external constituencies. On the inside, Eisner holds regular "synergy" meetings comprising top managers from each division. The purpose of the meetings is to plan how each division can promote other divisions. Innovation, perhaps Disney's key competitive advantage, is managed through Walt Disney's Imagineering division. From an external perspective, few companies rival Disney's ability to create profitable alliances. Tokyo Disneyland, the best-attended theme park in the world, is a joint venture with Oriental Land Company, Ltd. An alliance with McDonald's makes the fast food giant the primary promotional partner in the restaurant business. Another deal with Canada's Royal Mounties allows Disney to sell officially licensed Mounties souvenirs. Indeed, the project on 42nd Street is being financed largely through local government loans at only 3% interest.[1]

Why are companies like Disney successful, while so many businesses fail? Although luck may play a small role, the most successful organizations are able to acquire and manage resources, capabilities, and strategic alliances with other organizations that provide competitive advantages. For example, in addition to its successful alliances with a multitude of firms, Disney enjoys almost unparalleled brand recognition, world-class human resource management, and an unequaled ability to create. Disney management carefully fosters these resources and capabilities and applies them to all of Disney's business areas. The processes associated with acquiring and managing organizational resources and establishing strategic alliances all fall within the management area generally referred to as strategic management.

WHAT IS STRATEGIC MANAGEMENT?

Strategic management is the process through which organizations analyze and learn from their internal and external environments, establish strategic direction, create strategies that are intended to help achieve established goals, and execute those strategies, all in an effort to satisfy key organizational constituencies, which are called stakeholders. A simple model of the strategic management process is illustrated in Figure 1.1. The two-headed arrows demonstrate that organizations often cycle back to earlier activities during the strategic management process. Consequently, the model is not rigid, but simply represents a useful sequence in which to discuss the central topics of strategic management. Strategic restructuring, which will be discussed in the last chapter, typically involves all of the strategic management processes.

Figure 1.1 *The Strategic Management Process*

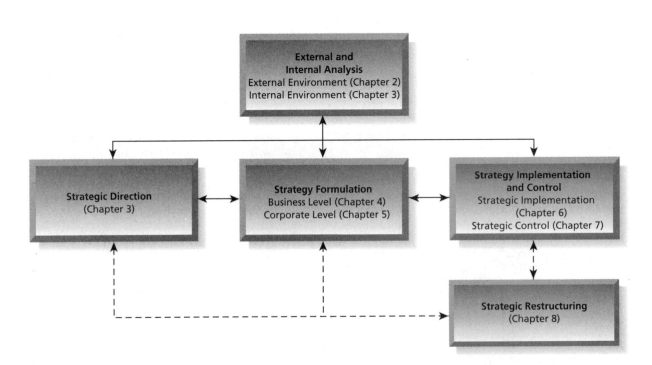

External and Internal Environmental Analysis

External environmental analysis, discussed in Chapter 2, involves evaluation of the broad and task environments to determine trends, threats, and opportunities and to provide a foundation for strategic direction. The **broad environment** consists of domestic and global environmental forces such as sociocultural, technological, political, and economic trends. The broad environment forms the context within which the firm and its task environment exist. The **task environment** consists of **external stakeholders,** groups or individuals outside the organization that are significantly influenced by or have a major impact on the organization.[2] External stakeholders include customers, suppliers, competitors, government agencies and administrators, and a variety of other external groups that have a stake in the organization. Many of the stakeholders and forces that have the potential to be most important to organizations are shown in Figure 1.2. All of the external stakeholders should be analyzed at both the domestic and international levels. In each of the countries in which a company operates, managers must interact with government agencies, competitors, and activist groups to manage the organization within each country's sociocultural, political, economic, and technological context. Thus, Figure 1.2 contains both a global and a domestic dimension.

    Internal stakeholders, which include managers, employees, and the owners and their representatives (e.g., the board of directors), also have a stake in the organization's outcomes. A fully developed internal analysis also includes a

Figure 1.2 *The Organization and Its Environments*

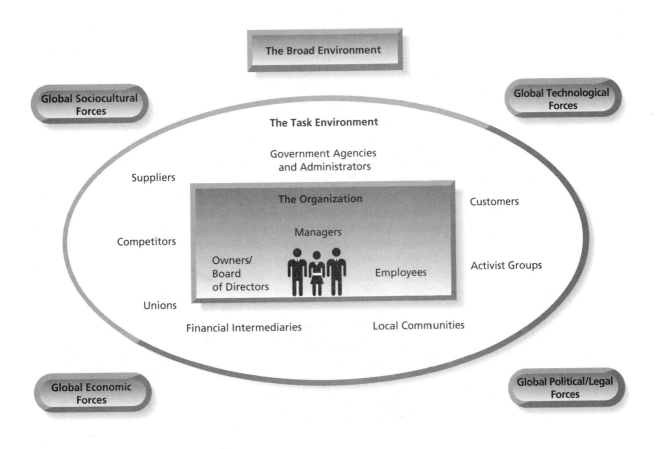

broader evaluation of all of the organization's resources and capabilities to determine strengths, weaknesses, and opportunities for competitive advantage and to identify organizational vulnerabilities that should be corrected. Internal analysis is the subject of Chapter 2.

As illustrated by the downward pointing arrows in Figure 1.1, analysis of the external and internal environments provides an organization with a foundation for all of the other tasks of strategic management. For example, an organization's managers should formulate strategies based on internal strengths and weaknesses and in the context of the opportunities and threats found in its external environment. In addition, strategic direction is an outcome of melding the desires of key organizational stakeholders with environmental realities.

Strategic Direction

Strategic direction pertains to the longer-term goals and objectives of the organization. At a more fundamental level, strategic direction defines the purposes for which an organization exists and operates. This direction is often contained in a **mission** statement. Unlike shorter-term goals and strategies, the mission is an enduring part of planning processes within the organization. Missions often describe the areas or industries in which an organization operates. For example, the mission of the New York Stock Exchange is as follows:

Support the capital-raising and asset-management processes by providing the highest-quality and most cost-effective, self-regulated marketplace for the trading of financial instruments; promote confidence in and understanding of that process; and serve as a forum for discussion of relevant national and international policy issues.[3]

A well-established strategic direction provides guidance to the managers and employees who are largely responsible for carrying it out. It also provides the external stakeholders with a greater understanding of the organization with which they interact. Since strategic direction is an important part of the internal organization, it is also discussed in Chapter 3.

Business and Corporate Strategy Formulation

A **strategy** is an organizational plan of action that is intended to move an organization toward the achievement of its shorter-term goals and, ultimately, toward the achievement of its fundamental purposes. As shown in Figure 1.3, strategy formulation is often divided into three types: corporate, business, and functional.

Corporate strategy formulation, the subject of Chapter 5, refers primarily to domain definition, or the selection of business areas in which the organization will compete. Although some firms, such as McDonald's, are involved in one basic business, diversified organizations are involved in several different businesses and serve a variety of customer groups. **Business strategy formulation**, discussed in Chapter 4, pertains to domain direction and navigation, or how businesses compete in the areas they have selected. **Functional strategy formulation** contains the details of how functional areas such as marketing, operations, finance, and research should work together to achieve the business-level strategy. Thus, functional strategy is most closely associated with strategy implementation, the topic of Chapter 6.

Another way to distinguish among the three strategies is to determine the organizational level at which decisions are made. Corporate strategy decisions are typically made at the highest levels of the organization by the CEO or board of

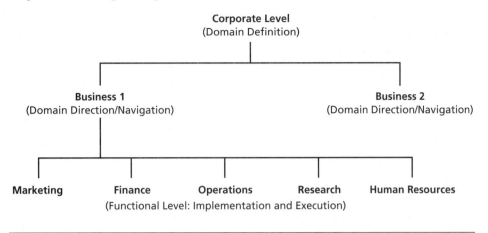

Figure 1.3 *Strategy Formulation in a Multibusiness Organization*

directors, although these individuals may receive input from managers at other levels. If an organization is only involved in one area of business, then business strategy decisions tend to be made by the same people. In organizations that have diversified into many areas, the different areas may be represented by different operating divisions or lines of business. In those situations division heads or business unit managers make the business strategy decisions. Functional decisions are made by functional managers, who represent organizational areas such as operations, finance, personnel, accounting, research and development, or information systems.

Strategy Implementation and Control

Strategy formulation results in a plan of action for the organization and its various levels. On the other hand, strategy implementation represents a pattern of decisions and actions that are intended to carry out the plan. **Strategy implementation** (Chapter 6) involves creating the functional strategies, systems, structures, and processes that organizations need for achieving strategic ends. Functional strategies outline the specific actions that each function must undertake to convert business- and corporate-level strategies into actions. Unless all of the plans are translated into specific actions, nothing will change. Organizational systems are developed to train and compensate employees, assist in the planning efforts, reinforce organizational values, and gather, analyze and convey information. Structures reflect the way people and work are organized, which includes reporting relationships and forming into work groups, teams, and departments. Processes, such as standard operating procedures, are developed to create uniformity across the organization and promote efficiency. Strategy implementation may require changes to any of these factors as the organization pursues new strategies over time.

Good control also is critical to organizational success. **Strategic control,** the topic of Chapter 7, refers to the processes that lead an organization to adjust its strategic direction, strategies, or the implementation plan when necessary. Managers may collect new information that leads them to reevaluate their assessment of the environment. They may determine that the organizational mission is no longer appropriate or that the organizational strategies are not leading to the desired outcomes. On the other hand, the strategic control system may tell managers that the environmental assumptions, mission, and strategies are appropriate, but the strategies have not been well executed. In such an instance, adjustments should be made in the implementation process.

As noted earlier, the strategic management process is usually not as sequential or linear as the previous discussion implied. The activities are usually performed simultaneously, and assumptions, direction, strategies, and processes are constantly adjusted as new information is learned and new assessments are made.

Strategic Restructuring

At some point in the life of every organization, growth will slow and some stakeholders will begin to feel dissatisfied. Wal-Mart is an excellent example. After two decades of phenomenal growth in sales, earnings, and stock value, Wal-Mart has begun to level off. Some assert that Sam Walton's death triggered the decline. Others argue that Wal-Mart is suffering from inevitable market saturation. Regardless of the reason, organizations eventually feel the need to reevaluate their strategies and the ways they are executing them. **Restructuring**, discussed in Chapter 8, typically involves a renewed emphasis on the things an organization does well, combined with a variety of tactics to revitalize the organization and strengthen its competitive position. Currently popular restructuring tactics include refocusing corporate assets on a more limited set of activities, retrenchment, Chapter 11 reorganization, leveraged buyouts, and changes to the organizational structure.

Now that we have described the strategic management process, we will establish a theoretical foundation for the rest of the book, followed by a brief discussion of the social responsibilities of modern organizations. Then we will turn our attention to the trends that are moving organizations quickly into a global playing field.

ALTERNATIVE PERSPECTIVES ON STRATEGY DEVELOPMENT

The field of strategic management blends a wide variety of ideas representing many functional areas of business. This diversity may be one reason that scholars and practitioners have not been able to agree on a standard set of theories (i.e., a paradigm) to guide the field. Nevertheless, some ideas are more widely adopted than others. The next several sections contain brief explanations of some of the major theories and ideas that form the basis for our model of the strategic management process. These theories are summarized in Table 1.1. Other important theories are woven into the chapters where they are most applicable.

Determinism versus Enactment

The traditional process for developing strategy consists of analyzing the internal and external environments of the organization to arrive at organizational strengths, weaknesses, opportunities, and threats (SWOT). The results from this **situation analysis**, as this process is sometimes called, form the basis for developing missions, goals and strategies.[4] In general, an organization should select strategies that (1) take advantage of organizational strengths and external opportunities or (2) neutralize or overcome internal weaknesses and external threats.

The traditional approach to strategy development is conceptually related to **environmental determinism**. According to this view, good management is asso-

Situation Analysis	The traditional process for developing strategy, consisting of analyzing the internal and external environments of the organization to arrive at organizational strengths, weaknesses, opportunities, and threats (SWOT). The results form the basis for developing missions, goals, and strategies.
Environmental Determinism	Management's task is to determine which strategy will best fit environmental, technical, and human forces at a particular point in time and then work to carry it out.
Principle of Enactment	Organizations do not have to submit to existing forces in the environment. They can, in part, create their environments through strategic alliances with stakeholders, advertising, political lobbying, and a variety of other activities.
Deliberate Strategy	Managers plan to pursue an intended strategic course. Strategy is deliberate.
Emergent Strategy	Strategy simply emerges from a stream of decisions. Managers learn as they go.
Stakeholder Management	The organization is viewed from the perspective of the internal and external constituencies that have a stake in the organization. Stakeholder analysis is used to guide the strategy process. Stakeholder management is central to the development of mutually beneficial relationships and alliances with external stakeholders.
Resource-Based View	An organization is a bundle of resources. The most important management function is to acquire and manage resources in such a way that the organization achieves sustainable competitive advantages leading to superior performance.

Table 1.1 *Ideas and Theories Supporting the Strategic Management Model*

ciated with determining which strategy will best fit environmental, technical, and human forces at a particular point in time and then working to carry it out.[5] From this perspective, the most successful organization will be the one that best *adapts* to existing forces. In other words, the environment is the primary determinant of strategy. After a critical review of environmental determinism, a well-known researcher once argued:

There is a more fundamental conclusion to be drawn from the foregoing analysis: the strategy of a firm cannot be predicted, nor is it predestined; the strategic decisions made by managers cannot be assumed to be the product of deterministic forces in their environments. . . . On the contrary, the very nature of the concept of strategy assumes a human agent who is able to take actions that attempt to distinguish one's firm from the competitors.[6]

The principle of enactment assumes that organizations do not have to submit to existing forces in the environment—they can, in part, create their environments through strategic alliances with stakeholders, advertising, political lobbying, and a variety of other activities.[7] Of course, smaller organizations are somewhat limited in their ability to influence independently some components of their external environments, such as national government agencies and administrators; however, they typically can have more influence on forces in the their local task environments.

It is not necessary to completely reject determinism and the view that organizations should adapt to their environments or the more modern view that organizations can alter their environments through enactment. In reality, the best-run organizations engage in both processes simultaneously, enacting those parts of the environment over which the firm can exercise some control and adapting to environmental circumstances that are either uncontrollable or too costly to influence. For instance, Disney altered its environment by buying a major customer of its television programs and movies with the acquisition of Capital Cities/ABC. On the other hand, Disney has canceled several large projects, most recently an "Americana" themed park and a Rocky Mountain ski resort, in response to pressure from social groups.

Deliberate versus Emergent Strategy Formulation

The traditional school of thought concerning strategy formulation also supports the view that managers respond to the forces discussed thus far by making decisions that are consistent with a preconceived strategy. In other words, strategy is deliberate. **Deliberate strategy** implies that managers *plan* to pursue an *intended* strategic course. On the other hand, in some cases strategy simply emerges from a stream of decisions. Managers learn as they go. An **emergent strategy** is one that was not planned or intended. According to this perspective, managers *learn* what will work through a process of trial and error.[8] Supporters of this view argue that organizations that limit themselves to acting on the basis of what is already known or understood will not be sufficiently innovative to create a sustainable competitive advantage.[9]

The story of the small Honda motorcycle supports the concept of emergent strategy. When Honda executives decided to market a small motorcycle, they had no idea it would be so successful. In fact, the prevailing wisdom was that small motorcycles would not sell very well. But Honda executives broke the rules and decided to market a small motorcycle. As sales expanded, they increased marketing and ultimately captured two-thirds of the U.S. motorcycle market. In another example, General Motors had a minivan on the drawing boards long before Chrysler. On the basis of rational analysis, GM decided that the minivan probably would not sell.[10] Chrysler's minivan introduction was extremely successful, and redefined the look of family vehicles. GM's subsequent attempts to enter the market have been largely unsuccessful. In spite of the strength of these examples concerning emergent strategy, it is not a good idea to reject deliberate strategy either. One of the strongest advocates of learning and the emergent strategy recently confessed, "we shall get nowhere without emergent learning alongside deliberate planning."[11] Both processes are necessary if an organization is to succeed.

Stakeholder Analysis and Management

The stakeholder view of strategic management considers the organization from the perspective of the internal and external constituencies that have a strong interest in the organization. These stakeholders should be managed in such a way that the organization can achieve its goals and objectives, which are themselves determined by the desires of key stakeholders. One of the common criticisms of the stakeholder approach is that it leads to a situation in which all (or most) stakeholders are equally weighted in the decision-making process. However, this is a misconception. One of the first activities associated with any well-done stake-holder analysis is the establishment of priorities given to each stakeholder. For example, in most organizations owners and customers would have higher man-agement priority than financial intermediaries or special interest groups.

It is helpful to draw a distinction between stakeholder analysis and stake-holder management. **Stakeholder analysis** involves identifying and prioritizing key stakeholders, assessing their needs, collecting ideas from them, and integrat-ing this knowledge into strategic management processes such as the establish-ment of strategic direction and the formulation and implementation of strategies. Organizations can use the information they collect from stakeholders to develop and modify their strategic direction, strategies, and implementation plans. Organizations can also use information from stakeholders to predict their responses to planned actions at home and abroad.

Stakeholder management, on the other hand, involves communicating, nego-tiating, contracting, and managing relationships with stakeholders, and motivat-ing them to behave in ways that are beneficial to the organization and its other stakeholders. In reality, the processes associated with stakeholder analysis and management overlap. For example, a firm may use a survey both to collect infor-mation on customer needs and to communicate information about a new service. This book describes many strategies firms are using to manage their stakeholders. A central theme is that many successful organizations have learned that coopera-tive strategies with external stakeholders can lead to competitive advantages in the global economy.

The Resource-Based View of the Firm

Finally, in recent years another perspective on strategy development has been gaining wider acceptance. It is called the **resource-based view of the firm**, and it has its roots in the work of the earliest strategic management theorists.[12] According to this view, an organization is a bundle of resources, which fall into the following general categories: (1) financial resources, including all of the mon-etary resources from which a firm can draw; (2) physical resources, such as plant, equipment, location, and access to raw materials; (3) human resources, which per-tain to the skills, background, and training of individuals within the firm; and (4) general organizational resources, which include a variety of factors that are pecu-liar to specific organizations. Organizational resources include the formal report-ing structure, management techniques, internal systems for planning and control-ling, culture, reputation, and relationships within the organization as well as relationships with external stakeholders.[13]

From a resource-based perspective, **strengths** are firm resources and capabili-ties that can lead to a competitive advantage. **Weaknesses** are resources and capa-bilities that the firm does not possess but that are necessary, resulting in a com-petitive disadvantage. **Opportunities** are conditions in the broad and task environments that allow a firm to take advantage of organizational strengths, overcome organizational weaknesses, or neutralize environmental threats. **Threats** are conditions in the broad and task environments that may stand in the way of organizational competitiveness or the achievement of stakeholder satisfaction.

If a resource that a firm possesses allows the firm to take advantage of oppor-tunities or neutralize threats, if only a small number of firms possess it, and if it is costly or impossible to imitate, then it may lead to a **sustainable competitive advantage**. A sustainable competitive advantage is an advantage that is difficult for competitors to imitate and thus leads to higher-than-average organizational performance over a long time period.[14] For example, the success of the Marriott hotel chain is largely attributable to advantages created by resources that have been difficult for other companies to duplicate in the hotel industry. The first is financial controls. Marriott can determine and anticipate construction and operating costs with nearly exact precision. Second, Marriott has developed a distinctive competence in customer service or "becoming the provider of choice." Looking to the future, Marriott is actively engaged in creating a third organizational capability as the "employer of choice." Marriott executives reason that with fewer people entering the labor force in the 18-to-25-year age group, good workers will become increasingly difficult to attract. Also, good workers are especially important in a service business like the hotel industry because they interact directly with customers.[15]

Many strategy scholars believe that the effective development of organizational resources is the most important reason that some organizations are more successful than others. Most of the resources that a firm can acquire or develop are directly linked to its stakeholders. For example, financial resources are closely linked to the establishment of good working relationships with financial intermediaries. Also, the development of human resources is associated with internal stakeholder management. Finally, organizational resources reflect the organization's understanding of the expectations of society and the linkages it has established with internal and external stakeholders.

The strategic management process model upon which this book is based relies, to some degree, on each of the theories and ideas described in these sections. The sections dealing with analysis of the internal and external environments draw heavily from stakeholder theory, as do the sections dealing with the formation of alliances. The entire book is guided by resource-based theory, as even relationships with external stakeholders are viewed as a resource upon which the organization can draw. The other perspectives are also interwoven into the fiber of the book where appropriate. This balanced approach will provide you with a set of tools that you can apply to a wide variety of organizational circumstances.

All of the popular strategic management perspectives recognize that strategic management entails the direction of large amounts of organizational resources—human, physical, financial, and intangible. As organizations conduct their daily business, they affect and influence many stakeholders, including owners, employees, customers, suppliers, and communities. Over time, these stakeholders develop expectations of the organization and often depend on the organization, to some degree, for their welfare. Consequently, organizational decisions often have an ethical dimension. Some decisions that are legal within society may be viewed as unethical by some people because they compromise an implied trust between the organization and its stakeholders. The next section provides a brief discussion of ethics and social responsibility.

ETHICS AND SOCIAL RESPONSIBILITY

As they relate to individuals, **ethics** are a personal value system that help determine what is right or good. These values are typically associated with a system of beliefs that supports a particular moral code or view.[16] **Organizational ethics** are a value system that has been widely adopted by members of an organization. For example, Wal Mart's values emphasize the worth of customers and employees, whereas Motorola's values focus on participation and patriotism. To determine what the ethics of an organization are, a student can simply study the pattern of decisions in the organization to discover what or who is given priority.[17]

Sometimes the stated ethics of an organization differ from the actual values that guide organizational decisions. For example, an organization may publish an affirmative action statement that condemns prejudice in hiring and promotion decisions on the basis of sex or race. However, that same organization may not have a single minority member or female on its top management team. Thus, studying the pattern of promotion decisions over a few years can determine whether the stated ethical position differs from the actual behavior within the organization.

Embedded within the application of ethics found here is the notion of social responsibility. Social responsibility contains four major components: (1) economic responsibilities, such as the obligation to be productive, profitable, and to meet the consumer needs of society; (2) legal responsibilities to achieve economic goals within the confines of written law; (3) moral obligations to abide by unwritten codes, norms, and values implicitly derived from society; and (4) discretionary responsibilities that are volitional or philanthropic in nature.[18]

Research evidence does not unequivocally support the idea that firms that rank high on social responsibility, based on the four components described, are necessarily any more or less profitable than firms that rank low.[19] However, firms that have an overall high rank in the four areas listed (one of which includes productivity and profitability) have achieved an end in itself. The old belief, espoused primarily by economists, that the only valid objective of a corporation is to maximize profits regardless of social consequences is no longer considered acceptable by many, if not most, members of modern societies. This sort of philosophy can lead to, at best, shortsightedness and, at worst, disaster, to the extent that organizations forget their other obligations in the pursuit of short-run financial rewards. In addition, one business ethics expert argued that

there is a long-term cost to unethical behavior that tends to be neglected. That cost is to the trust of the people involved. Companies today—due to increasing global competition and advancing technological complexity—are much more dependent than ever upon the trust of workers, specialists, managers, suppliers, distributors, customers, creditors, owners, local institutions, national governments, venture partners, and international agencies. People in any of those groups who believe that they have been misgoverned by bribes, sickened by emissions, or cheated by products tend, over time, to lose trust in the firm responsible for those actions.[20]

The logic continues that trust leads to commitment, which leads to increased effort on the part of everyone associated with the firm. Committed effort is precisely what is needed to prosper in a complex world in which interdependence is increasing.

In summary, organizations that exhibit trustworthy behavior enjoy good reputations, a more committed effort by internal and external stakeholders to the organization, and an eagerness on the part of stakeholders to conduct business. On the other hand, behavior that violates trust can lead to a poor reputation, lawsuits, walkouts, and boycotts, as well as avoidance on the part of stakeholders to participate in transactions with the organization. The Manville case is illustrative of this point.

Nearly fifty years ago, employees and managers of Manville (then Johns-Manville) started to receive information that asbestos inhalation was associated with various forms of lung disease. Manville chose to ignore this information and suppress research findings. The company even went so far as to conceal chest X-rays from employees in their asbestos operations. When confronted about this tactic, a Manville lawyer was quoted as saying that they would let their employees work until they dropped dead, all in the interest of saving money. Eventually, this neglect of research findings and their own employees led to financial ruin for Manville.[21]

Concerning ethical decision making, the approach of many business organizations seems to be to wait until someone complains before taking action. This is the type of attitude that resulted in the savings and loan crisis, the Bhopal explosion tragedy in India, and the explosion of the space shuttle *Challenger*. In each of these situations, the organizations involved could have avoided problems by being more responsive to warning signals from key stakeholders. History has taught us that many human-induced disasters and crises could be avoided if organizations are more sensitive to what their stakeholders tell them.

Social responsibility and ethics become even more complicated as organizations cross international borders. Nevertheless, global forces are causing organizations to increase their international involvement. The final section of this chapter discusses some of these forces.

THE CASE FOR GOING GLOBAL

Most successful organizations find that their domestic markets are becoming saturated or that foreign markets offer opportunities for growth and profitability that often are not available domestically. Many forces are leading U.S. firms into the international arena (see Table 1.2). Several of these forces are quite remarkable. Concerning profitability, Coca-Cola makes substantially higher profits in its foreign operations than it does at home.[22] Hasbro, the toy maker, also enjoys much higher prices and higher margins in other countries than it does in the United States. McDonald's expects to see much greater growth in international markets than in U.S. markets. Some smaller, start-up firms find they can enter growing international markets more easily than they can fight for market share in saturated U.S. markets.

Changes in European markets, such as falling trade barriers, are among the most significant global changes. Although the process of unification in Europe is proceeding slowly, it is expected to lead eventually to increased productivity and reduced costs for European businesses. Furthermore, strategic alliances in the sector are expected to increase.[23] Eastern Europe, despite political turmoil, still offers substantial investment opportunities due to low labor rates and untapped consumer markets.[24] Latin America, some authors have suggested, also offers substantial business opportunities.[25] Of course, Japan is already an economic superpower. Now that Japanese consumers have gained purchasing power, the world economy is dominated by three regions, called the "Triad" regions: North America, Europe, and the Pacific Rim. Some researchers have suggested that in order to remain competitive, larger organizations should be involved in all three regions.[26]

Going global offers many new management challenges. The fact is that Europeans and the Japanese have different views of business and manage differently than American managers, although management techniques are slowly converging.[27] Most of the larger companies described in this book have substantial international business assets.

Saturated domestic markets

Profitability of foreign markets

Falling trade barriers (i.e., EC 1992)

Newly industrialized countries (i.e., Korea, Taiwan, Spain) leading to increasing global
competition and new market opportunities.

Growing similarity of industrialized nations

Shift toward market economies (i.e., East Germany)

English becoming a universally spoken language

Globalization of capital markets

Availability of lower-cost resources (i.e., labor) in some foreign countries

Uniformity in technical standards

Opportunities to learn from foreign joint venture partners

Sources: Based on information contained in H. Henzler and W. Rall, "Facing Up to the Globalization Challenge," *McKinsey Quarterly* (Winter 1986): 52–68; T. Peters, "Prometheus Barely Unbound," *Academy of Management Executive* (November, 1990): 70–84; M. E. Porter, ed., *Competition in Global Industries* (Boston: Harvard Business School Press, 1986): 2–3.

Table 1.2 *Forces Favoring Globalization*

KEY POINTS SUMMARY

This chapter emphasized the important role of the strategic management process in modern organizations. Some of the most important points follow:

1. The strategic management process includes the activities of internal and external analyses, the establishment of strategic direction, the development of strategies for the corporate and business levels of the organization, the development and execution of an implementation plan, and the establishment of strategic controls.

2. The traditional process for developing strategy, sometimes called situation analysis, consists of analyzing the internal and external environments of the organization to arrive at organizational strengths, weaknesses, opportunities, and threats (SWOT). The results form the basis for developing missions, goals, and strategies.

3. A deterministic view of strategy argues that the key role of managers is to determine which strategy will best fit environmental, technical, and human forces at a particular point in time and then to work to carry it out. However, according to the principle of enactment, organizations do not have to submit to existing forces in the environment. They can, in part, create their environments through strategic alliances with stakeholders, advertising, political lobbying, and a variety of other activities.

4. The deliberate view of strategy is that managers plan to pursue an intended strategic course. On the other hand, the emergent view argues that strategy simply develops or evolves from a stream of decisions. Managers learn as they go.

5. Stakeholder theory views the organization from the perspective of the internal and external constituencies that have an interest in it.

6. According to the resource-based view of the firm, an organization is a bundle of resources. The most important management function is to

acquire and manage resources in such a way that the organization achieves sustainable competitive advantages leading to superior performance.

7. Social responsibilities include (1) economic responsibilities, (2) legal responsibilities, (3) moral obligations, and (4) discretionary responsibilities.

8. Many trends and influences are pushing firms to increase their involvement in international markets. Most larger firms have substantial global investments.

9. Ultimately, a firm's strategy is reflected in what the firm actually does, rather than what it says it will do. Strategic management processes are concerned with aligning intention with action.

REFERENCES

1. F. Rose, "Can Disney Tame 42nd Street?" *Fortune* (June 24, 1996):95–104; Reuter, "McDonalds, Disney, as Expected, Cinch Extensive Marketing Pact," *Investor's Business Daily* (May 24, 1996); The Walt Disney Company, *1995 Annual Report.*

2. R. E. Freeman, *Strategic Management: A Stakeholder Approach* (Boston: Pitman Publishing, 1984); M. Pastin, *The Hard Problems of Management: Gaining the Ethics Edge* (San Francisco: Jossey-Bass, 1986).

3. *Annual Report*, New York Stock Exchange, 1990, 1.

4. C. W. Hofer and D. E. Schendel, Strategy Formulation: *Analytical Concepts* (St. Paul, West Publishing, 1978).

5. J. Bourgeois, III, "Strategic Management and Determinism," *Academy of Management Review* 9 (1984): 586–596; L. G. Hrebiniak and W. F. Joyce, "Organizational Adaptation: Strategic Choice and Environmental Determinism," *Administrative Science Quarterly* 30 (1985): 336–349.

6. Bourgeois, "Strategic Management and Determinism," 589.

7. L. Smirchich and C. Stubbart, "Strategic Management in an Enacted World," *Academy of Management Review* 10 (1985): 724–736.

8. H. Mintzberg and A. Mchugh, "Strategy Formation in an Adhocracy," *Administrative Science Quarterly* 30 (1985): 160–197.

9. H. Mintzberg, "The Design School: Reconsidering the Basic Premises of Strategic Management," *Strategic Management Journal* 11 (1990): 171–196.

10. H. Mintzberg, "Learning 1, Planning 0: Reply to Igor Ansoff," *Strategic Management Journal* 12 (1991): 463–466.

11. Mintzberg, "Learning 1, Planning 0," 465.

12. N. J. Foss, C. Knudsen, and C. A. Montgomery, "An Exploration of Common Ground: Integrating Evolutionary and Strategic Theories of the Firm," in *Resource-Based and Evolutionary Theories of the Firm*, ed. C. A. Montgomery, (Boston: Kluwer Academic Publishers, 1995).

13. J. B. Barney, "Firm Resources and Sustained Competitive Advantage," *Journal of Management* 17 (1991): 99–120; J. B. Barney, *Gaining and Sustaining Competitive Advantage* (Reading, Mass: Addison-Wesley, 1997); J. S. Harrison, M. A. Hitt, R. E. Hoskisson, & R. D. Ireland, "Synergies and Post-Acquisition Performance: Differences versus Similarities in Resource Allocations,"*Journal of Management* 17 (1991): 173–190; J. T. Mahoney and J. R. Pandian, "The Resource-Based View within the Conversation of Strategic Management," *Strategic Management Journal* 13 (1992): 363–380; B. Wernerfelt, "A Resource-Based View of the Firm," *Strategic Management Journal* 5 (1984): 171–180.

14. Barney, "Firm Resources and Sustained Competitive Advantage"; Mahoney and Pandian, "The Resource-Based View."

15. Ulrich and Lake, "Organizational Capability," 79.

16. L. T. Hosmer, *The Ethics of Management*, 2nd ed. (Homewood, Ill.: Irwin, 1991), 103.

17. This entire discussion of ethics as ground rules was strongly influenced by M. Pastin, *The Hard Problems of Management*, (San Francisco: Jossey-Bass, 1986), 40–42.

18. A. B. Carroll, "A Three-Dimensional Model of Corporate Social Performance," *Academy of Management Review* 4 (1979): 497–505.

19. K. E. Aupperle, A. B. Carroll, and J. D. Hatfield, "An Empirical Examination of the Relationship between Corporate Social Responsibility and Profitability," *Academy of Management Journal* 28 (1985): 446–463.

20. L. T. Hosmer, "Response to 'Do Good Ethics Always Make for Good Business?'" *Strategic Management Journal* 17 (1996): 501. See also L. T. Hosmer, "Strategic Planning as If Ethics Mattered," *Strategic Management Journal*, Summer Special Issue, 15 (1994): 17–34.

21. S. W. Gellerman, "Why 'Good' Managers Make Bad Ethical Choices," *Harvard Business Review* (July / August 1986): 85–90.

22. "As a Global Marketer, Coke Excels by Being Tough and Consistent," *The Wall Street Journal*, December 19, 1989, 1.

23. H. Weihrich, "Europe 1992: What the Future May Hold," *Academy of Management Executive* (May 1990): 7–18.

24. E. T. Yon, "Corporate Strategy and the New Europe," *Academy of Management Executive* (August 1990): 61–65.

25. J. I. Martinez, J. A. Quelch, and J. Ganitsky, "Don't Forget Latin America," *Sloan Management Review* (Winter 1992): 78–82.

26. K. Ohmae, "Becoming a Triad Power: The New Global Corporation," in ed. H. Vernon-Wortzel and L. H. Wortzel *Global Strategic Management: The Essentials*, 2nd ed., (New York: John Wiley and Sons, 1991), 62–74.

27. R. Calori and B. Dufour, "Management European Style," *Academy of Management Executive* (August 1995): 61–73.

2

The External Environment

General Motors

The following are excerpts taken from a statement by John F. Smith, Jr., chief executive officer of General Motors, as published in the company's special environmental report: "Global businesses must act responsibly in regard to their business and to the natural environments in which they operate.

As we pursue our strategies worldwide, we accept a social and environmental responsibility as well. These responsibilities include the promotion of a sustainable global economy and recognition of the accountability we have to the economies, environments, and communities where we do business around the world. It is important to work for environmental protection in balance with economic objectives and to establish national policies to foster development that can be sustained over the long term. Indeed, sustainable development is supported by the fact that economic growth and environmental protection can be collectively achieved through cooperative efforts—and that's a key philosophy at General Motors.

In January 1994, a GM representative was appointed by President Clinton to the President's Council on Sustainable Development. Through this council, GM has collaborated with government and environmental organizations to develop action plans that will foster U.S. economic vitality and support the international directives that are outlined in Agenda 21, a document adopted by participants at the United Nations Conference on Environment and Development which describes the roles and responsibilities of transnational corporations and industrial activities in a sustainable world.

We at GM have many challenges ahead in defining sustainable development within the context of the global automotive industry. One thing is certain: The managerial skills and technology that a global enterprise such as GM can mobilize provide considerable potential for sustainable development initiatives."[1]

Why would the world's largest automaker devote resources to publishing an environmental report and becoming involved in environmental initiatives, especially considering the performance problems GM has experienced in the last two decades? Top executives are thinking long term. They realize that the environmental movement that began with a few special-interest groups half a century ago has become a part of mainstream social opinion, especially in the United States. GM is also establishing alliances with government and other organizations that keep it in this mainstream. GM realizes, as do many other organizations, that staying aware of and responding to forces in the broad environment can provide benefits, some of which are hard to quantify.

This chapter is about the influence of the external environment on organizations. Although an organization cannot have much direct influence on its broad environment, it can buffer itself from threats and take advantage of opportunities. On the other hand, the external stakeholders that compose an organization's task environment are subject to substantial firm influence. We will now discuss the broad environment, followed by the task environment.

THE BROAD ENVIRONMENT

The broad environment can have a tremendous impact on a firm and its task environment; however, individual firms typically have only a marginal impact on this environment. In rare cases, individual firms can influence trends in the broad environment, as when Intel influences technological trends in the microprocessor, microcomputer, and software industries. In general, however, it is virtually impossible for one independent firm to dramatically influence societal views on abortion, drug abuse, free trade with China, migration to the Sun Belt, or even the desirability of particular clothing styles. Consequently, although firms may be able to influence the broad environment to some degree, the emphasis in this book generally will be on analyzing and responding to this segment of the environment. The most important elements in the broad environment, as it relates to a business organization and its task environment, are global sociocultural, economic, technological, and political/legal forces.

Global Sociocultural Forces

A few of the major sociocultural issues currently facing the United States are shown in Table 2.1. Analysis of societal trends is important from at least four perspectives. First, because most of the other stakeholder groups are also members of society, some of their values and beliefs are derived from broader societal influences, which can create opportunities and threats for organizations. For example, societal interest in fitness has led to business opportunities in the home fitness industry, whereas concerns about teenage smoking has set the stage for a regulatory backlash against the tobacco companies.

Second, firms may reduce the risk of gaining a bad "ethical" reputation by anticipating and adjusting for sociocultural trends. For example, the Denny's restaurant chain was known for many years as one of America's most racist companies. However, Ron Petty, Denny's CEO, introduced initiatives that turned the company into a model of multicultural sensitivity:

The percentage of minority officers, vice presidents and above, has risen from zero in 1993 to 11% today. Minorities hold 20% of the jobs directly below vice president, a category

Role of government in health care and child care
Declining quality of education
Legality of abortion
Increasing levels of crime
Importance and role of the military
Levels of foreign investment/ownership in the United States
Social costs of restructuring, especially layoffs
Pollution and disposal of toxic and nontoxic wastes
General increase in environmental awareness
Drug addiction
Continued migration toward the Sun Belt states
Graying of America
AIDS and other health problems
Major global issues
Immigration restrictions

Table 2.1 *Major Social Issues in the United States*

called director; there were no nonwhites in 1993. Of Denny's 512 franchises, 27 are African American, vs. one in 1993; the goal is 65 by the end of 1997..."Denny's has jumped out in front and taken a positive approach to solving its problems, unlike most companies that do the minimum required by law," says Terry Demchak, a partner at Saperstein Goldstein Demchak & Baller, the California law firm that represented black customers in one of two class-action suits against the chain.[2]

Shoney's, one of Denny's major competitors, is also involved in major initiatives to erase its racist stigma.[3]

Third, correct assessment of sociocultural trends can help businesses avoid restrictive legislation. Industries and organizations that police themselves are less likely to be the target of legislative activity. For example, the United States Sentencing Guidelines (USSG), compulsory guidelines courts must use to determine fines and penalties when corporate illegalities are proven, were a direct response to public outcry over negligence on the part of businesses in preventing white-collar crime.[4]

The fourth reason that analysis of sociocultural values is important is that demographic and economic changes in society can create opportunities for and threats to the revenue growth and profit prospects of an organization. For example, many baby boomer couples had babies later in life than their counterparts in past generations, causing a demographic trend toward older couples with children. The higher levels of income of these more established "30- and 40- something" parents have led to the development of higher quality baby accessories, clothing, and supplies, as well as new business opportunities in child care and specialized education. Seemingly unrelated industries, such as the motion picture and television industries, have taken advantage of these trends by producing many movies and television shows that center on birth, babies, and children. Demographic changes such as this one can help direct organizational planning and are often at the core of any forecast of industry demand.

Not only must an organization assess the potential effects of sociocultural forces on its business, it must manage its relationship and reputation with society at large. The media acts as a watchdog for society. It is a commanding force in managing the attitudes of the general public toward organizations. Executives have nightmares about their organizations being the subjects of the next *20/20* program or some other news show. On the other hand, a well-managed media can have a significant positive impact on a firm's image. To manage relations with the media, large organizations typically employ public relations (PR) experts.

Global Economic Forces

Economic forces can have a profound influence on organizational behavior and performance. Economic growth, interest rates, the availability of credit, inflation rates, foreign exchange rates, and foreign trade balances are among the most critical economic factors. Economic growth can also have a large impact on consumer demand for products and services. Consequently, organizations should consider forecasts of economic growth in determining when to make critical resource allocation decisions such as plant expansions. Inflation and the availability of credit, among other factors, influence interest rates that organizations have to pay. High interest payments can constrain the strategic flexibility of firms by making new ventures and capacity expansions prohibitively expensive. Volatile inflation and interest rates, such as those experienced in the United States in the 1970s and in South American and Eastern European countries, increase the uncertainty associated with making strategic decisions.

Foreign exchange rates are another major source of uncertainty. For global organizations, profit earned in a foreign country may turn into a loss due to unfavorable exchange rates. Finally, foreign trade balances are highly relevant to both domestic and global organizations because they are an indication of the nature of trade legislation that might be expected in the future. For example, the United States has a large trade surplus with the European Union (EU). As a result, American manufacturers who export to the EU are concerned about new protectionist legislation, such as high tariffs that may be enacted to reduce the trade imbalance.[5]

The sociocultural forces discussed in the last section often are interdependent with the economic forces. In the United States, birthrates (a sociocultural force) are low and, because of improved health care and lifestyles (another sociocultural force), more people are living longer. This demographic shift toward an older population is influencing the economic forces in society. For example, the older population means that demand for premium services are high but, simultaneously, there are shortages of young workers to fill the service jobs, which drives up wage rates and can lead to inflation. So, for example, a service firm tracking these trends may project that its demand will go up as it sells its services to the older customers; but its wage rates will go up as well, leading to lower unit profitability.

To assess the effect of the interdependent sociocultural and economic forces, organizations often model their business environments using different scenarios. The scenarios are composed of optimistic, pessimistic, and most likely assumptions and interpretations of various economic and sociocultural trend data collected for the process. Continuing with the previous example, the service firm may develop demand and wage rate scenarios as a way of considering several different possible future business environments. These scenarios can be updated as information becomes more firm, and they may be used for evaluating different courses of action, such as capacity expansions or investments in labor-saving technologies.

   This brief discussion of economic forces indicates the importance of monitoring and forecasting events in the global economy. We now turn our attention to the role that technological forces play in the strategic management of organizations.

Global Technological Forces

Technological change creates new products, services, and, in some cases, entire new industries. It also can change the way society behaves and what society expects. Notebook computers, compact discs and players, direct satellite systems, and cellular telephones are technological innovations that have experienced extraordinary growth in recent years, leaving formerly well-established industries stunned, creating whole new industries, and influencing the way many people approach work and leisure. Computers and telecommunications technologies, for example, have played an essential role in creating the increasingly global marketplace.

   Technology refers to human knowledge about products and services and the way they are made and delivered. Technologies typically evolve through a series of steps, and each step has its own set of implications for managers. When a new idea or technology is proven to work in the laboratory, it is called an **invention**. New inventions are made every day—corporate research laboratories, universities, and individuals invent new products, new processes, and new technologies all of the time. Only a handful of those inventions, however, are ever developed past the laboratory stage. When an invention can be replicated reliably on a meaningful scale, it is referred to as an **innovation**. Most technological innovations take the form of new products or processes, such as fax machines, airbags, and cellular phones. A **basic innovation**, such as the microprocessor, lightbulb, and fiber optics, impacts much more than one product category or one industry.

   To avoid being blindsided by a new technology, organizations should monitor technological developments in industries other than their own and conduct brainstorming sessions about the possible consequences for their own products and markets. To help identify trends and anticipate their timing, organizations may participate in several kinds of technological forecasting efforts. In general, organizations may monitor trends by studying research journals, government reports, and patent filings. Another more formal method of technological forecasting is to solicit the opinion of experts outside of the organization. These experts may be interviewed directly or contacted as part of a formal survey, such as a Delphi study. A third method is to develop scenarios of alternative technological futures, which capture different rates of innovation and different emerging technologies. Scenarios allow an organization to conduct what-if analyses and to develop alternative plans for responding to new innovations.

   In addition to forecasting, some organizations establish strategic alliances with universities to engage in joint research projects, which allows the companies to keep abreast of new trends. Other organizations simply donate funds to universities for research in exchange for information about findings. The Partnership Data Net, a Washington-based information center on partnerships, lists about 3,000 partnerships between schools and businesses.[6] Akzo NV, the Dutch chemical giant with more than 11,000 employees at 161 locations in North America alone, created a massive partnership with 12 U.S. colleges that has paid healthy dividends in terms of new products.[7]

With a well-thought-out plan for monitoring technological trends, an organization can better prepare itself to receive early warnings about trends that will create opportunities and threats. Now we will turn our attention to the global political and legal forces in the broad environment of organizations.

Global Political/Legal Forces

Political forces, both at home and abroad, are among the most significant determinants of organizational success. The stakes are often high. For instance, a newly revised pact among the governments of Kazakhstan, Russia, and Oman may allow Chevron to recover a $715 million investment in the Tengiz oil field.[8] In another example, Israel recently asked the White House to limit the ability of U.S. satellite companies to survey Israel from space. However, an Israeli company that is about to enter the same business would not face similar restrictions.[9] In the U.S., a Supreme court ruling allows liability lawsuits against manufacturers of medical devices even though the devices are regulated by law.[10] Also, recent court rulings have made banks liable when *their customers* pollute.[11]

Governments provide and enforce the rules by which organizations operate. Even in the United States, which is considered a "free" market economy, no organization is allowed the privilege of total autonomy from government regulations. Governments can encourage new business formation through tax incentives and subsidies; they can restructure organizations, as in the case of the AT&T breakup; and they can totally close organizations that do not comply with laws, ordinances, or regulations. Furthermore, alliances among governments provide an additional level of complexity for organizations with significant foreign operations. Nonprofit organizations are as subject to government intervention and regulation as for-profit organizations.

Although all organizations face some form of regulation, the trend is toward deregulation and privatization of industries worldwide. In Portugal, for example, the previously regulated, government-owned banking industry is moving toward privatization. In Eastern Europe, many industries are struggling to survive and prosper in an emerging free market economy. In the United States, the last twenty years has brought the deregulation of airline, banking, long-distance telephone communication, and trucking industries. The once highly regulated utility industry is undergoing partial deregulation, which is opening up new opportunities but creating competitive threats as well. Regulation protected these industries from competition, but required set prices and strict operating procedures. With deregulation, existing industry competitors face turbulence and unpredictability. However, deregulation also provides opportunities for new firms to enter the market.

The amount of time and effort organizations should devote to learning about regulations, complying with them, and fostering good relationships with regulatory agencies and their representatives depends, in part, on the industry. Some laws and regulations pertain to only one industry, such as nuclear energy. Many regulations, however, are cross-cutting, in that they apply to organizations in general. In the United States, two of the most widely known regulatory agencies are the Occupational Safety and Health Administration (OSHA) and the Environmental Protection Agency (EPA).

In summary, social forces, the global economy, technology and the global political/legal forces make up the broad environment, the context in which the firm and its task environment exist. The next section will discuss the task environment.

THE TASK ENVIRONMENT

The task environment consists of stakeholders with whom organizations interact on a fairly regular basis. These stakeholders include domestic and international customers, suppliers, competitors, government agencies and administrators, local communities, activist groups, unions, and financial intermediaries. Michael Porter, an economist at Harvard University, assimilated years of economic research into a simple model that helps determine the influence of the first three of these stakeholders—suppliers, customers, and competitors—on competition in an industry. His model will be presented in the next section.[12]

Competitive Forces

Michael Porter integrated the theory of industrial organization economics into a "user friendly" model of the forces that drive industry competition. **Industries** are often difficult to define, but in general they refer to a group of organizations who compete directly with each other to win orders or sales in the marketplace. Porter's model includes suppliers, customers, and industry competitors. Competitors are further divided into three types: existing competitors, potential competitors, and indirect competitors. The influence of potential competitors on industry competition is determined by the strength of entry barriers, in other words, the forces that discourage new firms from entering the industry. Indirect competitors sell products that can be substituted for products sold by existing competitors, such as contact lenses as a substitute for glasses. According to Porter, the five forces largely determine the type and level of competition in an industry and, ultimately, the industry's profit potential.[13] These forces are illustrated in Figure 2.1.

An entire industry (as opposed to a single organization) is placed in the center of the model. One of the most common errors made by new students of strategic management is placing an organization in the middle of the model instead of an industry group. When this happens, substitutes are treated as competing products, which is inconsistent with Porter's ideas concerning the power of substitutes in influencing competition in an industry. Next we will discuss the factors that determine the strength of each of these five forces.

Customers. Although all customers are important, some are more important than others. For instance, when retail giant Home Depot announced that it would no longer buy carpet from Shaw Industries (because Shaw, a carpet manufacturer, was moving into retail), Shaw's stock dropped by 11% in one day.[14] According to Porter, customers tend to exhibit a powerful force on competition in an industry if the following conditions exist:

1. There are a small number of customers. In this case, losing one customer makes a big difference.
2. The customers make high-volume purchases.

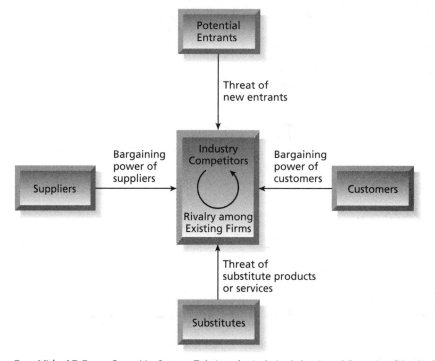

Figure 2.1 *Porter's Five-Forces Model of Industry Competition*

3. The purchases customers make from the industry are large relative to the amount expended for items from other industries. Here customers will expend considerable effort to shop for the best price.
4. The products customers are buying are undifferentiated (also known as standard or generic). This means that customers are not concerned about which company they buy from.
5. The customers earn low profits. Customers who earn low profits are under constant pressure to keep the costs of their purchases down.
6. The customers can easily get accurate information on the selling industry's costs and demand. This gives them a real edge during negotiations.
7. The customers can easily integrate backward and become their own suppliers. Both Sears and General Motors have been known to buy supplier companies when they are unhappy with pricing.
8. Customers can easily switch from one seller to another.

In combination, these forces determine the bargaining power of customers, that is, the degree to which customers exercise active influence over pricing and the direction of product development efforts. The discount retail industry (especially large competitors such as Wal-Mart, KMart, and Target) is an example of a customer industry that is powerful because of high volume purchases and the ease with which retailers can switch from one manufacturer to another for many products.

Suppliers. Suppliers to industries provide equipment, supplies, component parts, and raw materials. The labor and capital markets from which firms draw their employees and investment funds are also a source of supply. Powerful suppliers can raise their prices and therefore reduce profitability levels in the buying industry. They can also exert influence and increase uncertainty for the buying industry by *threatening* to raise prices, reducing the quality of goods or services provided, or not delivering supplies when needed. In general, supplier power is greater under the following circumstances:

1. Only a few suppliers are available.
2. Few substitutes exist for the product or service that is supplied. (These first two conditions limit the ability of the buying industry to use alternative supply sources as a bargaining tool.)
3. Suppliers are not dependent on the buying industry for a large percentage of their total sales. This means that the loss of one sale is not very important.
4. Suppliers know that the buying industry must have the product or service that suppliers provide to manufacture their own products.
5. Suppliers have differentiated their products, which means that the buying industry is willing to pay more for certain brands.
6. Suppliers make it costly to switch suppliers. IBM built its mainframe business by making IBM mainframes incompatible with other brands, thus preventing buyers from switching.
7. Suppliers can easily integrate forward and thus compete directly with their former buyers.

These forces combine to determine the strength of suppliers and the degree to which they can exert influence over the profits earned by firms in the industry. The notebook computer industry, for instance, is one that is particularly susceptible to the power of suppliers. Most of the industry competitors purchase microprocessors, batteries, operating system software, and flat-panel displays from suppliers. Consequently, the manufacturing costs, performance characteristics, and innovativeness of the notebook computer are largely in the hands of suppliers.

Existing Competitors. In most industries, competitive moves by one firm affect other firms in the industry, which may incite retaliation or countermoves. In other words, competing firms have an economic stake in each other. Some of the major forces that lead to high levels of competition include the following:

1. Slow industry growth, which means that competitors must steal market share if they intend to grow.
2. High fixed costs, which mean that firms are under pressure to increase sales to cover their costs and earn profits.
3. Lack of product differentiation, which puts a lot of pressure on prices and often leads to price-cutting strategies.
4. A large numbers of competitors, which means that the total market must be divided in more ways.
5. High exit barriers, which means that firms may lose all or most of their investments in the industry when they withdraw from it. Therefore, they are more likely to remain in the industry even if profits are low.

In many industries, competition is so intense that profitability suffers, as has been the case in the airline, small computer, and fast food industries.

Potential Competitors/Entry Barriers. Several forces determine the ease with which new competitors can enter an industry and, therefore, how many new entrants can be expected. New entrants increase competition in an industry, which may drive down prices and profits. They may add capacity, introduce new products or processes, and bring a fresh perspective and new ideas—all of which can drive down prices, increase costs, or both. Forces that keep new entrants out, providing a level of protection for existing competitors, are called **entry barriers**.

Examples of entry barriers that are found in many industries include the following:

1. Economies of scale, which occur when it is more efficient to produce a product in a larger facility at higher volume.
2. Large capital requirements, also known as start-up costs, can prevent a small competitor from entering an industry.
3. High levels of product differentiation, which means that some firms enjoy a loyal customer base, making it harder for a new firm to draw away customers.
4. High switching costs, which apply not only to suppliers, can also serve as an entry barrier protecting established firms in an industry.
5. Limited access to distribution channels, which may prevent new companies from getting their products to market.
6. Government policies and regulations that limit entry into an industry, effectively preventing new competition.
7. Other advantages that are difficult to duplicate in the short term, such as patents, favorable locations, proprietary product technology, government subsidies, or access to scarce raw materials.
8. A past history of aggressive retaliation by industry competitors toward new entrants.

Taken together, these forces can result in high, medium, or low barriers. In industries with high entry barriers, few new firms enter the industry, which reduces the competitive intensity. When entry barriers are low, new firms can freely enter the industry, which increases rivalry and depletes profits. Examples of industries that are traditionally associated with high barriers to entry are aircraft manufacturing (due to technology, capital costs, and reputation) and automobiles manufacturing (due to capital costs, distribution, and brand names). Medium-high barriers are associated with industries such as household appliances, cosmetics, and books. Low-entry barriers are found in industries such as apparel manufacturing and most forms of retailing.[15]

Indirect Competitors/Substitutes. If organizations provide goods or services that readily substitute for the goods and services provided by an industry, those organizations become indirect competitors. For example, aspirin, ibuprofen, and acetaminophen are all substitute pain relievers. In the service sector, credit unions are substitutes for banks and bus travel is a substitute for airline travel.

Close substitutes can place a ceiling on the price that an industry can be charge for a good or service.[16] For example, if the price of artificial sweeteners becomes too high, many consumers who typically prefer artificial sweeteners would probably switch back to sugar.

Although Porter does not explicitly address other factors in his original model, other stakeholder groups exist that can influence an industry's profitability. Special-interest groups and government agencies, for example, take actions that cause organizations to invest money, which can influence cost structures and profits. For example, improvements in automotive fuel efficiency and safety are largely the result of pressures from consumer groups and regulators.

An analysis of the five forces is useful from several perspectives. First, by understanding how the five forces influence competition and profitability in an industry, a firm can better understand how to position itself relative to these forces, determine any sources of competitive advantage now and in the future, and estimate the profits that it can expect. Firm managers may also decide to alter the influence of the five forces by actions such as erecting higher entry barriers through large-scale economies or greater product differentiation, or by creating switching costs to encourage customer loyalty.

An organization can also analyze the five forces within an industry prior to entry or as a basis for deciding to leave the industry. As a result of such an analysis, a firm may conclude that an industry is not attractive because of low entry barriers, powerful suppliers or buyers, close substitutes, or the number and strength of current competitors. In general, a thorough understanding of the forces within an industry can help a firm better understand the industry's overall profit potential, and those forces most likely to create opportunities and threats.

This completes our discussion of Porter's model, which we used to consider the power of several important stakeholder groups. The next section provides ideas concerning how to manage external stakeholders.

External Stakeholders and Environmental Uncertainty

By establishing the priority of stakeholders, an organization gains direction as to the amount of attention it should give stakeholders as it develops its corporate direction, strategies, and implementation plans. Also, prioritizing stakeholders provides clues concerning the types of strategies that may be appropriate in managing them. High-priority stakeholders are those that have a strong influence on the outcomes of the organization. For example, a customer may have a large influence on next year's profits due to the large orders that it places, or a strong government regulator may be able to dramatically alter the way a firm will operate. These types of stakeholders powerfully influence the environmental uncertainty that an organization faces.

Environmental uncertainty reduces a firm's ability to predict with confidence the future state of its environment. If the environment were highly predictable, the management task would be fairly simple and profits would be relatively easy to achieve. On the other hand, high levels of environmental uncertainty reduce an organization's ability to chart an effective course into the future. From this perspective, stakeholders that (1) contribute to the environmental uncertainty facing a firm or (2) are able to reduce the environmental uncertainty facing a firm should be given higher strategic priority. Figure 2.2 indicates that organizations should use strategic partnering tactics with these types of stakeholders in an effort to reduce uncertainty. A recent example in the space industry demonstrates this point:

Lockheed Space Operations Company (LSOC), a division of what is now Lockheed Martin, recently experienced a very high level of environmental uncertainty. The U.S. government has

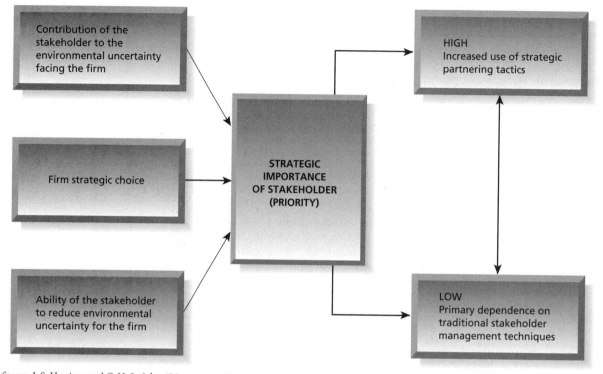

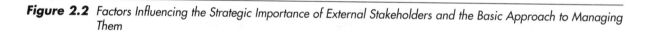

Source: J. S. Harrison and C. H. St. John, "Managing and Partnering with External Stakeholders," *Academy of Management Executive* (May 1996): 50. Used with permission.

Figure 2.2 *Factors Influencing the Strategic Importance of External Stakeholders and the Basic Approach to Managing Them*

been putting increasing pressure on government agencies to reduce costs. Under a recent cost initiative, the government decided that the many contracts associated with the space shuttle and rocket operations at Kennedy Space Center should be managed by one prime contractor.

Executives at LSOC, who were largely responsible for the space shuttle launch operations, were concerned about the political clout of Rockwell. Rockwell had built the space shuttle and trained many of the astronauts who were now high-level government officials. To reduce the uncertainty associated with this situation, LSOC formed a joint venture with Rockwell to run the Kennedy Space Center. The joint venture proposal was selected by the government among several other contenders.

Priority is also a matter of strategic choice, as indicated in Figure 2.2. For example, an organization may give high priority to a particular special-interest group such as a church or environmental group because of the values of the CEO. For instance, Ben and Jerry's, the ice cream maker, gives high priority to environmental concerns because the founders value those issues.

The first column in Table 2.2 (on pp. 32–33) lists some traditional stakeholder management techniques, grouped by type of external stakeholder. These techniques are both common and essential, and they should be used where appropriate. However, recently the emphasis in stakeholder management has been shifting away from protecting the organization from the influence of external stakeholders toward treating stakeholders almost as if they are part of the internal organization (see the second column of Table 2.2). Partnering tactics are not new. What is new is that they are being used with increasing frequency. The rest of this chapter presents a few examples that demonstrate how organizations can manage their task environments.

Partnering with External Stakeholders

Efforts to partner with customers and suppliers often provide significant benefits. Many firms are involving strategically important customers and suppliers in product and process design, in quality training sessions, and in on-line production scheduling. For example, Digital Equipment Corporation (DEC) and Hewlett-Packard include suppliers on their product planning teams. DEC also asks managers to evaluate its suppliers as if they were part of the internal organization.[17] G&F Industries, a plastic components manufacturer, has dedicated an employee to Bose, one of its major customers. The employee works full time inside the Bose facility.[18]

To combat collapsing product and process life cycles and to get a jump on new emerging technologies, competitors also are joining forces in increasing numbers. Rival organizations are forming alliances for technological advancement, for new product development, to enter new or foreign markets, and to pursue a wide variety of other opportunities.[19] In oligopolies, where a few major rivals dominate an industry, the major firms may cooperate with each other in setting prices. Formal price-setting cooperation is called **collusion**, and it is illegal in the United States and many other countries. However, firms may still cooperate informally by being careful not to drop prices enough to start a price war.

In Japan and elsewhere, organizations may participate in powerful cooperative alliances called **keiretsu**. These alliances are composed of manufacturers, suppliers, and finance companies who often own stock in each other. Although keiretsu are often accused of collusion and other competition reducing actions, they also lead to greater efficiency for keiretsu members.

Organizations may form alliances with rivals in an effort to influence common stakeholders such as government agencies, activist groups, unions, or local communities. These alliances then become a part of the organization's **political strategy**, which includes all organizational activities that have as one of their objectives the creation of a friendlier political climate for the organization. Lobbying is part of a political strategy, but it is only a small part of the bigger political picture. Collective activity may include membership in trade associations, chambers of commerce, and industry and labor panels. Firms join associations to gain access to information and to obtain legitimacy, acceptance, and influence.[20] Finally, many organizations form alliances directly with government agencies and officials to pursue a wide variety of objectives, including basic research, finding answers to social problems, and establishing trade policies.

Although this section has focused primarily on stakeholders that are likely to be high priority, such as customers, suppliers, competitors, and government agencies and administrators, partnerships with some of the other stakeholders listed in Table 2.2 have brought equally impressive results. For example, the New England Electric System (NEES) utility formed a partnership with the Conservation Law Foundation, a New England–based environmental organization, to deal with conservation, load management, and regulatory and rate adjustments. As a result of this collaboration, it is estimated that one third of the planned power plants in the region will not have to be built until the year 2010, releasing this capital for other uses. New England Electric saved capital and the Conservation Law Foundation

Stakeholders	Traditional Management Tactics	Partnering Tactics
Customers	Customer service departments Marketing research Advertising On-site visits 800 numbers Long-term contracts Product/service development Market development	Customer involvement on design teams Customer involvement in product testing Joint planning sessions Enhanced communication linkages Joint training/service programs Sharing of facilities Financial investments in customer Appointments to board of directors
Suppliers	Purchasing departments Encourage competition among suppliers Sponsor new suppliers Threat of vertical integration Long-term contracts	Supplier involvement on design teams Integration of ordering system with manufacturing (i.e., just-in-time inventory) Shared information systems Joint development of new products Coordinated quality control (i.e., TQM) Simultaneous production Appointments to board of directors
Competitors	Competing on the basis of product and service differentiation, technological advances, innovation, speed, price cutting, market segmentation Intelligent systems Corporate spying and espionage*	Keiretsu* Joint ventures for R&D or market development Collective lobbying efforts Informal price leadership or collusion* Industry panels to deal with labor or other problems Mergers (horizontal integration)
Government Agencies- Administrators	Legal departments Tax departments Government relations departments Lobbying/political action committees Campaign contributions Self-regulation Personal gifts to politicians*	Consortia on international trade and competitiveness Joint or government sponsored research Joint ventures to work on social problems Joint foreign development projects Panels on product safety Appointment of retired government officials to the board of directors

Table 2.2 *Examples of Tactics for Managing and Partnering with External Stakeholders*

helped reduce, among other things, air pollution and respiratory problems in the affected areas. It was a win-win situation.[21]

Unions are also being treated as partners instead of adversaries in some of the companies that have had the greatest success with programs such as self-managed work teams. For example, since 1982 Xerox has implemented three teamwork programs with its 6,200 copier assemblers, represented by the Amalgamated Clothing and Textile Workers Union (ACTWU). The efforts have worked so well that Xerox is now bringing 300 jobs from abroad to a new home plant in Utica, where it expects to save $2 million a year. Xerox shares internal financial documents with union leaders and provides the unions with executive development through use of the company's own managers. CEO Paul Allair commented on the success of these programs: "I don't want to say we need unions if that means the old, adversarial kind. But if we have a cooperative model, the union movement will be sustained and the industries it's in will be more competitive."[22]

Stakeholders	Traditional Management Tactics	Partnering Tactics
Local Communities- Governments	Community relations offices Public relations advertising Involvement in community service/politics Local purchases of supplies/local employment Donations to local government organizations Donations to local charities Gifts to local government officials*	Task force to solve skilled-labor shortages Joint urban renewal programs Cooperative training programs Development committees/boards Employment programs for workers with special needs, such as the handicapped Joint education programs
Activist Groups	Internal programs to satisfy demands Public/political relations efforts to offset or protect them from negative publicity Financial donations	Consultation with members on sensitive issues Joint ventures for research/research consortia Appointment of group representatives to board Jointly sponsored public relations efforts
Unions	Avoid unions through high levels of employee satisfaction Avoid unions by thwarting attempts to organize Hiring of professional negotiators Public relations advertising Chapter XI protection	Mutually satisfactory (win-win) labor contracts Contract clauses that link pay to performance (i.e., profit sharing) Joint committees on safety and other issues Joint employee development programs Joint industry/labor panels Labor leaders appointed to board of directors and included in major decisions
Financial Intermediaries	Financial reports Close correspondence Finance and accounting departments High-level financial officer Audits	Inclusion in decisions requiring financial backing Contracts and linkages with other clients of the financial intermediary Appointments to the board of directors Shared ownership of new projects

*These tactics are of questionable ethical acceptability to some internal and external stakeholders in the United States and elsewhere.

Source: Adapted from J. S. Harrison and C. H. St. John, "Managing and Partnering with External Stakeholders, *Adacemy of Management Executive* (May 1996), 53. Used with permission.

Table 2.2 (continued) *Examples of Tactics for Managing and Partnering with External Stakeholders*

KEY POINTS SUMMARY

This chapter dealt with the external environment, which consists of the broad and task environments. The following are key points from this discussion:

1. The most important elements in the broad environment, as it relates to a business organization and its task environment, are sociocultural forces, global economic forces, technological forces, and global political/legal forces. Organizations use a variety of techniques, including brainstorming, scenario development, surveys, and expert opinion to forecast changes in this environment.

2. One important distinction between the task and broad environments is that the task environment is subject to a high level of organizational influence, whereas the broad environment is not.

3. The task environment includes external stakeholders such as customers, suppliers, competitors, government agencies and administrators, local communities, activist groups, unions, and financial intermediaries.

4. The five primary forces that determine the nature and level of competition in an industry include the strength of customers, the strength of suppliers, the availability of substitutes, the strength of entry barriers, and forces that determine the nature of existing competition.

5. Organizations should use partnering tactics to manage external stakeholders that have a large influence on the environmental uncertainty facing the organization, but they should do so without threatening their own core competencies. On the other hand, traditional monitoring techniques can be used to anticipate the needs of lower-priority stakeholders.

6. Important partnering tactics include joint ventures and other forms of strategic alliances, the establishment of mutually beneficial contracts, various forms of stakeholder involvement in organizational processes and decisions, and the development of political alliances to promote a favorable task environment.

REFERENCES

1. General Motors, *Environmental Report*, 1995.

2. F. Rice, "Denny's Changes Its Spots," *Fortune* (May 13, 1996): 133–134.

3. D. J. Gaiter, "How Shoney's, Belted by a Lawsuit, Found the Path to Diversity," The *Wall Street Journal*, April 16, 1996, A1, A6.

4. D. R. Dalton, M. B. Metzger, and J. W. Hill, "The 'New' U.S. Sentencing Commission Guidelines: A Wake-up Call for Corporate America," *Academy of Management Executive* (February 1994); 7–16.

5. R. A. Melcher, "Europe, Too, Is Edgy about Imports—From America," *Business Week* (January 27, 1992): 48–49.

6. S. A. Waddock, "Building Successful Social Partnerships," *Sloan Management Review* (Summer 1988): 18.

7. J. Vleggaar, "The Dutch Go Back to School for R&D," The *Journal of Business Strategy* (March/April, 1991): 8.

8. A. Reifenberg, "Caspian Pact May Bolster Chevron Effort," *The Wall Street Journal*, March 11, 1996, A3, A6.

9. J. J. Fialka, "Israel Asks White House to Place Curbs on 3 U.S. Satellite-Surveillance Firms," *The Wall Street Journal*, June 17, 1996, A2.

10. "Business and Finance," *The Wall Street Journal*, June 27, 1996, A1.

11. G. Hector, "A New Reason You Can't Get a Loan," *Fortune* (September 21, 1992): 107–112.

12. M. E. Porter, *Competitive Strategy: Techniques for Analyzing Industries and Companies* (New York: The Free Press, 1980); see also D. F. Jennings and J. R. Lumpkin, "Insights between Environmental Scanning Activities and Porter's Generic Strategies: An Empirical Analysis," *Journal of Management*, 18 (1982): 791–803.

13. This section on competitive forces draws heavily on the pioneering work of Michael Porter. See Porter, *Competitive Strategy*, 1–33.

14. "Retail," *Orlando Sentinel*, February 1, 1996, C1.

15. J. S. Bain, *Barriers to New Competition* (Cambridge, Mass.: Harvard University Press, 1956); H. M. Mann, "Seller Concentration, Barriers to Entry and Rates of Return in Thirty Industries, 1950–1960," *Review of Economics and Statistics* 48 (1966): 296–307.

16. Porter, *Competitive Strategy*, 23.

17. R. M. Kantar, "The New Managerial Work," *Harvard Business Review* (November/December 1989): 85–92.

18. F. R. Bleakley, "Some Companies Let Suppliers Work on Site and Even Place Orders," *The Wall Street Journal*, January 13, 1995, A1, A6.

19. A good review of this literature is found in J. Hagedoorn, "Understanding the Rationale of Strategic Technology Partnering: Interorganizational Modes of Cooperation and Sectoral Differences," *Strategic Management Journal* 14 (1993): 371–385; see also E. R. Auster, "International Corporate Linkages: Dynamic Forms in Changing Environments," *Columbia Journal of World Business* 22 (1987): 3–13; K. R. Harrigan, "Joint Ventures and Competitive Strategy," *Strategic Management Journal* 9 (1988): 141–158.

20. W. R. Scott, *Organizations: Rational, Natural, and Open Systems*, 3rd ed (Englewood Cliffs, N.J.: Prentice Hall, 1992).

21. T. A. Hemphill, "Strange Bedfellows Cozy Up for a Clean Environment," *Business and Society Review* (Summer 1990): 38–45.

22. A. Bernstein, "Why America Needs Unions But Not the Kind It Has Now," *Business Week* (May 23, 1994): 70–82.

APPENDIX 2

Strategic Groups

In some industries, groups of competitors are constrained by similar resource positions and follow similar strategies. The groups or clusters of similar competitors are called **strategic groups**. For example, in the steel industry, domestic steel companies are of two general types: integrated continuous mills and minimills. Traditionally, the two groups of competitors faced very different cost structures and competed in largely different market segments. In recent years, the integrated mills have invested in minimill technology and the minimill firms have developed new technologies to enter previously inaccessible market segments. Over time, the resource positions and strategies are converging, and the sharp differences between strategic groups are eroding.

One way to keep track of strategic groups and their behavior over time is with the use of a strategic group map such as the one in Figure 2A.1 on the next page. A **strategic group map** is constructed by plotting industry rivals based on two or more strategic dimensions that are important to an industry's strategy. The axes of a strategic group map should describe strategy and not performance. Therefore, variables such as pricing strategy, customer service approach, level of advertising, and product mix are appropriate, whereas return-on-assets and earnings-per-share, variables are not. Furthermore, to reveal more about the industry, the dimensions should not be highly correlated with one another. Members of the same strategic group should end up in the same general location on the map.

Strategic group maps can help an organization understand the strategies of competitors. They may also highlight an area in the industry in which no firms are presently competing (an opportunity). Another helpful use is in tracking the evolution of an industry over time. If movement from one group to another is difficult, then it is likely that mobility barriers exist. Mobility barriers are similar to entry barriers, but they exist between strategic groups within one industry.

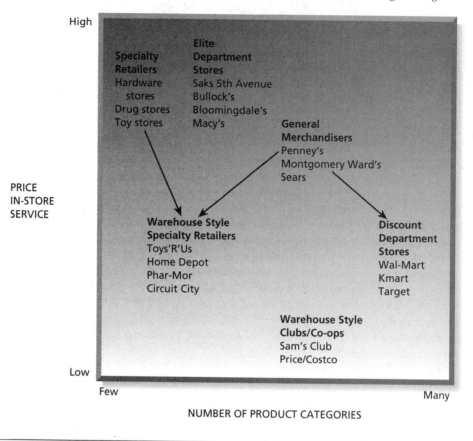

Figure 2A.1 *Strategic Group Map of Department Store and Specialty Retailing*

chapter 3

The Internal Environment
and Strategic Direction

Compaq Computer

Compaq Computer CEO Eckhard Pfeiffer has convinced his employees that they can dominate the world of computing. Under the leadership of this perfectionist, Compaq has proved itself a master of what may be the most critical task of business in the Nineties: doing everything fast. Since 1991, when the board ousted co-founder Rod Canion and put Pfeiffer in the driver's seat, annual revenues have nearly quadrupled, from $3.3 billion to $14.8 billion. Pfeiffer sets outsized goals and meets them. In late 1993 he said he wanted Compaq to be the leading PC maker in the world by 1996 (at the time it was third). Compaq got there in 1994.

Now Pfeiffer is giving his charges even more audacious targets. He wants Compaq to own at least twice as much share as its nearest competitor in every market it enters. He wants Compaq to become one of the top three computer companies in the world. In 1996 it was fifth, behind IBM, Fujitsu, Hewlett-Packard and NEC.[1]

In this chapter we turn our attention inside the organization: to the organization's resources and the managers who are responsible for developing those resources into capabilities and sources of competitive advantage. A manager such as Eckhard Pfeiffer can have a profound influence on the way internal resources are used to build sustainable competitive advantages. The most successful organizations typically have excellent resources and managers and, like Compaq, have a strong sense of direction. We will first discuss how internal resources and managers contribute to the strategic competitiveness of organizations and then we will describe the tools organizations use to develop and communicate strategic direction.

THE INTERNAL ENVIRONMENT

Internal stakeholders include managers, employees, and owners, which in public corporations are represented by a board of directors. One of the most significant internal stakeholders is the chief executive officer (CEO). Most of the research indicates that CEOs have a significant impact on the strategies and performance of their organizations.[2] Certainly, CEOs like Michael D. Eisner at Disney, Bill Gates at Microsoft, or Andy Grove at Intel leave little doubt that much of an organization's success depends on the person at the top.

The Chief Executive Officer

The highest ranking officer in a large organization can be called by a number of titles, but the most common is **chief executive officer**, or CEO. The CEO has the primary responsibility of setting the strategic direction of the firm, although larger organizations are typically led by several high-ranking officers, such as chief operating officers and vice presidents, who form the **top management team**.

Top executives and managers perform a variety of functions both inside and outside of their organizations. Based on in-depth observations of managers at work, strategy scholar Henry Mintzberg concluded that these functions include serving as a figurehead, spokesperson, leader, resource allocator, monitor, liaison with outside groups, disseminator of information to internal stakeholders, disturbance handler, entrepreneur, and negotiator.[3] Most of these functions deal specifically with managing stakeholders.

The CEO's most important responsibility is to exercise strategic leadership, which encompasses many of the functions Mintzberg identified. The traditional view of leaders in organizations is that they set direction, make the important decisions, and rally the followers (usually employees). According to Peter Senge, a professor at MIT, this traditional view is particularly common in the West where leaders are often equated with heroes.[4] There are many examples of visionary decision makers throughout political and business history. Lee Iaccoca of Chrysler; Steven Jobs, the founding CEO of Apple Computer; Bill Gates of Microsoft; and Ross Perot of Electronic Data Systems are just a few of the CEOs who are widely viewed as visionary leaders. It is common for organizations to incorporate stories about their great leaders in the myths and rituals that form the organizational culture.[5]

In the traditional model of leadership, the CEO decides where to go and then, through a combination of persuasion and edict, directs others in the process of implementation.[6] For many organizational scholars, the traditional view of the CEO and upper management as brilliant, charismatic leaders with employees who are "good soldiers" is no longer valid in many organizational settings. Turbulent global competitive environments and multibusiness organizations are far too complex for one person to stay on top of all the important issues.

Many organizational scholars believe that the true role of the CEO is to harness the creative energy of individual employees, so that the organization as a whole learns over time.[7] In this capacity, the CEO has four primary responsibilities. First, he or she must create or design the organization's purpose, vision, and core values. Second, the CEO must oversee the creation of policies, strategies, and structure that translate purpose, vision, and core values into business decisions. These first two responsibilities are consistent with what we expect of organizational leaders: they establish direction and purpose and then install the management systems that coordinate decisions and actions.

It is with the third responsibility of leadership that a new role begins to emerge. Rather than directing, the CEO should create an environment for organizational learning by serving as a coach, teacher, and facilitator.[8] The CEO creates this learning environment by helping organizational members question their assumptions about the business and its environment: what customers want, what competitors are likely to do, which technology choices work best, and how to solve a problem. For learning to take place, members must understand that the organization is an interdependent network of people and activities. Furthermore, learning requires that members keep their work focused on creating patterns of behavior that are consistent with strategy rather than reacting haphazardly to problems. Leaders play the essential role in creating an environment where employees question assumptions, understand interdependency, see the strategic significance of their actions, and are empowered to lead themselves.[9]

Finally, CEOs and other managers must serve as stewards for their organizations: they must care about the organization and the society in which it operates. Organizational leaders must feel and convey a passion for the organization, its contribution to society, and its purpose. They should feel that "they are part of changing the way businesses operate, not from a vague philanthropic urge, but from a conviction that their efforts will produce more productive organizations, capable of achieving higher levels of organization success and personal satisfaction than more traditional organizations."[10] This concept is best illustrated with a statement made by Stanley Gault shortly after he took over the struggling Goodyear Tire and Rubber Company:

People would say, "Why would you undertake this challenge?" Well, frankly, the decision was 98% emotional because Goodyear is the last major American-owned tire company . . . Therefore, I decided that I was willing to change my life for three years if there was any way I could lead the charge to rebuild Goodyear.[11]

An ongoing debate questions whether it is appropriate to try to match particular manager attributes to the type of strategy the firm is pursuing.[12] Some research suggests that strategies focused on cost reduction are best implemented by managers with production/operations backgrounds because of the internal focus on efficiency and engineering. The research also suggests that strategies focused on developing differences that customers will value need to be managed by marketing and R&D-trained executives because of the innovation and market awareness that are needed.[13] Also, some tentative evidence suggests that strategic change or innovation in organizations is more likely to occur under the leadership of managers who are younger (both in age and in time in the organization) but well educated.[14] Growth strategies may be best implemented by managers with greater sales and marketing experience, willingness to take risks, and tolerance for ambiguity. However, those same characteristics may be undesirable in an executive managing the activities of a retrenchment strategy.[15] Finally, when radical restructuring is required, a less biased outsider may be needed.[16] Unfortunately, until additional research confirms or disproves these various findings, adherence to these prescriptions may be risky.

Boards of Directors and Agency Costs

Most larger companies, as well as smaller companies needing funds for growth, have issued stock. Therefore, their owners are the shareholders. If all of the stock is owned by a few individuals, often within the same family, the company is referred to as closely held or private. On the other hand, in larger, publicly owned companies, the interests of shareholders are protected by a board of directors that has been elected by the voting shareholders. The board of directors is responsible for hiring, firing, supervising, advising, and compensating top managers within the firm. Boards typically also reserve the right to reject major strategic decisions, such as the development of a new line of business, mergers, acquisitions, or entrance into foreign markets.

One of the major strategic issues with regard to boards of directors is the role they play in monitoring potential conflicts of interest. As soon as ownership and management are separated, as is the case in most public organizations, the potential for conflicts of interest exists. Top managers become **agents** for the owners of the firm—they have a fiduciary duty to act in the owners' best interests. On occasion, top managers, as human beings, attempt to maximize their own self-interests at the expense of shareholders. When this occurs it is called an **agency problem.**[17] Some examples of agency problems are shown in Table 3.1.

One responsibility of boards is to monitor and prevent the potential for agency problems. For example, boards need sufficient power both to monitor and to discipline CEOs. Vigilant boards are widely regarded as the best defense against conflicts of interest.[18] Even so, some business experts believe that many boards are negligent in their fiduciary duties associated with reprimanding or replacing top managers who are not acting in the best interests of shareholders, and they point to increasing incidence of shareholder suits against boards of directors as evidence of that concern.[19] In addition, big investors are putting lots of pressure on board members and directly on CEOs to initiate sweeping organizational changes that will lead to more accountability and higher performance.[20]

Many boards have responded to these and other forces by taking a more active role in corporate governance. Some years ago, John G. Smale, past CEO of Procter & Gamble and a ten-year veteran of General Motors' board of directors, was dissatisfied with GM's lackluster performance. He convinced other board members to elect him to the position of chairman of the executive committee, which effectively put him in control of GM. In what is now called a board revolt, he initiated the replacement of the CEO, which set GM on a new strategic course.[21] The GM board coup was followed by a wave of similar actions in several large companies, including IBM, Time Warner, American Express, and Westinghouse.[22]

The inclusion of several nonemployees (outsiders) on the board can help ensure that shareholder interests are well served. Outsiders were an important factor in the board revolt at GM. In fact, research indicates that the percentage of outsiders on the board of directors is increasing.[23] However, the inclusion of outsiders may not be a potent force in reducing agency problems if external board

The following are a few commonly mentioned problems that may be evidence of agency conflicts:

High Salaries
It is in the best interests of CEOs to draw a high salary; however, these high salaries reduce the amount of earnings available to the shareholders. CEO compensation packages for the largest U.S. companies typically reach into the millions of dollars annually.

Current Expenses versus Future Investments
Since research and development expenditures reduce current earnings and often do not provide financial benefits for many years, CEOs who are compensated based on profitability levels have a built-in incentive not to approve research projects.

Status and Growth
 Some power-hungry or status-conscious top managers may expand the size of their empires at the expense of organizational shareholders. For example, a few years ago Harding Lawrence led Braniff Airways to financial ruin through overzealous growth.

CEO Duality
CEO duality means that the CEO is also the chair of the board of directors. As chair, the CEO is in a strong position to ensure that personal interests are served even if the other stakeholders' interests are not.

Table 3.1 *Evidence of Agency Problems*

members are personal friends of the CEO or other top managers. These types of relationships often limit the objectivity of outsiders.

The previous discussion demonstrated the importance of boards of directors in governing the behavior of top managers. However, boards can also play other important strategic roles, such as playing a part in deciding an organization's strategic direction and in forming strategic alliances. Two recent studies, in fact, discovered higher performance in companies with boards that participated more actively in organizational decisions than in companies with "caretaker" boards.[24] For example, **interlocking directorates** can lead to a more active board and important strategic alliances. Interlocking directorates occur when the CEO of one company sits on the board of another company, which is a common practice in many countries, especially Japan (i.e., keiretsu). Although it is typically illegal in the United States to have the CEO of a direct competitor on the board (e.g., Coca-Cola could not include the CEO of Pepsi on its board), firms often include suppliers or customers. Such links as these can facilitate contract negotiations and the transfer of information and technology.

Employees and Culture

Employees and the way they are managed can be important sources of competitive advantage. The Council on Competitiveness determined that well-trained employees will be a key to the future competitiveness of U.S. companies but discovered that training programs in the United States are inadequate.[25] These trends make the effective management of employees critical to strategic success.

In general, research has shown that more sophisticated human resource planning, recruitment, and selection strategies are associated with higher labor productivity, especially in capital-intensive organizations.[26] Also, a large-sample study of nearly one thousand firms indicated that "High Performance Work Practices" are associated with lower turnover, higher productivity, and higher long- and short-term financial performance.[27]

An organization's culture, the system of shared values that guides employees, is another important component of the internal environment. An organization's culture often reflects the values and leadership styles of the executives and managers and results, to a great degree, from past human resource management practices, such as recruitment, training, and rewards.

An organization's culture can be its greatest strength or its greatest weakness. Some organizations have succeeded in creating cultures that are completely consistent with what the organization is trying to accomplish—high-performance cultures. At Nucor Steel, the company's stated commitment to a low-cost strategy is supported by a culture that expects efficiency and tight fiscal policy. At Johnson & Johnson, the company's commitment to customers as its primary stakeholder is reflected in policy statements and adopted by employees. In other organizations, poor morale and a cynical attitude toward customers often undermines organizational performance.

The first three sections of this chapter have described the human side of the internal environment. CEOs, other managers, the board of directors, employees and the culture that ties these people together can all be sources of strength or weakness to an organization. The next section is a broader discussion of organizational resources in general and, specifically, how resources and resource management can lead to a sustainable competitive advantage.

Internal Resources and Competitive Advantage

The resources and capabilities that lead to a competitive advantage differ in each industry and can also change over time. For example, researchers discovered that high-performing film studios during the period from 1936 to 1950 possessed superior property-based resources, such as exclusive long-term contracts with stars and theaters. However, during the period from 1951 to 1965 knowledge-based resources in the form of production and coordinative talent and budgets were associated with high performance. Researchers attributed these findings to the capabilities needed to deal with increasing uncertainty in the film industry.[28] Their study also demonstrates that organizational resources only result in a competitive advantage if they are uniquely valuable in the external environment. Chapter 1 introduced the concept of competitive advantage from uniquely valuable resources. We now continue the discussion.

Uniquely Valuable Resources. Chapter 1 described internal resources and capabilities as falling into four general categories: financial, physical, human, and organizational. In general, capabilities and resources become strengths leading to a *competitive advantage* if three conditions are met:

1. *The resources and capabilities are valuable.* They allow the firm to exploit opportunities or neutralize threats. For example, Sony has developed the capability to design, manufacture and sell miniaturized electronics. This capability has value to external stakeholders—namely customers. Sony has applied this capability to numerous market opportunities such as stereos, tape players, compact disc players, televisions, and video cameras.

2. *The resources and capabilities are unique.* If an organization is the only one with a particular capability, then that capability may be the source of competitive advantage. If numerous organizations possess a particular resource or capability, then the situation is described as one with competitive parity—no company has the advantage. Note that uniqueness does not imply that only one organization possesses a capability or resource—only that few firms do.

3. *The resources and capabilities are hard to imitate.* Competing firms face a cost disadvantage in imitating a resource or capability. The more difficult or costly a resource or capability is, the more valuable it is in producing a sustainable competitive advantage. In the case of a patent or a trademark, competing firms face an absolute cost disadvantage.[29]

Figure 3.1 demonstrates how resources and capabilities become potential sources of sustainable competitive advantage. McDonald's, for example, has outperformed its competitors for many years because of superior locations (a physical resource) and a highly efficient operations system that delivers a consistent product at low cost (an organizational resource).

For a firm to realize an advantage from unique and valuable resources, the firm must also be organized to take advantage of them. For example, Xerox formed a research laboratory called PARC which, in the late 1960s and 1970s, developed an amazing assortment of technological innovations, including the personal computer, the computer mouse device, the laser printer, and Windows-type software. However, the company did not take advantage of many of PARC's innovations because it did not have an organization in place to do so. For instance, poor communications prevented most Xerox managers from knowing what PARC was doing, and a highly bureaucratic system mired a lot of the innovations in red tape.

If a resource or capability is valuable, unique, hard to imitate, *and* it also can be applied to more than one business area, it is called a **core competence** or **distinctive competence**.[30] Companies like Wal-Mart and Disney are masters at exploiting their sources of competitive advantage across different businesses. Disney has extended its unique and valuable animated characters through books, movies, theme parks, and television, showing a distinctive competence in creativity and "imagineering."

Most of the resources and capabilities that have been described are tangible. They can be seen, touched, or quantified.[31] However, some of the most important resources are hard to quantify. For many firms, the key to competitive advantage is to combine resources and develop capabilities that are hard to imitate. For example, a patent, which is tangible, may provide an organization with an advantage for a while. But the capability to develop and introduce new products quickly and accurately involves integrating the efforts of several resources: marketing (determining need), design and development engineers (creating the product, specifying raw materials), operations (arranging for raw materials and producing the product), and many others. These integrated resources and capabilities are particularly difficult for competitors to observe and imitate.

Other examples of intangible resources and capabilities are positive relationships with external stakeholders, a good organizational reputation, and a well-known corporate brand. John Reed, CEO of Citicorp, would like to turn Citibank into "a worldwide consumer brand," establishing it, in effect, as the Coca-Cola or

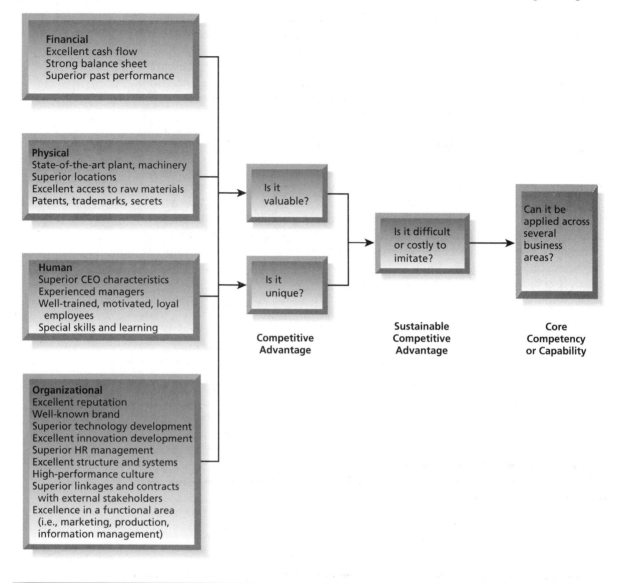

Figure 3.1 *Organizational Resources and Capabilities Leading to Competitive Advantage*

McDonald's of financial services. What goes with the brand equity that those companies have, and that he covets, is the ability to set themselves above the competition, either by the prices they can obtain, by the quantities sold, or both.[32] Disney also takes full advantage of its brand, which is one of its core competencies. According to Michael Eisner, CEO:

> We are fundamentally an operating company, operating the Disney Brand all over the world, maintaining it, improving it, promoting and advertising it with taste. Our time must be spent insuring that the Brand never slides, that we innovate the Brand, nurture the Brand, experiment and play with it, but never diminish it. Others will try to change it, from outside and from within. We must resist. We are not a fad! The Disney name and products survive fads![33]

Financial Resources. Financial resources also can be a source of advantage, although they rarely qualify as unique or difficult to imitate. Nevertheless, strong cash flow, low levels of debt, a strong credit rating, access to low-interest capital, and a reputation for creditworthiness are powerful strengths that can serve as sources of strategic flexibility. Firms that are in a strong financial position can be more responsive to new opportunities and new threats and are under less pressure from stakeholders than their competitors who suffer financial constraints. Financial analysis, a tool for evaluating the financial resources of a firm and their fit with the organization's strategy, is discussed in Table 3.2.

Assessing Internal Strengths and Weaknesses

In evaluating the resources and capabilities of the organization, it is important to consider all of the various activities of the business and to understand the role they play in building advantage and implementing strategies. Strategy should be based on what the organization does well relative to competitors *or* on the capabilities or resources the firm *wants to develop* that will create a competitive advantage in the future. Organizational constraints should be considered but should not place absolute limits on strategy. Instead, long-term organizational success often depends on developing new competencies.

Value Chain Analysis. Michael Porter developed a framework, called the value chain, which allows systematic study of the various value-adding activities of a business (see Figure 3.2 on p. 50).[34] Value chain analysis may be used to identify key resources and processes that represent strengths, areas that need improvement, and opportunities to develop a competitive advantage.

The **value chain** divides organizational processes into distinct activities that create value for the customer. The primary activities include inbound logistics, operations, outbound logistics, marketing and sales, and service. **Inbound logistics** includes activities associated with acquiring inputs that are used in the product, such as warehousing, materials handling, and inventory control. **Operations** refers to transforming inputs into the final product through activities such as machining, assembly, molding, testing, and printing. **Outbound logistics** are activities related to storing and physically distributing the final product to customers, such as finished goods warehousing, order processing, and transportation. **Marketing and sales** include processes through which customers can purchase the product and through which they are induced to do so, such as advertising, the distribution of catalogs, direct sales, distribution channeling, promotion, and pricing. Finally, **service** refers to providing services that will enhance or maintain product value, such as repairing, supplying parts, or providing installation.

Organizations also engage in activities that support these primary functions. These activities are placed above the primary activities in Figure 3.2. **Procurement** refers to the actual purchase of inputs and not to the inputs themselves or to the way they are handled once they are delivered. All of the primary processes need purchased inputs, many of which are not raw materials. Examples of these inputs include typewriters, accounting firm services, and computers. **Technology development** refers to learning processes that result in improvements in the way organizational functions are performed.

Human resource management includes human-based activities such as recruiting, hiring, training, and compensation. Finally, **administration** consists of general management activities such as planning and accounting. The dotted lines connecting most of the support activities with the primary activities demonstrate that they can be associated with each of the primary activities as well as support

Financial analysis is used to indicate the ability of the firm to finance growth. For example, managers of a firm that has very high leverage (long-term debt) may have to be less ambitious in their strategies for taking advantage of opportunities. On the other hand, an organization with a strong balance sheet is well poised to pursue a wide range of opportunities. Strong financial resources are often hard to imitate in the short term.

Financial analysis is also an important strategic tool that managers use to assess performance and identify strengths, weaknesses, and trends. In general, financial analysis involves making two essential comparisons: (1) a comparison of the firm to its competitors, to determine relative financial strengths and weaknesses, and (2) a comparison of the firm to itself over time, to show trends.

Competitor Comparisons. Firms often attempt to compare their expenses, investments, sources of income, and resulting profitability to competitors as a way of assessing the success of their strategies. A firm may observe that competitors are making more aggressive investments in R&D or paying higher wages to employees, which may heighten competitive intensity in the future. The findings from a competitor comparison must always be weighed against the goals of the firm. For example, a firm's investment in inventories may be higher than that of competitors for one of three reasons: (1) the firm is not as effective at managing inventories as competitors, which would be a cause for concern; (2) higher levels of inventories support the firm's particular strategy (e.g., fast delivery and guaranteed availability); or (3) the items in inventory or accounting conventions are different, making a meaningless "apples and oranges" comparison.

Organization Trends. Firms regularly track their own expenses and sources of income over time as a way of identifying trends. Poor financial trends are sometimes symptoms of greater problems. For example, a firm may discover that administrative costs are increasing at a faster rate than sales. This could indicate diseconomies of scale or the need for tighter controls on overhead costs, or, on the contrary, part of the firm's deliberate attempt to position itself now for future sales growth. The most common ratios used in financial analysis are as follows on the next page:

Table 3.2 *Analyzing Financial Resources*

---

the complete chain. Administration is the only exception, since it applies to the complete chain instead of to any one unit. Margin, which is on the right-hand side of the Figure 3.2, indicates that firms can achieve higher profit margins through the development of competencies and superior resources based on their value chain activities.

An organization can develop a competitive advantage (1) in any of the primary or support activities, (2) in the way they are combined or (3) in the way internal activities are linked to the external environment. The cumulative effect of value chain activities and the way they are linked inside the firm and with the external environment determine organizational strengths, weaknesses, and performance relative to competitors.

Functional Analysis. A thorough profile of the strengths and weaknesses of the major value-adding activities requires in-depth study of the specific actions, resources, and capabilities at the functional level. For example, an evaluation of marketing's value-adding performance and potential would consider the number and type of target customers, product positioning, product line mix, product line breadth, pricing strategies, promotion practices, and distribution channels. Each aspect would be characterized as a strength or weakness, then it would be evaluated for its fit with current and future strategic plans. By identifying the specific strengths and weaknesses within each category of value-adding activities, an

Ratio	Calculation	What It Measures
Profitability Ratios		
Gross profit margin	$\dfrac{\text{Sales} - \text{COGS}}{\text{Sales}} \times 100$	Efficiency of operations and product pricing
Net profit margin	$\dfrac{\text{Net profit after tax}}{\text{Sales}} \times 100$	Efficiency after all expenses are considered
Return on assets (ROA)	$\dfrac{\text{Net profit after tax}}{\text{Total assets}} \times 100$	Productivity of assets
Return on equity (ROE)	$\dfrac{\text{Net profit after tax}}{\text{Stockholders' equity}} \times 100$	Earnings power of equity
Liquidity Ratios		
Current ratio	$\dfrac{\text{Current assets}}{\text{Current liabilities}}$	Short-run debt-paying ability
Quick ratio	$\dfrac{\text{Current assets} - \text{inventories}}{\text{Current liabilities}}$	Short-term liquidity
Leverage Ratios		
Debt to equity	$\dfrac{\text{Total liabilities}}{\text{Stockholders' equity}}$	The relative amount of debt and equity financing (common measure of financial risk)
Total debt to total assets (debt ratio)	$\dfrac{\text{Total liabilities}}{\text{Total assets}}$	Percentage of assets financed through borrowing (also a common risk measure)
Activity Ratios		
Asset turnover	$\dfrac{\text{Sales}}{\text{Total assets}}$	Efficiency of asset utilization
Inventory turnover	$\dfrac{\text{COGS}}{\text{Average inventory}}$	Management's ability to control investment in inventory
Average collection period	$\dfrac{\text{Receivables} \times 365 \text{ days}}{\text{Annual credit sales}}$	Effectiveness of collection and credit policies
Accounts receivable turnover	$\dfrac{\text{Annual credit sales}}{\text{Receivables}}$	Effectiveness of collection and and credit policies

Table 3.2 (continued) *Analyzing Financial Resources*

organization can develop plans for correcting or avoiding weaknesses and for cultivating and building strengths. A detailed framework for profiling organizational strengths and weaknesses is shown in the case analysis appendix.

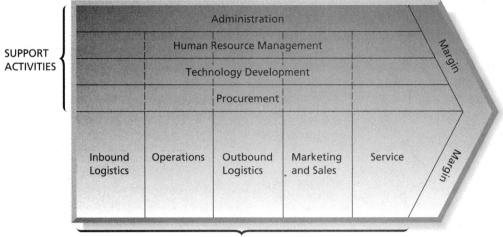

Source: Adapted from Michael E. Porter, *Competitive Advantage: Creating and Sustaining Superior Performance*, (New York: The Free Press, 1985), 37. Adapted with permission of The Free Press, a division of Simon & Schuster. Copyright © 1985 by Michael E. Porter.

Figure 3.2 *The Value Chain Including Support Activities*

We have concluded our discussion of organizational resources and capabilities, value creation and competitive advantage, and processes for assessing strengths and weaknesses. We now turn our attention to a discussion of strategic direction.

ESTABLISHMENT OF STRATEGIC DIRECTION

High-performing companies tend to have an organizational identity that both internal and external stakeholders understand. On the inside, a well-established organizational identity can guide managers at all levels as they make strategic decisions.[35] In addition, communicating strategic direction to external stakeholders can increase their understanding of the motives of the organization's management and may also facilitate the creation of alliances, since potential alliance partners have a greater ability to judge the existence of common goals. Strategic direction is established and communicated through tools such as missions, visions, business definitions, and enterprise strategies. Strategic direction also includes a general orientation toward growth.

Organizational Mission

An organization's mission, whether written down or just apparent from the organization's pattern of decisions and actions over time, provides an important vehicle for communicating ideals and a sense of direction and purpose to internal and external stakeholders. It also can help guide organizational managers in making resource allocation decisions. Sometimes students of strategic management confuse the terms *mission* and *vision*. In general, an organizational mission is what the organization is and its reason for existing, whereas a vision is a forward-looking

view of what the organization wants to become. However, when mission statements are written down, a vision statement is often included or embedded in the
formal mission statement. In fact, a formal written mission statement often
includes many or all of the elements of strategic direction: vision, business definition, enterprise strategy, and goals. Consequently, a mission is a catchall statement of organizational purpose.

Organizations often prepare written mission statements as a way of communicating with the public. For example, mission statements are frequently included
in annual financial reports to shareholders. Table 3.3 contains the mission statement for Rhone Poulenc Rorer, a global pharmaceutical organization that resulted
from the 1990 merger of Rhone Poulenc and Rorer. On the other hand, some missions are never written down, even in the most successful companies. In these situations the organization's purpose is made clear through its actions or through
other, less formal statements, often by the CEO. For example, Walt Disney does
not have a formal mission statement. However, the organization's actions over
time as well as the statements made by Michael Eisner and those found in a recent
annual report (reproduced in Table 3.4) make Disney's mission very clear.

Business Definition

Derek Abell has argued that clear business definition is the starting point of all
strategic planning and management.[36] A clear business definition provides a
framework for evaluating the effects of planned change and for planning the steps
needed to move the organization forward.

When defining the business, the question "What is our business?" should be
answered from three perspectives: (1) Who is being satisfied? (2) What is being
satisfied? (3) How are customer needs satisfied?[37] The first question refers to the
markets that the organization serves, the second question deals with the specific
functions provided to the customers identified in question 1, and the third question refers to the **resource conversion processes and capabilities** that the firm

---

Our Mission is to become the BEST pharmaceutical company in the world by dedicating
our resources, our talents and our energies to help improve human health and the quality
of life of people throughout the world.

Being the best means:
• Being the BEST at satisfying the needs of everyone we serve: Patients, healthcare profes-
  sionals, employees, communities, governments and shareholders;
• Being BETTER AND FASTER than our competitors at discovering and bringing to market
  important new medications in selected therapeutic areas;
• Operating with the HIGHEST professional and ethical standards in all our activities,
  building on the Rhone-Poulenc and Rorer heritage of integrity;
• Being seen as the BEST place to work, attracting and retaining talented people at all
  levels by creating an environment that encourages them to develop their potential to the
  fullest,
• Generating consistently BETTER results than our competitors, through innovation and a
  total commitment to quality in everything we do.

Source: Annual report.

Table 3.3 *Sample Mission Statement of Rhone Poulenc Rorer*

Although Walt Disney Company does not have a formal written mission statement, these statements from Michael Eisner, CEO, make Disney's purpose very clear. They are found at the beginning of one of Disney Company's recent annual reports.

Our goal is to increase wealth for our shareholders. We must do this while never forgetting the value of our Brand, never forgetting our responsibility to our cast members, never forgetting the communities in which we serve and never forgetting the high quality standards of our work. We must always operate in an ethical way and never take the expedient or slippery path.

Our goal is to increase creative productivity through superior work. We will build upon our conviction that doing it better pays off, that short cuts lead to short earnings and that setting the highest standards drives the highest results. The rush to mediocrity, the rush to short-term results, and the acceptance of the lowest common entertainment denominator do not work for us. We believe in always striving for excellence. We believe we have an obligation to carry on the Disney tradition.

We must concentrate on continuing to lead creatively. We must throw out mediocrity. Our only criteria for our products should be excellence and fiscal viability. We must not commit to anything that is cheap and average or expensive and average. *Average is awful.* We must, however, not commit to any venture, no matter how great, unless the project can promise a good fiscal return.

Our strategic direction is quality and innovation. We know our audience, and predominantly it is a family audience. We should not lament that others appeal more strongly to the disenfranchised teenage audience. They always come back when they become re-enfranchised adults with children.

Source: Walt Disney Company, *1995 Annual Report*, 6–7.

Table 3.4 *Disney's "Unwritten" Mission*

uses to provide the functions identified in question 2. In actuality, most mission statements also identify specific **products or services** provided by the organization. In this regard, a fourth question, which is an extension of the third question, can be stated: "What are our products and services?" This approach is, admittedly, marketing oriented. Its greatest strength is that it focuses on the customer, a very important external stakeholder for most firms.

The **scope** of an organization is the breadth of its activities across markets, functions, resource conversion processes, and products. Some large organizations, such as PepsiCo and Nestle, have a very broad scope. Other firms, including L.L. Bean and Nucor, have a narrower scope. Also, firms such as McDonald's are very broad on one dimension (markets served) but narrow on all the rest.

Table 3.5 contains three examples of firms and their business definitions, organized around the four areas of a business definition—products and services, markets, functions served, and resource conversion processes (Church and Dwight is the 150-year old manufacturer of Arm & Hammer baking soda). Notice that the concepts discussed thus far apply equally well to both product and service firms.

Organizational Vision

Peter Drucker suggested that the business definition question should be stated not only as "What is our business?" but also as "What will it be?" and "What should it be?"[38] The second question refers to the direction that the organization is heading at the current time. In other words, where will the organization end up if it

	Church & Dwight	Toys 'R' Us	Delta Airlines
Products and Services	Baking soda and related consumer products	Toys and clothing for children	Air transportation
Markets	Grocery stores and bakeries	Children, grandparents, and parents	Business travelers, vacationers, and infrequent travelers
Functions Served	Odor absorbency, baking, cleaning	Availability, entertainment, clothing	Fast, long-distance transportation
Resource Conversion Processes	Chemical processing-packaging, promotion, and advertising	Buying, inventory management, distributing, limited service, promotion, and advertising	Flying, logistics, fleet management, baggage handling, reservations, promotion, and advertising

Table 3.5 *Business Definitions of Well-Known Companies*

continues in its current course? The third question, "What should it be?" allows the existing strategy to be modified in order to move the organization in an appropriate direction.

Unlike a mission, which addresses an organization's purpose at the present time, an organization's vision is very future oriented. An organization with a vision has a clear sense of what it wants to be in the future. For example, Bill Gates has a clear vision of how he expects his industry to evolve and the role he wants to play in it. He wants Microsoft to dominate the software systems that link all digital transactions and communications in business, entertainment, and leisure. That vision, which involves a very different business definition for the future, provides the framework for creating new businesses and forming new partnerships.

For many years, Wal-Mart's vision was to become the largest discount retailer in the United States, a vision that was achieved shortly before Sam Walton's death. In the case of Wal-Mart, the organizational vision did not require a departure from the existing business definition, although it did require continued growth along the "markets served" dimension as the company entered new regions. More importantly, Sam Walton and Wal-Mart illustrate how a well-articulated vision of what the company wants to be in the future can be a strong motivational tool. Once it is stated, it may be used to focus the efforts of the entire organization.[39] For example, plans, policies, or programs that are inconsistent with the corporate vision may need to be altered or replaced. A well-understood vision can help managers and employees believe that their actions have meaning. As we will discuss in later chapters, organizations develop specific goals, objectives, and action plans to focus their efforts on those areas that fit the business vision.

Enterprise Strategy and Ethics

One fundamental question an organization should ask in determining its purpose is "What do we stand for?" This question is the critical link between ethics and strategy. **Enterprise strategy** is the term used to denote the joining of ethical and strategic thinking about the organization.[40] It is the organization's best possible reason (assuming there is a reason) for the actions it takes. An enterprise strategy can contain statements concerning a desire to maximize stockholder value, satisfy the interests of all or a subset of other stakeholders, or increase social harmony or the common good of society.[41] For example, in the mission statement of Rhone Poulenc Rorer (Table 3.3), the enterprise strategy is to "help improve human health and the quality of life of people throughout the world." Some researchers have found that organizational mission statements containing elements of an enterprise strategy are more likely to be found in high-performing corporations than in low-performing corporations.[42]

Enterprise strategy is a natural extension of the ethics of the organization, which are an extension of the values of key managers. The ethics of an organization are not just a matter of public statements. Ethical decision making is a way of doing business. An organization that specifically works to build ethics into its business practice, to develop and implement an enterprise strategy, will have a frame of reference for handling potential ethical problems.

Many organizations create a code of ethics to communicate the values of the corporation to employees and other stakeholders. For example, the code of ethics of United Technologies states the following:

Our code of ethics, comprised of corporate principles and standards of conduct, governs our business decisions and actions. The integrity, reputation, and profitability of United Technologies ultimately depend upon the individual actions of our employees, representatives, agents and consultants all over the world. Each employee is personally responsible and accountable for compliance with our code.[43]

The United Technologies code of ethics, which is quite long, addresses specific standards of conduct the organization will exhibit in its dealings with customers, suppliers, employees, shareholders, competitors, and worldwide communities. Employees are encouraged to report violations to their supervisors or the vice president for business practices. Clearly, a company like United Technologies expects members to maintain standards of ethical behavior that transcend minimum legal standards. To ensure that employees abide by the corporate code of ethics, some companies establish an ethics system, including an audit process to monitor compliance.

KEY POINTS SUMMARY

This chapter described internal stakeholders and the important roles they play in strategic management processes, followed by a discussion of strategic direction. The following are some of the chapter's most important points:

1. The chief executive officer (CEO) is the primary orchestrator of organizational vision and strategies. CEOs perform interpersonal, informational, and decisional functions in organizations and influence the organization through their personal values and styles of strategic leadership.

2. Owners in a for-profit, publicly held corporation, the shareholders, are typically represented by a board of directors, which is responsible for

overseeing the activities of organizational managers and ensuring that shareholder interests are protected.

3. Agency problems can exist when boards of directors are weak in carrying out their supervisory responsibilities, when CEOs also serve as chairs of their own boards (e.g., CEO duality), or any time CEOs of other managers act in their own personal interests at the expense of shareholders.

4. Organizations need highly qualified employees if they are going to succeed in the global economy. Training and other human resource management activities are crucial to long-term competitiveness.

5. Other tangible resources that can lead to a competitive advantage include superior financial resources, excellent physical resources, and organizational resources such as excellent management systems and structures. Intangibles such as brands, business relationships, culture, and reputation are harder to quantify but are some of the most important sources of competitive advantage.

6. For each potential resource or capability, the following questions should be asked: "Is it valuable?" "Is it unique?" "Is it difficult or expensive for competitors to imitate?" Finally, for potential sources of competitive advantage to become real, firms should be organized in such a manner that the full potential is realized.

7. The value chain may be used to determine the strengths and weaknesses of the different value-adding activities of the business and to indentify sources of competitive advantage.

8. A mission often contains statements concerning the organization's basic purposes and broad goals, as reflected in its enterprise strategy, a vision of what it can become, and a definition of its business or businesses.

REFERENCES

1. D. Kirkpatrick, "At Compaq," *Fortune* (April 1, 1996): 121–122.

2. S. Finkelstein and D. C. Hambrick, *Strategic Leadership: Top Executives and Their Effects on Organizations* (Minneapolis: West Publishing Company, 1996): Chapter 2.

3. H. Mintzberg, *The Nature of Managerial Work* (New York: Harper and Row, 1973).

4. P. M. Senge, "The Leader's New Work: Building Learning Organizations," *Sloan Management Review* 32 no. 1, (Fall 1990): 7–24.

5. E. H. Schein, *Organization Culture and Leadership* (San Francisco: Jossey-Bass, 1985).

6. P. Nutt, "Selecting Tactics to Implement Strategic Plans," *Strategic Management Journal* 10 (1989):145–161.

7. Senge, "The Leader's New Work"; C. C. Manz and H. P. Sims, "SuperLeadership," *Organization Dynamics* 17 no. 4 (1991): 8–36.

8. Senge, "The Leader's New Work."

9. Senge, "The Leader's New Work"; Manz and Sims, "SuperLeadership."

10. Senge, "The Leader's New Work," 13.

11. J. M. Graves, "Leaders of Corporate Change," *Fortune* (December 14, 1992); 104–114..

12. J. G. Michel and D. C. Hambrick, "Diversification Posture and Top Management Team Characteristics," *Academy of Management Journal* 35 (1992): 9–37; S. F. Slater, "The Influence of Style on Business Unit Performance," *Journal of Management* 15 (1989): 441–455; A. S. Thomas, R. J. Litschert, and K. Ramaswamy, "The Performance Impact of Strategy-Manager Coalignment: An Empirical Examination," *Strategic Management Journal* 12 (1991): 509–522.

13. V. Govindarajan, "Implementing Competitive Strategies at the Business Unit Level: Implications of Matching Managers to Strategies, *Strategic Management Journal* 10 (1989): 251–269.

14. K. A. Bantel and S. E. Jackson, "Top Management and Innovations in Banking: Does the Composition of the Top Team Make a Difference?" *Strategic Management Journal* 10 (1989): 107–124; C. M. Grimm and K. G. Smith, "Management and Organizational Change: A Note on the Railroad Industry," *Strategic Management Journal* 12 (1991): 557–562; M. F. Wiersema and K. A. Bantel, "Top Management Team Demography and Corporate Strategic Change," *Academy of Management Journal* 35 (1992): 91–121.

15. A. K. Gupta and V. Govindarajan, "Business Unit Strategy, Managerial Characteristics, and Business Unit Effectiveness at Strategy Implementation," *Academy of Management Journal*, 27 (1984): 25–41.

16. B. Brenner, "Tough Times, Tough Bosses: Corporate America Calls in a New, Cold-Eyed Breed of CEO," *Business Week* (November 25, 1991): 174–180.

17. S. Weisbach, "Outside Directors and CEO Turnover," *Journal of Financial Economics* 20 (1988): 431–460.

18. E. F. Fama and M. C. Jensen, "Separation of Ownership and Control," *Journal of Law and Economics* 26 (1983): 301–325.

19. I. F. Kesner and R. B. Johnson, "Crisis in the Boardroom: Fact and Fiction," *Academy of Management Executive* (February 1990): 23–35.

20. M. Magnet, "Directors, Wake Up!" *Fortune* (June 15, 1992): 86–92.

21. A. Taylor III, "The Road Ahead at General Motors," *Fortune* (May 4, 1992): 94–95; J. B. Treece, "The Board Revolt," *Business Week* (April 20, 1992): 31–36.

22. J. A. Byrne, "Requiem for Yesterday's CEO," *Business Week* (February 15, 1993): 32–33; C. J. Loomis and D. Kirkpatrick, "The Hunt for Mr. X: Who Can Run IBM?" *Fortune* (February 22, 1993): 68–72; A. A. Morrison, "After the Coup at Time Warner," *Fortune* (March 23, 1992): 82–90.

23. I. F. Kesner, B. Victor, and B. T. Lamont, "Board Composition and the Commission of Illegal Acts: An Investigation of Fortune 500 Companies," *Academy of Management Journal* 29 (1986): 789–799; I. B. Kesner and R. B. Johnson, "An Investigation of the Relationship between Board Composition and Shareholder Suits," *Strategic Management Journal* 11 (1990): 327–336.

24. W. Q. Judge, Jr., and C. P. Zeithaml, "Institutional and Strategic Choice Perspectives on Board Involvement in the Strategic Decision Process," *Academy of Management Journal* 35 (1992): 766–794; J. A. Pearce II and Shaker A. Zahra, "The Relative Power of CEOs and Boards of Directors: Associations with Corporate Performance," *Strategic Management Journal* 12 (1991): 135–153.

25. "Analysis of U.S. Competitiveness Problems," In *America's Competitive Crisis: Confronting a New Reality* a report by the Council on Competitiveness (April 1987): 121–126.

26. M. J. Koch and R. G. McGrath, "Improving Labor Productivity: Human Resource Management Policies Do Matter," *Strategic Management Journal* 17 (1996): 335–354.

27. M. A. Huselid, "The Impact of Human Resource Management Practices on Turnover, Productivity and Corporate Financial Performance," *Academy of Management Journal* 38 (1995): 635–672.

28. D. Miller and J. Shamsie, "The Resource-Based View of the Firm in Two Environments: The Hollywood Film Studios from 1936 to 1965," *Academy of Management Journal* 39 (1996): 519–543.

29. J. B. Barney, "Looking Inside for Competitive Advantage," *Academy of Management Executive* (November 1995): 49–61.

30. Barney, "Looking Inside for Competitive Advantage."

31. M. A. Hitt, R. D. Ireland, and R. E. Hoskisson, *Strategic Management: Competitiveness and Globalization* (Minneapolis: West Publishing Company, 1995): 73.

32. C. L. Loomis, " Citicorp: John Reed's Second Act," *Fortune* (April 29, 1996): 90.

33. Walt Disney Company, *1995 Annual Report*, 6–7.

34. M. E. Porter, *Competitive Advantage: Creating and Sustaining Superior Performance* (New York: The Free Press, 1985), Chapter 2.

35. L. J. Bourgeois, "Performance and Consensus," *Strategic Management Journal* 1 (1980): 227–248; G. G. Dess, "Consensus on Strategy Formulation and Organizational Performance: Competitors in a Fragmented Industry," *Strategic Management Journal* 8 (1987): 259–277; L. G. Hrebiniak and C. C. Snow, "Top Management Agreement and Organizational Performance," *Human Relations* 35 (1982): 1139–1158.

36. D. F. Abell, *Defining the Business: The Starting Point of Strategic Planning* (Englewood Cliffs, N.J.: Prentice Hall, 1980), 169.

37. Ibid.

38. P. F. Drucker, *Management—Tasks, Responsibilities, Practices* (New York: Harper and Row, 1974): 74–94.

39. D. J. Isenberg, "The Tactics of Strategic Opportunism," *Harvard Business Review* (March/April 1987): 92–97.

40. L. T. Hosmer, "Strategic Planning as if Ethics Mattered," *Strategic Management Journal* 15 (1994): 17–34; D. Schendel and C. Hofer, *Strategic Management: A New View of Business Policy and Planning* (Boston: Little, Brown, 1979).

41. R. E. Freeman and D. R. Gilbert, Jr., *Corporate Strategy and the Search for Ethics* (Englewood Cliffs, N.J.: Prentice Hall, 1988).

42. J. A. Pearce, II, and F. David, "Corporate Mission Statements: The Bottom Line," *Academy of Management Executive* (May 1987): 109–115.

43. *Code of Ethics*, United Technologies, 1991.

4

Business Strategy

Pep Boys

P ep Boys wants to annihilate other auto parts retailers. When intense competition from Pep Boys forces chains like Auto Zone, Western Auto, or Genuine Parts to abandon a location, CEO Mitchell Leibovitz adds a snapshot of the closed-down store to his collection. He burns and buries baseball caps bearing their corporate logos and videotapes the ritual to show his 14,500 employees. "I don't believe in friendly competition," he says. "I want to put them out of business."

Pep Boys participates in the $125-billion-a-year after-market for automobile parts and servicing. Alone among its major competitors, Pep Boys can install what it sells. Nearly all its stores have ten or so service bays that keep long hours. They stay open 13 hours a day Monday through Sunday, no appointment needed. To curb the overcharging and superfluous repairs that are endemic in auto service, Leibovitz mixes sticks with carrots. Mechanics get a percentage of their labor charge, but—contrary to common practice—no share of the price of the parts they install. If work has to be done over, they may forfeit their cut. Customers can register complaints and compliments through an 800 "squeal" number and postage-paid feedback cards that Leibovitz reads himself. Says Leibovitz: "The service business is hard to manage. But if it were easy, everyone would do it."[1]

Business-level strategy defines an organization's approach to growth and competition in its chosen markets. Pep Boy's competitive strategy can be described as a combination of low-cost leadership and differentiation, an increasingly popular combination called "best cost." Pep Boys achieves low cost through high volume and a massive distribution network. However, Pep Boys also differentiates its service in the eyes of the consumer through an innovative pricing policy, a huge supply of hard-to-get parts, convenient hours, and an 800 number.

Some of the major strategic management responsibilities of business-level managers are listed in Table 4.1. They include establishing the overall direction of the business unit, performing an ongoing analysis of the changing business situation, selecting strategies for growth and for competitive positioning, and then managing resources to produce a sustainable competitive advantage. These responsibilities and the methods for carrying them out are similar in for-profit and nonprofit organizations.[2] They also apply well to organizations that are oriented toward services, as the Pep Boys example illustrates. This chapter focuses on selecting specific business-level strategies and developing distinctive competencies that lead to competitive advantages.

Within single business firms, and within each business unit of multibusiness firms, managers must decide how to position the business to achieve its growth and profit targets. Business managers develop two categories of strategies: growth strategies and competitive strategies. **Growth strategies** are concerned with

Table 4.1 *Major Business-Level Strategic Management Responsibilities*

Major Responsibilities	Key Issues
Direction setting	Establishment and communication of mission, vision, ethics, and long-term goals of a single business unit.
	Creation and communication of shorter term goals and objectives
Analysis of business situation	Compilation and assessment of information from stakeholders and other sources
	Identification of strengths, weaknesses, opportunities, threats, sources of sustainable competitive advantage
Selection of strategy	Determination of growth strategy—internal strategies, external strategies, and level of aggressiveness
	Selection of a generic approach to competition—cost leadership, differentiation, focus, or best cost
	Selection of a strategic posture—specific strategies needed to carry out the generic strategy
Management of resources	Acquisition of resources or development of competencies leading to a sustainable competitive advantage
	Development of functional strategies and an appropriate management structure to support business strategy

increasing the size and viability of the business over time. In planning growth strategies, managers are concerned with answering three key questions: (1) Where do we allocate resources within our business in order to achieve growth?, (2) What changes in business scope do we see as compatible with growth and overall strategic direction? and (3) How do we *time* our growth moves compared to competitors? **Competitive strategies**, on the other hand, are concerned with how the firm intends to position itself to create value for its customers in ways that are different from those of competitors. Strategies that involve the organization in new industries and new businesses are called corporate strategies. Corporate strategies are the subject of the next chapter.

GROWTH STRATEGIES

In designing growth strategies for a single business, managers must decide where to allocate resources and how to alter the scope (products, markets, functions served, and resource conversion activities) of the business if, indeed, the scope should be altered at all. In general, single businesses may choose to pursue growth through internal or external investment or to stabilize their growth through restricted investment. Internal growth, external growth, and stability strategies, as well as their implications for resource allocations and business scope, are the topics of the next three sections. All of these approaches are outlined in Table 4.2.

Internal Growth Strategies

By investing its resources (i.e., time, money, and people) internally, a business can pursue market penetration, market development, or product/service development. **Market penetration** entails investing in advertising, capacity expansion or the sales force with the intent of increasing market share in the current business. This strategy requires no changes in the scope of the organization. On the other hand, **market development**, in which the organization seeks new market segments, or **applications development**, which involves creating new applications for products, both require a broadened definition of the markets or functions served. To support market development, firms may need to invest in market research, new marketing approaches, and a new sales force. In applications development, firms will invest in market research, product testing and qualifications, and new market strategies. For example, a nylon fabric manufacturer who sells fabric to windsuit manufacturers would likely have to invest in market and applications development in order to sell nylon fabric to tent or sleeping bag manufacturers.

Firms pursuing **product/service development** seek to *modify* existing products or *develop* new products or services for the purpose of selling more to existing customers or creating new market segments. In addition to changes in the scope of products or services, this type of development may require expanded definitions in markets, functions served, or the resource conversion process. Resource allocations focus on product/service development, applications development, basic research and development, and perhaps process development or market development, depending on the nature of new or modified products or services. For example, pharmaceutical companies continuously invest in new and improved products. For the treatment of colon cancer, Johnson & Johnson manufactures an effective drug that started out as a sheep wormer sold through veterinarians! Through product and applications development, the drug now serves a

Internal Growth Options
1. Market Penetration
   - Tactic: Increase market share in current business through advertising, promotions, stepped-up sales effort
   - Change in scope: None
2. Market Development
   - Tactic: Identify new market segments or new applications for products/services.
   - Change in scope: Broaden definition of markets or functions served by products/services
3. Product/Services Development
   - Tactic: Modify existing products/services or develop new products/ services for existing or potential customers
   - Change in scope: Definite change in products/services; possible changes in markets, functions served, or resource conversion processes

External Growth Options
1. Horizontal Integration
   - Tactic: Purchase company in same line of business
   - Change in scope: Extend market base; may also include other changes, depending on the company acquired
2. Strategic Alliances
   - Tactic: Create alliances with other organizations to achieve market position, product development, or process development
   - Change in scope: Extend products/services, markets, and functions served or alter resource conversion process

No-Growth or Slow-Growth Option
1. Stability
   - Tactic: Maintain the status quo (some firms may pursue this strategy temporarily during restructuring)
   - Change in scope: None

Table 4.2 *Growth Strategy and the Scope of the Business*

very different function and a completely different customer group. Consequently, the types of customers served and the functions served by a particular company's product or service line may change over time.

Virtually all business organizations follow internal growth strategies of some type. In general, market penetration strategies are successful in the early stage of an organization's life cycle when many customers are untapped. However, with growth and success, the organization must cast a wider net to find more customers and to sustain growth. At that point, organizations usually begin more aggressive investments in market development and product development to broaden their appeal to more and more customers. To fuel growth and supplement their products and markets, some businesses look outside of the organization for investment opportunities and ideas. These external growth strategies are the subject of the next section.

External Growth Strategies

External growth strategies involve investing organizational resources in another company or business to achieve growth targets, and these strategies include horizontal integration and joint ventures or alliances. As with internal growth strategies, external growth strategies involve an allocation of resources and have implications for the scope of the single business or business unit.

Horizontal integration involves the acquisition of an organization in the same line of business. Typically, horizontal integration is accomplished for the purpose of gaining market share in a particular market, expanding a market geographically, or augmenting product or service lines. It involves acquisition of the capability, market segments, or products lines, rather than developing these resources internally. This was the motivation behind Delta Airlines' acquisition of Western Airlines. However, the products or services of the firm that is purchased may be different enough to require a broader definition of products or services, functions served, or the resource conversion process. Horizontal integration is particularly common in industries that are undergoing consolidation, where new product and market opportunities are scarce and growth must come by taking a share of a competitor's market.

The second external mechanism for achieving growth within a single business or business unit is through joint ventures or strategic alliances formed with other organizations to penetrate new domestic or foreign markets, develop new products and services, or improve existing processes for producing products and services. Formal contractual joint ventures, as well as less formal strategic alliances, are common in situations in which individual competing firms believe they are lacking a skill, technology, or capability that is needed to develop new products or markets. For example, a joint venture between General Motors and Toyota led to the Geo. Also, Corningware cookware was developed through a joint venture between Corning Glass Works and Dow Chemical. The company is now known as Dow-Corning.

Ventures that penetrate new markets require a broadening of the market definition, whereas ventures to develop new products or services require changes to the products or services and perhaps to their functions also. Finally, ventures that seek to improve processes probably require changes in the resource conversion process.

The external growth strategies may involve a significant investment in or acquisition of another firm, and may involve creation of a new business division or business unit. Acquisitions and changes in organizational structure are usually managed at the corporate level, even if the intention is to grow an individual business. Therefore, we will return to a discussion of mergers and acquisitions in Chapter 5 "Corporate Strategy."

Stability Strategies

Though most for-profit organizations actively seek growth, some organizations do not. They may be family-owned businesses, nonprofit organizations that are satisfied with the current level of operations, or simply business organizations that are content with their share of a mature market. Organizations such as these do not take any overt actions to achieve growth. For them, the prevalent theme of operations is "business as usual." These types of organizations maintain fairly level investments in marketing, operations, and services and only engage in enough R&D to maintain their share of the market.

Although this strategy may seem passive, in many situations it is perfectly logical and an appropriate use of investment funds. Many situations exist in which investing for the objective of growth is ineffective. For instance, a firm may find itself in a mature, declining, or rigidly segmented market in which efforts to increase sales would cost more than they are worth. This situation is typical of industries with low profits, no growth, and high **exit barriers**. Exit barriers exist when the capital equipment and skills an organization possesses are not applicable to other businesses.[3] For example, the plants and equipment used by steel companies have almost no potential for other uses. Consequently, many steel companies are barely able to survive against the more successful minimill firms, but they do not close down because their entire investment would be lost.

Timing of Growth Strategies

A key issue in planning growth strategies is to determine their timing relative to competitors. Based on field studies in four industries, Raymond Miles and Charles Snow classified firms into one of four categories based on the rate at which they changed their products and markets.[4] **Prospectors** pursue what could be termed an offensive strategy. They aggressively seek new market opportunities and are willing to take risks. **Defenders**, on the other hand, are turf protectors that engage in little or no new product/market development. Their strategic actions are intended to preserve market share by reducing the impact of offensive moves by competitors. **Analyzers** occupy a position in between prospectors and defenders. They attempt to maintain positions in existing markets while waiting to see what happens when a competitor introduces a new product or enters a new market. They then follow the competitor when the opportunity and the parameters for success are clearer. **Reactors** do not have a distinct strategy. They simply react to environmental situations.

The Miles and Snow classifications illustrate two fundamentally different positions with respect to growth. Prospectors aggressively pursue growth, whereas defenders tend to pursue stability. Analyzers pursue growth in areas that show substantial promise, usually after others have made an initial entry. In planning growth strategies, it is important to identify not only 'what should be done, but *when* it should be done as well. We will now turn our attention to a discussion of competitive strategies.

GENERIC COMPETITIVE STRATEGIES

In addition to planning the resource allocations necessary for growth, managers must select a general approach to the market. Growth and competitive strategies are tightly linked: only through successful competitive strategies will an organization have the fuel necessary to make the growth strategies successful.

The strategies used for products and services are as different as the organizations that create them. However, classifying competitive strategies into generic types helps firms identify common strategic characteristics. In general, according to Michael Porter, firms seek a competitive advantage by offering either (1) products or services that differ from those of competitors in ways that are valued by customers or (2) products or services that are standard but are produced at lower cost.[5] Porter combined these two bases for competitive advantage with the scope of the market in which a firm competes to form the generic strategies of cost leadership, differentiation, and focus. Focus is further divided into cost focus and differentiation focus, because a firm can focus on a particular segment of the market through either low-cost leadership or differentiation. These divisions are illustrated in Figure 4.1.

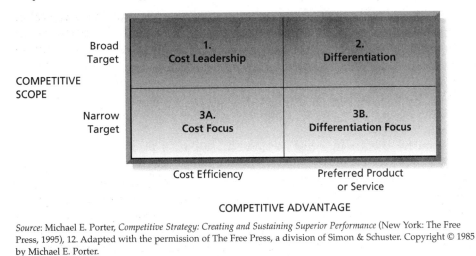

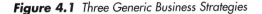

COMPETITIVE ADVANTAGE

Source: Michael E. Porter, *Competitive Strategy: Creating and Sustaining Superior Performance* (New York: The Free Press, 1995), 12. Adapted with the permission of The Free Press, a division of Simon & Schuster. Copyright © 1985 by Michael E. Porter.

Figure 4.1 *Three Generic Business Strategies*

Since Porter's original work describing the generic strategies, increasing global competition has made a hybrid strategy increasingly popular. In this book, we refer to it as "best cost," which means that an organization pursues both cost leadership and differentiation simultaneously. We now describe these generic strategies in detail.

Cost Leadership

Firms pursuing cost leadership set out to become the lowest-cost providers of a good or service. The broad scope of cost leaders means that they attempt to serve a large percentage of the total market. Firms pursuing cost leadership include McDonald's and Panasonic.

To fully appreciate the significance of the low-cost-producer strategy, it is important to understand the factors that underlie cost structures in firms. Firms pursuing a low-cost-producer strategy typically employ one or more of the following factors to create their low-cost positions: (1) accurate demand forecasting combined with high-capacity utilization, (2) economies of scale, (3) technological advances, or (4) learning/experience effects.[6]

High-Capacity Utilization. When demand is high and production capacity is fully utilized, a firm's fixed costs are spread over more units, which lowers unit costs. However, when demand falls off, the fixed costs are spread over fewer units so that unit costs increase. This basic concept suggests that a firm capable of maintaining higher levels of **capacity utilization**—either through better demand forecasting, conservative capacity expansion policies, or aggressive pricing—will be able to maintain a lower cost structure than a competitor of equal size and capability.

Economies of Scale. The second major factor with the potential to lead to cost advantages is **economies of scale**. Economies of scale are often confused with increases in the "throughput" of a manufacturing plant or other facility. As described earlier, increases in capacity utilization that spread fixed expenses can lead to lower unit costs. However, true economies of scale are associated with *size* rather than capacity utilization. The central principle of economies of scale is that in some industries production costs per unit are less in a large facility than in a small facility. For example, the cost of constructing a 200,000-unit facility will not necessarily be twice the cost of building a 100,000-unit facility, so the initial fixed cost per unit of capacity will be lower for the larger facility.

Other scale economies are evident in many industries. Continuing with the previous example, the manager of the larger facility will not generally receive double the salary of the manager of the smaller facility. Also, activities such as quality control, purchasing, and warehousing typically do not require twice as much time or twice as many laborers. In addition, the purchasing manager of the larger facility may be able to negotiate better volume discounts on orders. In summary, the larger firm may be able to achieve per-unit savings in fixed costs, indirect labor costs, and materials costs. If per-unit costs are not lower in the larger plant, then the company has *not* achieved economies of scale. In fact, **diseconomies of scale** occur when a firm builds facilities that are so large that the sheer administrative costs and confusion associated with the added bureaucracy overwhelm any potential cost savings.

Technological Advances. Companies that make investments in cost-saving technologies are often trading an increase in fixed costs for a reduction in variable costs. If technological improvements result in lower total unit costs, then the firm has achieved a cost advantage from its investments, referred to as **economies of technology**. Although investments of this type are typically associated with the factory floor, it is just as common for investments to be made in office and service automation. For example, the automated distribution system at Wal-Mart, the automated ordering and warehouse system at Lands' End, and the reservation systems maintained by the major airlines all represent investments in technology that serve to lower overall costs and provide a degree of information and product control that was previously impossible.

Learning/Experience Effects. A final factor that influences cost structures is **learning effects**. You probably spent a long time registering for classes as a freshman. Now, as a veteran of several registrations, you know how to get through the process much faster. When an employee figures out through repetition how to do a job more efficiently, then learning is taking place. The learning curve effect says that the time required to complete a task will decrease as a predictable function of the number of times the task is repeated. In theory, the time required to complete the task will fall by the same percentage each time cumulative production doubles. For example, a firm might see a 10% reduction in the time required to manufacture its products between the first and second units of product, another 10% reduction between the second and fourth units, and another 10% reduction between the fourth and eighth units.

Clearly, dramatic time savings are achieved early in the life of a company. However, as the company matures, tangible cost savings from labor learning are harder to achieve because it takes longer to see a true doubling of cumulative volume. Also, learning effects do not just happen. They require a relatively labor-intensive process due to the fact that people learn but machines do not. Learning effects occur only when management creates an environment that is favorable to both learning and change and then rewards employees for their productivity improvements.

Experience effects are the same as learning effects but relate to indirect labor as well as direct production labor. For example, with experience a sales person becomes more efficient at identifying prospective clients and preparing sales presentations, and a purchasing manager becomes more efficient at negotiating supply agreements. In modern organizations, experience effects are even more important than direct labor learning effects, because direct labor often represents less than 15% of total product costs. Much of the middle management downsizing that we are seeing in industry today is an attempt to combine experience effects with economies of technology (networked computer systems) to achieve a higher level of organizational efficiency and effectiveness with fewer people.

Learning and experience effects can be described by a learning/experience curve, such as the one found in Figure 4.2.[7] Following from the logic of these two curves, the market share leader should enjoy a cost advantage relative to competitors because of the extra learning and experience that has occurred by producing the additional output. This concept has led many firms to fierce competitive pricing in an effort to obtain the highest market share and thus move right on the curve as far as possible. As the curve flattens, however, it becomes increasingly difficult to gain cost advantages from learning and experience effects. The same sort of phenomenon exists with respect to economies of scale.

Referenced Journals

Organizations that are able to achieve high-capacity utilization, economies of scale, economies of technology, or learning/experience effects may have the lowest cost, but they do not have to charge the lowest price. In other words, a *cost* leader does not have to be a *price* leader. If an organization is able to achieve the lowest cost while charging the same as competitors, it will still enjoy higher profits. However, if several customers switch to other brands and the loss of sales reduces capacity utilization, diminishes learning and experience effects, or undermines scale economies, this strategy could potentially lead to a loss of the lowest-cost position.

Several risks are associated with the low-cost strategy. First, firms pursuing cost leadership may not detect required product or marketing changes because of a preoccupation with cost. Second, these firms run the risk of making large investments in plants or equipment only to see them become obsolete because of technological breakthroughs by competitors. Their large investments make them reluctant to keep up with changes that are not compatible with their technologies.

Figure 4.2 A Typical Learning/Experience Curve

UNIT
COST

TOTAL CUMULATIVE OUTPUT

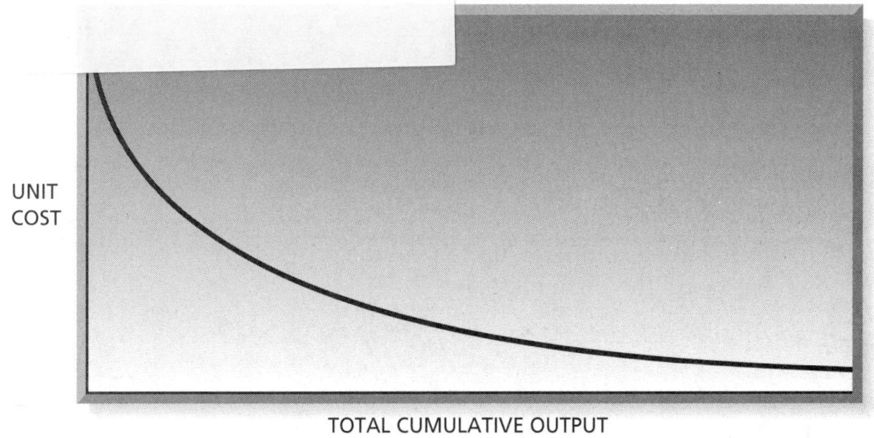

Third, efforts to seek low costs may just go too far. ValuJet's "penny-pinching" allowed it to achieve a very low cost position in the airline industry. ValuJet passed the savings on to consumers and experienced unprecedented growth. However, the airline's stinginess came under close scrutiny after the crash of ValuJet Flight 592 into the Florida Everglades. Federal investigators found some of ValuJet's procedures, especially maintenance procedures, unsafe and ultimately shut down the airline until safety concerns could be worked out.[8]

Differentiation

In differentiation strategies, the emphasis is on creating value through uniqueness, as opposed to lowest cost. Uniqueness can be achieved through product innovations, superior quality, superior service, creative advertising, better supplier relationships, or in many other ways. However, for a differentiation strategy to succeed, customers must be willing to pay more for the uniqueness of a product or service than the firm paid to create it. Competitive scope is still broad, which means that the differentiated product or service should be designed so that it has wide appeal to many market sectors. Examples of organizations that are pursuing differentiation strategies include Maytag through its highly reliable appliances, L.L. Bean through its mail-order services, BMW through its styling and performance, and Coca-Cola through its well-known brand name and reputation.

Firms pursuing differentiation strategies cannot ignore their cost positions. When costs are too high relative to competitors, a firm may not be able to recover enough of these additional costs through higher prices. Therefore, differentiators must attempt to reduce costs in the areas that are not directly related to the sources of differentiation. The only way a differentiation strategy will work is if buyers value the attributes that make a product unique enough to pay a higher price for it or choose to buy from that firm preferentially.

Consequently, the major risks associated with a differentiation strategy center on the difference between added costs and incremental price. One risk is that customers will sacrifice some of the features, services, or image possessed by a unique product or service because it costs too much. Another risk is that customers will no longer perceive an attribute as differentiating. For example, customers may come to a point at which they are so familiar with a product that brand image is no longer important.

Finally, imitation by competitors can eliminate perceived differentiation among products or services. This is what happened when a VCR manufacturer introduced the "HQ" (high quality) feature into VCRs. Within a few months, all VCRs had "HQ," thus eliminating any basis for higher prices based on the "HQ" feature. Rivalry in an industry can make it very difficult to sustain a competitive advantage from innovation for very long. For example, competitors are able to obtain detailed information on 70% of all new products within one year after development.[9] Consequently, staying ahead of the competition in product development requires *constant* innovation. As one business writer put it, "For outstanding performance, a company has to beat the competition. The trouble is the competition has heard the same message."[10]

Best Cost

Porter referred to firms that are not pursuing a distinct generic strategy as "stuck-in-the-middle."[11] According to Porter, these uncommitted firms should have lower performance than committed firms because they have no consistent basis for creating superior value and are not effective at implementing either strategy. He argued that firms that pursue one of the generic strategies exclusively perform better because they can center all of their resources on becoming good at that strategy.

However, in recent years, many firms have been successful at pursuing cost leadership and differentiation simultaneously. In some situations, the two strategies complement rather than detract from each other. It is well established that product quality and cost are complementary rather than conflicting strategies.[12] Furthermore, technological investments often allow firms to lower their costs while improving their performance on features that differentiate them in the eyes of customers, just as ATMs improve access and availability of teller services while driving down direct labor costs. Over time, the profits generated from the successful pursuit of one element of strategy (e.g., low cost) allow investment in other elements such as differentiating features.

Wal-Mart, for example, was successful at providing high-quality customer service in its industry at the lowest cost. A key part of Wal-Mart's strategy is a technologically advanced distribution system that allows the fast and efficient delivery of its products.[13] McDonald's seeks a low-cost position through its efficient, highly automated operations but also achieves the high levels of consistency over time that its customers value.

Some strategy scholars now argue that a combination of differentiation and low costs may be necessary to create a sustainable competitive advantage: "The immediate effect of differentiation will be to increase unit costs. However, if costs fall with increasing volume, the long-run effect may be to reduce unit costs."[14] Volume would be expected to increase because differentiation would make the product more attractive to the market. Then, as volume increases, costs will decrease. Jack Welch, CEO of General Electric, put it this way:

We're playing in a game where we'll show up and we'll be selling an engine against another engine competitor. Now, to get the deal, *you've got to have performance and all the other things*, but you'd better have low cost. And as you go around the world, and you want to sell turbines to developing countries, you'd better have a low cost base. Because in the end, you could have performance, you can have quality, but you'd better have cost [italics added].[15]

Anheuser-Busch has been very successful in creating brewing products that have a good image and high quality, yet the company is a cost leader due to efficiencies created by high-volume production, distribution, and advertising. Likewise, Kelloggs, best known for breakfast cereals, enjoys low-cost production due to economies of scale combined with higher prices made possible due to differentiation through advertising and new product development. Pep Boys, cited at the beginning of this chapter, is also pursuing a best-cost strategy.

The key to a best-cost strategy is simply supply and demand economics. For example, assume that three organizations manufacture hunting knives. The first firm pursues a low-cost strategy. It is able to produce a knife for $10 and sell 100,000 a year at $20, for a total profit of $1,000,000. The second firm uses a differentiation strategy. It produces a premium product with features that the market finds attractive. The premium product costs $40 to make, and the firm sells 50,000 at $60. The total profit is also $1 million, although the unit volume is half that of the low-price competitor. Both companies seem to be successful; however, they are each achieving success using a different generic strategy.

However, assume that a third company can create a very good knife, through a variety of product and process technological advances, for $20. Further suppose that this knife is almost as appealing as the product made by the second firm. If the firm can sell 75,000 at $50, the total profit will be more than $2 million and consumers will believe they are getting a great deal (saving $10). This is the essence of a best cost strategy—finding a level of differentiation that will bring a premium price while maintaining reasonable cost. Unlike a differentiation strategy in which the emphasis is on creating extra value or a low-cost strategy that stresses cutting costs, the best-cost strategy gives equal weight to both factors.

Focus

Focus strategies can be based on differentiation (differentiation focus) or lowest cost (cost focus). The key to a focus strategy is providing a product or service that caters to a particular segment in the market. A firm that is pursuing a focus strategy has to be able to identify its target market segment and both assess and meet the needs and desires of buyers in that segment better than any other competitor.

Cooper Tire and Rubber is an example of a company that pursues a cost focus strategy. Cooper is the only major tire company that does not sell tires to automobile manufacturers in the original equipment market (OEM). Instead, the company focuses on replacement tires. Cooper is very efficiency oriented: "Its low-rise corporate headquarters could pass for a 1950s suburban elementary school, right down to the linoleum floors and the flagpole out front. The annual report is printed in living black and white."[16] Cooper saves on R&D costs by copying the designs of OEM manufacturers instead of designing its own products. The cost focus strategy is so successful that Cooper provides the highest returns to its investors of any firm in the tire industry.

As another alternative, Japan Airlines (JAL) pursues a differentiation focus strategy by catering to wealthy passengers. For example, the airline has invested $95,000 each in luxury bathrooms for its first-class cabins on its routes between Tokyo and New York. According to a JAL spokesperson, "Especially on long-distance flights, the toilet is something that leaves a deep impression." The larger bathrooms will feature piped-in music, soft lighting, a three-sided mirror, a window, and faucets that stay on so that passengers can wash both hands at once. A first-class round-trip ticket from Tokyo to New York costs $9,300.[17]

The risks of pursuing a focus strategy depend on whether the strategy is cost focus or differentiation focus. The risks of each of these strategies are similar to the risks of the pure strategies themselves. However, the focus strategy has two risks that are not associated with the emphasis on low cost or differentiation. First, the desires of the narrow target market may become similar to the desires of the market as a whole, thus eliminating the advantage associated with focusing. Second, a competitor may be able to focus on an even more narrowly defined target and essentially outfocus the focuser.

A best-cost focus is another generic strategy that firms can pursue. However, this strategy is more difficult than a basic best-cost strategy because the narrow market focus means lower volume. At lower volume, it is hard to achieve low cost while still providing meaningful differentiation.

This completes our discussion of generic strategies. We have also devoted considerable attention to how to implement those strategies successfully. The final section examines how the product life cycle can be used in formulating and implementing business strategies.

CHANGES IN STRATEGY OVER TIME

The product life cycle describes the stages most products and industries evolve through from creation to maturation. Studying product life cycle concepts can help an organization's management understand the dynamic nature of strategy. As a product moves through the stages of the life cycle, different strategies and organizational resources are needed to compete effectively.

The **product life cycle** portrays how sales volume for a product changes over its lifetime. It is useful for managers involved in strategy formulation and implementation to understand the typical competitive and strategy changes that often accompany the different life cycle stages. As Figure 4.3 illustrates, demand for a product gradually builds during the **introduction stage**, as consumers come to understand the product and its uses. During the **growth stage**, demand greatly increases, which often attracts new competitors. Sales growth eventually begins to level off during the **maturity** stage of the life cycle. This slowing of growth can lead to a competitive "shake out," during which weaker producers retreat from the market, resulting in fewer competitors. During the **commodity** or **decline stage**, the demand curve can take many shapes. The traditional curve representing decline is labeled C in Figure 4.3. However, if the product becomes a commodity, which means that it is used in many other products or becomes a basic part of life for some consumers, demand may just level off, as in B, or may gradually increase over an extended time period, represented by A.[18]

Understanding the product life cycle not only helps management understand demand, but it can also help management to formulate strategies.[19] During the introduction stage, as demand for a product gradually builds, an organization's primary focus is on survival—producing the product at low enough cost and selling it at a high enough price so that the organization will be able to sustain operations and enter the next stage of the life cycle. The competitive environment at this stage is often turbulent. Often customer needs for the new product are not that well understood and new firms enter with different product versions and

Figure 4.3 The Product Life Cycle

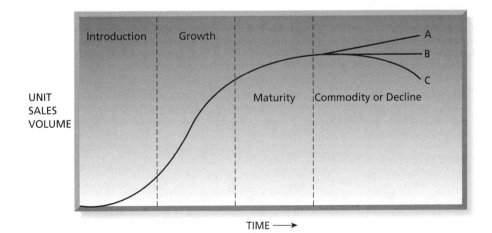

new methods. Because businesses often lose money during this stage, this is a difficult challenge.

In the introduction stage, firms also attempt to produce a product that is of sufficiently high quality that they will be able to establish a good reputation in the market. The emphasis is often on research and development. Early producers sometimes enjoy a "first-mover advantage," because of the experience they are gaining, the image they have the opportunity to build, and the opportunity they may have to create entry barriers, such as patents or exclusive distribution channels.[20] There is some evidence to support these ideas.[21] In fact, products sometimes come to be associated with early innovators, as in the case of Scott towels, Scotch tape, Linoleum floor coverings, and Xerox copy machines.

During the growth stage, as demand greatly expands and the number of competitors increases, existing competitors may attempt to erect entry barriers by building plants that are large enough to enjoy economies of scale, locking in contracts for supplies or product distribution, or differentiating products through advertising and new features or service. At this stage, products are much more standardized and competition tends to focus on product quality and availability. As growth begins to level off toward the end of the growth stage and as some firms fail to develop product characteristics that customers value or try to grow faster than their resources allow, a **competitive shakeout** usually occurs. Because market growth is no longer increasing, the weaker competitors discover that they can no longer generate enough sales or profits to sustain themselves. They sell off their assets, declare bankruptcy, or are acquired by stronger competitors.

During the maturity stage, as demand continues to level off, efficient, high-volume production tends to dominate the manufacturing strategy. A dominant design for the product has probably emerged; therefore, consumers typically focus on price and dependability. When an organization discovers a successful innovation, it is quickly incorporated into other firm's products. Consequently, product differentiation becomes increasingly difficult. Marketing, distribution efficiency, and low-cost operations gain importance during this stage.

Finally, during the commodity or decline stage, tight cost controls leading to efficiency are essential to success. Because the product has become highly standardized at this point, price is still a very important basis for competition. Competition is intense, and firms may begin to drop out again, especially if demand takes the shape of curve C in Figure 4.3 and if exit barriers are low. Examples of exit barriers that might motivate organizations not to drop out include owning a lot of assets that cannot be used for anything else, high costs of terminating contracts or tearing down buildings, or social costs such as laying off workers.[22]

To avoid the full effects of decline, firms may focus on a particular niche in the market that is still growing. Or innovative firms may be able to introduce a product that totally replaces the old product and makes it obsolete. For example, microcomputers are replacing typewriters and compact discs have replaced records. Finally, some organizations may just hang on until other firms have dropped out, at which time reduced competition can improve profitability and market share.[23] This is happening right now in the tobacco industry.

One of the lessons that we learn from the product life cycle is that organizations must adapt as their products move through the stages of evolution. Whereas product innovation and attempts to differentiate products may have value in the early stages, once a dominant design emerges, the focus of strategy must shift toward low costs and service, even if efforts to develop new products continue. For example, Tandem Computer was once a *very* loosely structured firm in a growing industry segment. However, as the computer industry matured, Tandem had to adapt to increasing competition by tightening its cost controls.[24]

The product life cycle concept also applies to whole industries that are identified by a basic product category such as automobiles or foods. Most industries in the United States have already matured and are represented by one of the three demand curves on the right side of Figure 4.3. This means that competition is fierce in most industries and that a careful analysis based on concepts found in this chapter is essential to success. However, even mature industries can experience growth in some product segments due to product innovations or other forms of differentiation that make older products undesirable or obsolete. Consequently, we come back to the notion that for the majority of firms, value creation through cost leadership or differentiation with controlled costs (or a focus strategy that emphasizes cost leadership or differentiation) is essential for higher-than-normal performance.

In summary, identifying the stage of the product/industry life cycle can provide strategic direction as firms develop their business-level strategies. As organizations fine-tune their strategies, they need to specify the distinctive competencies they will try to develop in order to achieve a competitive advantage.

KEY POINTS SUMMARY

This chapter dealt with business-level strategy, which defines an organization's approach to competing in its chosen markets. The following important points were examined in this chapter:

1. The responsibilities of business-level managers include establishing the overall direction of the business unit, analyzing the changing business situation, selecting growth and competitive strategies, and choosing a business-unit strategic posture.

2. Growth strategies are concerned with increasing the size and viability of the business over time. The primary issues with regard to growth are (1) where do we allocate resources within our business in order to achieve growth, (2) what changes in business scope do we see as compatible with growth and overall strategic direction, and (3) how do we *time* our growth moves compared to competitors?

3. The four generic competitive strategies discussed in this chapter are cost leadership, differentiation, best cost, and focus.

4. Firms that are cost leaders actively pursue ways to produce products and services at the lowest possible cost. A firm may achieve low cost through high capacity utilization, scale economies, technological advances, and learning or experience effects.

5. Organizations that pursue a differentiation strategy attempt to distinguish their products or services in such a way that they have greater value to their consumers. Differentiation is often pursued on the basis of satisfying customers through higher quality, state-of-the-art research and development, superior human resources, or establishing a strong reputation or brand through advertising.

6. Best-cost strategies combine elements from both differentiation and low-cost leadership.
7. Focus strategies apply one of the generic orientations to a specific market niche.
8. An understanding of the product life cycle can assist management in determining the distinct characteristics of a business-level strategy and how changes in industry growth rate and competitiveness will influence strategy choices.

REFERENCES

1. A. Taylor III, "How to Murder the Competition," *Fortune* (February 22, 1993): 87.
2. H. J. Bryce, *Financial and Strategic Management for Nonprofit Organizations* (Englewood Cliffs,N.J.: Prentice-Hall, 1987).
3. K. R. Harrigan, "Deterrents to Divestiture," *Academy of Management Journal* 24 (1981): 306–323.
4. R. E. Miles and C. C. Snow, *Organization Strategy, Structure and Process* (New York: McGraw-Hill, 1978); R. E. Miles, C. C. Snow, A. D. Meyer, and H. J. Coleman, Jr.,"Organizational Strategy, Structure and Process," *Academy of Management Review* 3 (1978): 546–562.
5. This discussion of generic strategies draws heavily from concepts found in M. E. Porter, *Competitive Strategy: Techniques for Analyzing Industries and Competitors* (New York: The Free Press, 1980): Chapter 2.
6. This discussion of factors leading to cost savings is based, in part, on R. Stagner, "Corporate Decision Making: An Empirical Study," *Journal of Applied Psychology* 53 (1969): 1–3.
7. W. J. Abernathy and K. Wayne, "Limits of the Learning Curve," *Harvard Business Review* (September/October 1974): 109–119; Boston Consulting Group, *Perspectives on Experience* (Boston: Boston Consulting Group, 1972); W. B. Hirschman, "Profit from the Learning Curve," *Harvard Business Review* (January/February, 1964): 125–139.
8. A. Paszton, M. Branningan and S. McCartney, "ValuJet's Penny-Pinching Comes under Scrutiny," *The Wall Street Journal,* May 14, 1996, A2, A4.
9. E. Mansfield, "How Rapidly Does New Industrial Technology Leak Out?" *Journal of Industrial Economics* (December 1985): 217.
10. P. Ghemawat, "Sustainable Advantage," *Harvard Business Review* (September/October 1986): 53.
11. Porter, *Competitive Strategy*.
12. M. Walton, *Deming Management at Work* (New York: G. P. Putnam's Sons, 1990).
13. T. C. Hayes, "Behind Wal-Mart's Surge, a Web of Suppliers," *The New York Times,* July 1, 1991: D1–D2.
14. C. W. L. Hill, "Differentiation versus Low Cost or Differentiation and Low Cost: A Contingency Framework," *Academy of Management Review* 13 (1988): 403. See also A. I. Murray, "A Contingency View of Porter's 'Generic Strategies,'" *Academy of Management Review* 13 (1988): 390-400.
15. "A Conversation with Roberto Goizueta and Jack Welch," *Fortune* (December 11, 1995): 98-99.
16. A. Talor III, "Now Hear This, Jack Welch!" *Fortune* (April 6, 1992): 94.
17. "Japan Airlines Puts Money in Toilet to Lure 1st-Class Travellers," *Orlando Sentinel* (May 8, 1996).
18. The term *commodity*, used to describe curves A and B, was borrowed from R. H. Hayes and S. C. Wheelwright, *Restoring Our Competitive Edge: Competing through Manufacturing* (New York: John Wiley and Sons, 1984): 203.
19. This discussion of strategy during the stages of product market evolution is based on C. R. Anderson and C. P. Zeithaml, "Stage of the Product Life Cycle, Business Strategy and Business Performance," *Academy of Management Journal* 27 (1984): 5–24; J. B. Barney and R. W. Griffin, *The Management of Organizations: Strategy, Structure, Behavior* (Boston: Houghton Mifflin, 1992): 229–230; Hayes and Wheelright, *Restoring Our Competitive Edge*, Chapter 7; C. W. Hofer and D. Schendel, *Strategy Formulation: Analytical Concepts* (St. Paul: West Publishing, 1978): Chapter 5.
20. M. B. Lieberman and D. B. Montgomery, "First-Mover Advantages," *Strategic Management Journal* 9 (1988): 41–58.
21. M. Lambkin, "Order of Entry and Performance in New Markets," *Strategic Management Journal* 9 (1988): 127–140.
22. K. R. Harrigan and M. E. Porter, "End-Game Strategies for Declining Industries," *Harvard Business Review* (July/August 1983): 111–120.
23. Harrigan and Porter, "End-Game Strategies for Declining Industries."
24. J. B. Levine, "How Jim Treybig Whipped Tandem Back into Shape," *Business Week* (February 23, 1987): 102–104.

5

Corporate Strategy

ABB

I f lean and mean could be personified, Percy Barnevik would walk through the door. A thin, bearded Swede, Barnevik is Europe's leading hatchet man. He is also the creator of what is fast becoming the most successful cross-border merger since Royal Dutch Petroleum linked up with Britain's Shell in 1907.

In four years, Barnevik, 51, has welded ASEA, a Swedish engineering group, to Brown Boveri, a Swiss competitor, bolted on 70 more companies in Europe and the United States, and created ABB, a global electrical equipment giant that is bigger than Westinghouse and can go head to head with GE. It is a world leader in high-speed trains, robotics, and environmental controls. Du Pont recently put Barnevik on its board. Says a senior executive at Mitsubishi Heavy Industries: "They're as aggressive as we are. I mean this as a compliment. They are sort of super-Japanese."

ABB isn't Japanese, nor is it Swiss or Swedish. It is a multinational without a national identity, though its mailing address is in Zurich. The company's 13 top managers hold frequent meetings in different countries. Since they share no common first language, they speak only English, a foreign tongue to all but one.[1]

This chapter deals with the functions top executives perform as they formulate corporate-level strategy, some of the tools they use, and theory concerning how corporate-level actions enhance the value of organizations. We discuss the way business units can be related to each other and provide a rationale for building distinctive competencies based on similarities among them. Then we describe specific tactics firms use to diversify.

At the corporate level, primary strategy formulation responsibilities include setting the direction of the entire organization, formulating a corporate strategy, selecting businesses in which to compete, choosing tactics for diversification and growth, and managing corporate resources and capabilities. These responsibilities and the key issues associated with each one are listed in Table 5.1.

DEVELOPMENT OF CORPORATE STRATEGY

The three broad approaches to corporate strategy are concentration, vertical integration, and diversification.

Single Business/Concentration

Most organizations begin with a single or small group of products and services and a single market. This type of corporate-level strategy is called **concentration**. For instance, McDonald's is only engaged in one line of business, with limited backward integration to ensure a high level of quality for some of its raw materials (e.g., potatoes). Because McDonald's operates worldwide, the only real diversity pursued by the company is geographic. However, the same basic operating strategy is pursued at every McDonald's location in the world (although some of the food ingredients may change). Other examples of companies that are pursuing a concentration, or single-business, strategy include Nucor, Federal Express, Domino's Pizza, Lands' End, and Delta Airlines.

Concentration strategies have sometimes been found to be more profitable than other types of corporate, or multibusiness strategies.[2] Of course, the profitability of a concentration strategy largely depends on the industry in which a firm is involved. When the industry conditions are attractive, the strengths of a concentration strategy are readily apparent. First, a single business approach allows an organization to master one business and industry environment. This specialization allows top executives to obtain in-depth knowledge of the business and industry, which should reduce strategic mistakes. Second, because all resources are directed at doing one thing well, the organization may be in a better position to develop the resources and capabilities necessary to establish a sustainable competitive advantage. By concentrating on a single business, firms are able to concentrate on a focused set of strategies developed to achieve growth and profitability, as discussed in Chapter 4. Third, a concentration strategy can prevent the proliferation of management levels and staff functions that are often associated with large multibusiness firms and that add overhead costs and limit the flexibility of business units. Fourth, a concentration strategy allows a firm to invest profits back into the business rather than competing with other corporate holdings for the investment funds.

On the other hand, concentration strategies entail several risks, especially when environments are unstable. Because the organization is dependent on one product or business area to sustain itself, change can dramatically reduce organizational performance. The airline industry is a good example of the effects of

Chapter 5 Corporate Strategy

Major Responsibilities	Key Issues
Direction setting	Establishment and communication of organizational mission, vision, enterprise strategy, and long-term goals
Development of corporate-level strategy	Selection of a broad approach to corporate-level strategy—concentration, vertical integration, diversification, international expansion
	Selection of resources and capabilities in which to build corporate-wide distinctive competencies
Selection of businesses and portfolio management	Management of the corporate portfolio
	Emphasis given to each business unit—allocation of resources for capital equipment, R&D, etc.
Selection of tactics for diversification and growth	Choice among methods of diversification—internal venturing, acquisitions, joint ventures
Management of resources	Acquisition of resources or development of competencies leading to a sustainable competitive advantage
	Development of business-level strategies and an appropriate management structure for the corporation
	Development of an appropriate corporate structure

Table 5.1 *Major Corporate-Level Strategic Management Responsibilities*

uncertainty on organizational performance. Prior to deregulation, most of the major airline carriers were profitable. They had protected routes and fixed prices. However, deregulation and the ensuing increase in competition hurt the profitability of all domestic carriers. Because most of the major carriers were pursuing concentration strategies, they did not have other business areas to offset their losses. Consequently, several airlines were acquired or went bankrupt.

Product obsolescence and industry maturity create additional risks for organizations pursuing a concentration strategy. If an organization's principal product becomes obsolete or matures, organizational performance can suffer until the organization develops another product that appeals to the market. Some organizations are never able to duplicate earlier successes. Furthermore, organizations that only have experience in one line of business have limited ability to switch to other areas when times get tough.

Concentration strategies can also lead to uneven cash flow and profitability. While the business is growing, the organization may find itself in a "cash poor" situation, because growth often entails additional investments in capital equipment and marketing. On the other hand, once growth levels off, the organization is likely to find itself in a "cash rich" situation, with limited opportunities for profitable investment in the business itself. In fact, this may be one of the most important reasons that organizations in mature markets begin to diversify.[3] Having exhausted all reasonable opportunities to reinvest cash in innovation, renewal, or revitalization, organizational managers may look to other areas for growth. Finally, a concentration strategy may not provide managers with enough challenge or stimulation. They may begin to tire of doing the same things year after year. This is less true in organizations that are growing rapidly, as growth typically provides excitement and promotion opportunities.

Many successful organizations abandon their concentration strategies at some point due to market saturation, increased competition, or some other reason. Corporate strategy typically evolves from concentration to some form of vertical integration or diversification of products, markets, or resource conversion processes (see Figure 5.1).[4] The final stage in Figure 5.1, restructuring, will be discussed in Chapter 7. Vertical integration and diversification are the topics of the next two sections.

Vertical Integration

Vertical integration is the term used to describe the extent to which a firm is involved in several stages of the industry supply chain. A typical industry supply chain, which is illustrated in Figure 5.2, begins with *extraction* of raw materials such as timber, ore, and crude oil. In *primary manufacturing*, these raw materials are converted into commodities such as wood pulp and iron. Primary manufacturing sometimes involves the creation of components that are used to assemble final products, such as the engine, transmission, and brake systems used in automobiles. *Final product manufacturing* involves the creation of a product that is in its

Figure 5.1 *The Development of Corporate-Level Strategy*

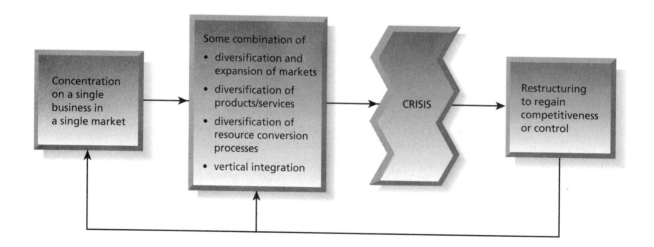

Source: Adapted from J. R. Galbraith and R. K. Kazanjian, *Strategy Implementation: Structure, Systems and Process*, 2nd ed. (St. Paul: West Publishing, 1986), 51.

Figure 5.2 *Industry Supply Chain for Manufacturing Firms*

final form prior to consumption, such as the final assembly of an automobile. At this point branding becomes very important, because consumers associate brand names of final products with particular levels of quality, service, and reliability. Finally, *wholesaling* entails channeling final products to retail outlets and *retailing* consists of selling these products to the ultimate consumers. Some products bypass the wholesaling or retailing stages because they are sold directly to the customer by the manufacturer.[5]

Some industries, such as steel and wood industries, contain firms that are predominantly vertically integrated. In other industries, such as the apparel industry, vertical integration is limited and most organizations are only involved in one or a few stages. Firms may pursue vertical integration for a variety of reasons, including increased control over the quality of supplies or the way a product is marketed, better or more complete information about supplies or markets, greater opportunity for product differentiation through coordinated effort, or simply because they believe they can enhance profits through assuming one of the functions that was previously performed by another company.[6] **Transaction cost economics**, which is the study of economic exchanges and their costs, described in Table 5.2, provides a cost perspective on vertical integration that helps explain when it may be appropriate.[7]

Research has not generally found vertical integration to be a highly profitable strategy relative to the other corporate-level strategies.[8] However, many of the firms that have been studied are old and large. They may have used vertical integration with success as their industries were forming. As one vertical integration expert explained, vertical integration can "lock firms in" to unprofitable adjacent businesses.[9] However, this does not mean that all vertical integration is unprofitable.

Furthermore, a recent study suggested that vertical integration may be associated with reduced administrative, selling, and R&D costs, although it may lead to higher production costs. The researchers believe that the higher production costs may result from a lack of incentive on the part of internal suppliers to keep their costs down. Because the internal suppliers have a guaranteed customer, they do not have to be as competitive.[10]

An important point to remember with regard to all of the strategies is that some companies are pursuing them successfully. Furthermore, vertical integration often requires substantially different skills than those the firm already possesses. In this regard, vertical integration is similar to unrelated diversification, a topic we will discuss later in this chapter.[11] A firm that can master one stage of the industry supply chain will not necessarily excel at other stages. For this reason, many firms avoid vertical integration and move directly into some form of diversification.

From a transaction cost perspective, firms can either negotiate on the open market for the products and services they need or they can produce these products and services themselves. If an organization can obtain required resources from a competitive open market without allocating an undue amount of time or other resources to the contracting process or contract enforcement, it is probably in its best interests to buy from the market instead of vertically integrating. However, when transactions costs are high enough to encourage an organization to produce a good or service in-house instead of buying it from the open market, a **market failure** is said to exist. The market is likely to "fail" under the following conditions:

• The future is highly uncertain. It may be too costly or impossible to identify all of the possible situations that may occur and to incorporate these possibilities into the contract.
• Only one or a small number of suppliers of a good or service exists, and these suppliers are likely to pursue their own self-interests.
• One party to a transaction has more knowledge about the transaction or a series of transactions than another.
• An organization invests in an asset that can only be used to produce a specific good or service, which makes use of the market difficult (asset specificity).

Sources: O. E. Williamson, *Markets and Hierarchies: Analysis and Antitrust Implications* (New York: The Free Press, 1975); O. E. Williamson, *The Economic Institutions of Capitalism* (New York: The Free Press, 1985).

Table 5.2 *Transaction Costs and Vertical Integration*

Diversification

Diversification, which is one of the most studied topics in all of strategic management, can be divided into two broad categories. **Related diversification** implies organizational involvement in activities that somehow relate to the organization's dominant or "core" business, often through common markets or similar technologies. **Unrelated diversification** does not depend on any pattern of relatedness. Some of the most common reasons for diversification are listed in Table 5.3.[12] They are divided into strategic reasons, which are frequently cited by executives in the popular business press, and personal motives that CEOs may have for pursuing diversification.

Unrelated Diversification.[13] Large, unrelated diversified firms, such as General Electric and Hitachi, are often called **conglomerates**, because they involve a conglomeration of unrelated businesses. Unrelated diversification as a way to grow a corporation became increasingly popular during the 1950s, 1960s, and early 1970s.[14] The increase in conglomerates was precipitated by several forces. Government antitrust laws were established to keep organizations from getting large and powerful enough in one industry to engage in monopoly pricing and other forms of noncompetitive or illegal behavior. Many organizational managers pursued unrelated diversification in an effort to use excess cash in ways that would not lead to conflicts with antitrust enforcement agencies. Another powerful force leading to unrelated diversification was an increase in the popularity of financial theories such as the Capital Asset Pricing Model (CAPM) that led managers to believe that they could reduce risk by purchasing companies with dissimilar return streams.[15] These financial theories apply well to portfolios of securities but not to buying and managing whole businesses.

Now, managers and researchers alike believe that unrelated diversification is not typically a good strategic option to pursue. Unrelated diversification places significant demands on corporate-level executives due to increased complexity

Strategic Reasons
Risk reduction through investments in dissimilar businesses
    or less dynamic environments
Stabilization or improvement in earnings
Improvement in growth
Cash generated in slower growing traditional areas exceeds
    that needed for profitable investment in those areas (organizational slack)
Application of resources, capabilities, and core competencies to related areas
Generation of synergy/economies of scope
Use of excess debt capacity (organizational slack)
Desire to learn new technologies
Increase in market power
Desire to turn around a failing business, leading to high returns

Motives of the CEO
Desire to increase power and status
Desire to increase compensation from running a larger enterprise
Desire to increase value of the firm
Craving for a more interesting and challenging management environment (boredom)

Table 5.3 *A Few Common Reasons for Diversification*

and technological changes across industries. In fact, it is very difficult for a manager to understand each of the core technologies and appreciate the special requirements of each of the individual units in an unrelated diversified firm. Consequently, the effectiveness of management may be reduced.

Most, but not all, research has demonstrated that unrelated firms have lower profitability than firms pursuing other corporate-level strategies.[16] There is also some evidence that unrelated diversification is associated with higher levels of risk than are other strategies.[17] Nevertheless, some firms have had success with unrelated diversification. Ford Motor Company is making literally billions of dollars each year in profits from its highly successful financial subsidiaries.[18] Also, General Electric, one of the biggest conglomerates in the world, has enjoyed many years of strong financial performance.[19]

The 1980s were marked with a dramatic *decrease* in unrelated diversification, accompanied by an increase in related diversification.[20] The Reagan administration's hands-off approach to antitrust policy supported the trend toward mergers among related firms. Related diversification, accompanied by sell-offs of unrelated businesses, is a continuing trend among U.S. firms.[21]

Related Diversification. When an organization's management chooses to diversify from its original core business into other businesses, it often enters an industry that seems to be similar or related to what it already knows. Most of the research on diversification strategies indicates that some form of relatedness among diversified businesses, rather than unrelatedness, leads to higher financial performance.[22] Also, a recent study demonstrated that related diversification is also associated with reduced risk.[23]

Related diversification is based on similarities that exist among the products, services, markets, or resource conversion processes of two businesses. These similarities are supposed to lead to synergy, which means that the whole is greater than the sum of its parts. In other words, one organization should be able to produce two related products or services more efficiently than two organizations each producing one of the products or services on its own. The same reasoning applies to similar markets and similar resource conversion processes. For example, Johnson & Johnson is involved in a wide variety of diversified businesses; however, virtually all of them are related to converting chemical substances into drugs and toiletries.

Relatedness comes in two forms; tangible and intangible.[24] **Tangible relatedness** means that the organization has the opportunity to use the same physical resources for multiple purposes. Tangible relatedness can lead to synergy through resource sharing. For example, if two similar products are manufactured in the same plant, operating synergy is said to exist. This phenomenon was referred to earlier during our discussion of economies of scope, which occur any time slack resources that would not have been used otherwise are put to good use.[25] Sharing production facilities can also lead to economies of scale through producing products or services in an optimally sized (typically larger) plant.[26]

Other examples of synergy resulting from tangible relatedness include (1) using the same marketing or distribution channels for multiple related products; (2) buying similar raw materials for related products through a centralized purchasing office to gain purchasing economies; (3) providing corporate training programs to employees from different divisions that are all engaged in the same type of work; and (4) advertising multiple products simultaneously, such as advertising Pepsi and Pizza Hut in the same television commercial (PepsiCo owns Pizza Hut).

Intangible relatedness occurs any time capabilities developed in one area can be applied to another area. It results in managerial synergy.[27] For example, Toys 'R' Us developed retailing skills that were directly applicable to Kids 'R' Us. Also, Campbell's Soup has applied skills attained from manufacturing and packaging soup to a variety of other products. Both of these companies make effective use of another intangible resource, image or goodwill. Goodwill means that a company with an established trade name can draw on this name to market new products. For instance, Singer, which has an established reputation for its sewing machines, also began marketing small consumer appliances and furniture under the same label. Also, Heinz enjoys a high quality reputation that is shared by all of its food varieties. Synergy based on intangible resources such as a brand name or management skills and knowledge may be more conducive to the creation of a sustainable competitive advantage, because intangible resources are hard to imitate and are never used up.[28]

Some types of relatedness are more imaginary than real. For example, the relatedness between oil and other forms of energy such as solar and coal proved illusive to several of the large oil companies, who experienced performance problems in these "related business ventures." In addition, even if relatedness is evident, synergy *has to be created*, which means that the two related businesses must fit together *and* that organizational managers must work at creating efficiencies from the combination process.[29] Two types of fit are required: strategic fit and organizational fit.

Strategic fit refers to the effective matching of strategic organizational capabilities. For example, if two organizations in two related businesses combine their resources, but they are both strong in the same areas and weak in the same areas, then the potential for synergy is diminished. Once combined, they will continue to exhibit the same capabilities. However, if one of the organizations is strong in R&D but lacks marketing power, while the other organization is weak in R&D but strong in marketing, then there is real potential for both organizations to be better off—if managed properly.

Organizational fit occurs when two organizations or business units have similar management processes, cultures, systems, and structures.[30] This is sometimes referred to as having a similar **dominant management logic.**[31] Organizational fit makes organizations compatible, which facilitates resource sharing, communication, and transference of knowledge and skills. Lack of fit is especially evident in mergers and acquisitions. For instance, two related companies may merge in an effort to create synergy but find that they are organizationally incompatible. Table 5.4 summarizes some of the most common problems that may undermine synergies.

In addition to the synergy that can sometimes be created through related diversification across a limited number of businesses, many corporations attempt to build core capabilities or competencies that can be applied across many or most businesses in the domestic market or globally. Organizations can develop core capabilities based on skills and resources that "(1) incorporate an integrated set of managerial and technological skills, (2) are hard to acquire other than through experience, (3) contribute significantly to perceived customer benefits, and (4) can be widely applied within the company's business domain."[32] For example, AT&T has developed a corporate-level core competence in benchmarking methods, Motorola in flexible manufacturing, and 3M in supplier management.[33]

This completes our discussion of the basic corporate-level strategies of concentration, vertical integration, unrelated diversification, and related diversification. In addition, we have argued for the development of corporate-level core capabilities. In the next section, we discuss the methods organizations use to implement their corporate-level strategies.

Table 5.4 *Forces that Undermine Synergies*

Management Ineffectiveness
Too little effort to coordinate between businesses means synergies will not be created.
Too much effort to coordinate between businesses can stifle creativity.

Administrative Costs of Coordination
Additional layers of management and staff add costs.
Executives in larger organizations are often paid higher salaries.
Delays from and expense of meetings and planning sessions necessary for coordination.
Extra travel and communications costs are needed to achieve coordination.

Poor Strategic Fit
Relatedness without strategic fit decreases the opportunity for synergy.
Overstated (or imaginary) opportunities exist for synergies.
Industry evolution undermines strategic fit.

Poor Organizational Fit
Cultures and management styles are incompatible.
Strategies, priorities, and reward systems are incompatible.
Production processes and technologies are incompatible.
Computer and budgeting systems are incompatible.

DIVERSIFICATION METHODS

This section emphasizes the techniques available to organizations to pursue diversification, once a decision concerning the desired type and level of diversification has been made. These techniques include internal venturing, acquisitions, and joint ventures. Companies like Exxon and Johnson & Johnson rely most heavily on internal venturing for diversification. Beatrice Foods and ITT, on the other hand, accomplish virtually all of their diversification through acquisitions. Procter & Gamble and Westinghouse favor a combination of joint ventures and acquisitions over internal venturing.[34]

Internal Venturing

Internal venturing can be viewed as an organizational learning process directed at developing the skills and knowledge necessary to compete in new domains.[35] It is entrepreneurship within an existing organization.[36] Internal venturing differs from market and product development activity within a business, as discussed in Chapter 4, because it is focused on entry into new or different industries or industry segments. Some organizations are very committed to internal venturing. At 3M, a corporate policy that supports internal venturing allows scientists to spend up to 15% of their time on personal research projects. Post-It notepads were invented through this program.[37]

The three basic types of diversification through internal venturing are (1) product line extension, refinement and repositioning that draws the organization into a new business opportunity; (2) introduction of new products related to an existing competence, which allows the firm to enter a new business; and (3) development of truly new-to-the-world products not related to the firm's core business.[38]

The most important strength an internal diversifier brings to a new business venture is the ability to make use of the combined resources and capabilities of its various operations, especially in the technological areas.[39] For example, IBM used its abundant resources in the computer industry to develop and market its very successful line of personal computers in the early 1980s. W. L. Gore and Associates has used its capabilities in Gore-Tex materials to venture into new businesses in health care, industrial applications, and outdoor apparel. Compared to joint venturing, internal venturing provides an organization with complete control over innovation and marketing processes, as well as the ability to fully exploit new innovations if the venture is a success.[40]

Nevertheless, research suggests that internal venturing is typically associated with slower growth than other diversification options, especially acquisitions. In fact, one researcher discovered that new ventures take, on average, eight years before they become profitable and generate a positive cash flow. Furthermore, it takes ten to twelve years before a new venture's return on investment equals that of existing product lines.[41] Also, another researcher found that only 12% to 20% of new R&D-based ventures ever become profitable.[42] However, if organizations can quickly learn which new ventures are going to be successful and respond to this knowledge before large amounts of resources have been expended, internal venturing can be a very successful approach to diversification.

The selection of an organizational design for pursuing an internal venture depends on the strategic importance of the venture and how closely the venture relates to current activities (see Figure 5.3).[43] Ventures that are considered strategically important to the future of the organization and are closely related to cur-

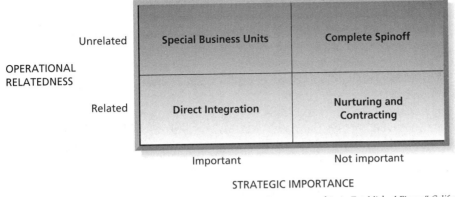

Unrelated	**Special Business Units**	**Complete Spinoff**
Related	**Direct Integration**	**Nurturing and Contracting**
	Important	Not important

OPERATIONAL RELATEDNESS

STRATEGIC IMPORTANCE

Source: Adapted from R. A. Burgelman, "Designs for Corporate Entrepreneurship in Established Firms," *California Management Review* 26, no. 3 (1994): 161. Copyright © 1984 by the Regents of the University of California. Reprinted by permission of the Regents.

Figure 5.3 *Internal Venturing Alternatives*

rent activities should probably be integrated into the mainstream of firm operations. Ventures that do not qualify as important or related should be spun off completely. However, the firm may want to create a special independent business unit to pursue a venture that is important but not operationally related. IBM used this approach by sending an independent research group to Boca Raton, Florida, to develop the original IBM personal computer.

Organizations may also encounter opportunities to pursue ventures that do not appear at the time to have much strategic importance yet are closely related to the firm's core operations. In these cases, the organization may provide another organization with the funds or other resources needed to pursue the venture, along with a contract that would allow both firms to share the outputs if the venture is successful. This strategy, which is called nurturing and contracting, keeps a firm's options open. Novell, the network software leader, nurtures and contracts with smaller companies that help develop software that is compatible with Novell's core network product, called Netware.

Acquisitions

As an alternative to corporate venturing, discussed in the last section, some organizations choose to buy diversification in the form of acquisitions. **Mergers** occur any time two organizations combine into one. **Acquisitions**, in which one organization buys a controlling interest in the stock of another organization or buys it outright from its owners, are the most common types of mergers. Acquisitions are a relatively quick way to (1) enter new markets, (2) acquire new products or services, (3) learn new resource conversion processes, (4) acquire needed knowledge and skills, (5) vertically integrate, (6) broaden markets geographically, or (7) fill needs in the corporate portfolio.[44] As mentioned briefly in the last chapter, mergers and acquisitions may be used to expand resources, markets, and products *within* a business as well as to diversify into new businesses.

Unfortunately, most of the research evidence seems to indicate that mergers and acquisitions are not, on average, financially beneficial to the shareholders of the acquiring firm.[45] In one study of 191 acquisitions in 29 industries, researchers found that acquisitions were associated with declining profitability, reduced research and development expenditures, fewer patents produced, and increases in financial leverage.[46] Perhaps the most condemning evidence to date concerning mergers and acquisitions was presented by Michael Porter.[47] He studied the diversification records of thirty-three large, prestigious U.S. companies over the 1950–1986 period and concluded that the corporate strategies of most companies reduced, rather than enhanced, shareholder value. Porter discovered that most of these companies divested many more of their acquisitions than they kept. For example, CBS, in an effort to create an "entertainment company," bought organizations involved in toys, crafts, sports teams, and musical instruments. All of these businesses were sold due to lack of fit with CBS's traditional broadcasting business. Table 5.5 provides several explanations for why acquisitions, on average, tend to depress profitability (at least in the short term).

Does this mean that all mergers are doomed to failure? Recently researchers have identified factors that seem to be associated with successful and unsuccessful mergers. Unsuccessful mergers were associated with large debt, overconfident or incompetent managers, poor ethics, changes in top management or the structure of the acquiring organization, and diversification away from the core area in which the firm is strongest. Successful mergers were related to low-to-moderate amounts of debt, a high level of relatedness leading to synergy, friendly negotiations (no resistance), a continued focus on the core business, careful selection of and negotiations with the acquired firm, and a strong cash or debt position.[48]

Furthermore, researchers have discovered that the largest shareholder gains from merger occurred when the cultures and the top management styles of the two companies were similar (organizational fit).[49] In addition, sharing resources and activities was found to be important to postmerger success.[50] However, it is fair to say that "there are no rules that will invariably lead to a successful acquisition."[51]

Many of the diversification objectives that organizations seek through acquisitions are also available through strategic alliances and joint ventures, which are the topic of the next section.

Strategic Alliances and Joint Ventures

A **strategic alliance** is formed by two or more organizations to develop new products or services, enter new markets, or improve resource conversion processes.[52] When the arrangement is contractual and the alliance operates independently of the organizations that form it, then the alliance typically is called a **joint venture**. Strategic alliances are becoming increasingly popular. Many of the partnerships with external stakeholders discussed in Chapter 2 are examples of strategic alliances and joint ventures.

AT&T has joint ventures with Philips, a leading European electronics and communications firm; Olivetti, a giant in European information processing; Lucky Goldstar, a manufacturer of communications equipment in Korea; Compania Telefonica Nacional de Espana, the Spanish telephone company; and three Taiwanese firms engaged in manufacturing switching equipment. Commenting on these alliances, James Olson, chairman of the board at AT&T, stated:

We can't do everything everywhere—we will need to cooperate and partner with other companies. And we will have to concentrate our resources on activities that contribute to the success of our business and our long-term strategy.

With partners that are established in the information industry overseas, AT&T will concentrate on bringing its evolving data networking capability to countries in the Triad (North America, Western Europe, and the Far East).[53]

High Financial Costs
1. High premiums typically paid by acquiring firms. If a company was worth $50/share in a relatively efficient financial market prior to an acquisition, why should an acquiring firm pay $75 (a typical premium) or more to buy it?
2. Increased interest costs. Many acquisitions are financed by borrowing money at high interest rates. Leverage typically increases during an acquisition.
3. High advisory fees and other transaction costs. The fees charged by the brokers, lawyers, financiers, consultants, and advisors who orchestrate the deal often cost millions of dollars. In addition, filing fees, document preparation, and legal fees in the event of contestation can be very high.
4. Poison pills. These antitakeover devices make companies very unattractive to a potential buyer. Top managers of target companies have been very creative in designing a variety of poison pills. One example of a poison pill is the "golden parachute," in which target firm executives receive large amounts of severance pay (often millions of dollars) if they lose their jobs due to a hostile takeover.

Strategic Problems
1. High turnover among the managers of the acquired firm. The most valuable asset in most organizations is its people, their knowledge, and their skills. If most managers leave, what has the acquiring firm purchased?
2. Short-term managerial distraction. "Doing a deal" typically takes managers away from the critical tasks of the core businesses for long durations. During this time period, who is steering the ship?
3. Long-term managerial distraction. Sometimes organizations lose sight of the factors that lead to success in their core businesses because they are too distracted running diversified businesses.
4. Less innovation. Acquisitions have been shown to lead to reduced innovative activity, which can hurt long-term performance.
5. No organizational fit. If the cultures, dominant logics, systems, structures, and processes of the acquiring and target firms do not fit, synergy is unlikely.
6. Increased Risk. Increased leverage often associated with mergers and acquisitions leads to greater financial risk. Acquiring firms also risk being unable to manage the newly acquired organization successfully.

Sources: Information in this table came from S. Chatterjee, M. H. Lubatkin, D. M. Schweiger, and Y. Weber, "Cultural Differences and Shareholder Value in Related Mergers: Linking Equity and Human Capital," *Strategic Management Journal* 13 (1992): 319–334; J. S. Harrison, "Alternatives to Merger—Joint Ventures and Other Strategies," *Long Range Planning* (December 1987): 78–83; J. P. Walsh, "Top Management Turnover Following Mergers and Acquisitions," *Strategic Management Journal* 9 (1988): 173–184; J. P. Walsh and J. W. Ellwood, "Mergers, Acquisitions, and the Pruning of Managerial Deadwood," *Strategic Management Journal* 12 (1991): 201–207.

Table 5.5 *A Few of Many Potential Problems with Mergers and Acquisitions*

Strategic alliances and joint ventures can help organizations achieve many of the same objectives that are sought through mergers and acquisitions. They can improve sales growth, increase earnings, or provide balance to a portfolio of businesses, which are some of the most commonly cited reasons for acquisitions.[54] For example, in 1980 Monsanto and General Electric formed a joint venture called Fisher Control International to make regulators and control valves. Within one year, their joint venture ranked second in sales in the growing process control equipment industry. Also, one of the largest and most profitable robot manufacturers in the world is a joint venture between General Motors and Fanuc Ltd. called GMF Robotics Corp.[55]

The strongest rationale for forming a joint venture is resource sharing. Because joint ventures involve more than one company, they can draw on a much larger resource base. The resources that are most likely to be transferable through a joint venture are the following:

1. *Marketing.* Companies can gain marketing information and resources not easily identified by outsiders, such as knowledge of competition, customer behavior, industry condition, and distribution channels.
2. *Technological.* Those participating in a joint venture can use technological skills and specific knowledge that is not generally available.
3. *Raw materials and components.* Some joint ventures are formed to give the organization access to different elements of the manufacturing process.
4. *Financial.* Companies can obtain external capital, usually in conjunction with other resources.
5. *Managerial.* Joint venture participants can use specific managerial and entrepreneurial capabilities and skills, usually in conjunction with other resources.
6. *Political.* Some joint ventures are obligated to enter developing countries; others are formed to gain political commitments.[56]

In addition to the advantages associated with resource sharing, joint ventures can enhance speed of entry into a new field or market because of the expanded base of resources from which ventures can draw. They also spread the risk of failure among all of the participants; that is, a failure will result in a smaller loss to each partner than it would to an organization that pursues the venture on its own. Consequently, compared to mergers or internal venturing, joint ventures are sometimes considered a less risky diversification option.

In spite of their strategic strengths, joint ventures are limiting, in that one organization only has partial control over the venture and enjoys only a percentage of the growth and profitability it creates. Joint ventures create high administrative costs associated with developing the multiparty equity arrangement and managing the venture once it is undertaken.[57] As in mergers and acquisitions, lack of organizational fit can reduce cooperation and lead to venture failure. Furthermore, joint ventures entail a risk of opportunism by venture partners. Good written contracts can help to alleviate but cannot eliminate this risk.

Successful joint ventures require careful planning and execution. Managers should communicate the expected benefits of the venture to the important external and internal stakeholders so they will understand the role the alliance will play in the organization.[58] Managers should also develop a strategic plan for the venture that consolidates the views of the partners about market potential, competitive trends, and potential threats. Several additional steps may be taken to improve the likelihood of success:

1. Through careful, systematic study, identify an alliance partner that can provide the capabilities that are needed. Avoid the tendency to align with another firm just because alliance-forming is a trend in the industry.
2. Clearly define the roles of each partner and ensure that every joint project is of value to both.
3. Develop a strategic plan for the venture that outlines specific objectives for each partner.
4. Keep top managers involved so that middle managers stay committed.
5. Meet often, informally, at all managerial levels.
6. Appoint someone to monitor all aspects of the alliance and use an outside mediator when disputes arise.

7. Maintain enough independence to develop the company's own area of expertise. Avoid becoming a complete "captive" of the alliance partner.
8. Anticipate and plan for cultural differences.[59]

In summary, all of the diversification tactics described in this section suffer from potential weaknesses. Internal venturing is slow, acquisitions are expensive and may stifle innovation, and strategic alliances/joint venturing leads to less control and the potential for opportunism. However, any one of these options can be used successfully, as long as basic strategic principles and good management are applied.

KEY POINTS SUMMARY

Corporate strategy focuses on the selection of businesses in which the organization will compete and on the tactics used to enter and manage those businesses and other corporate-level resources. Some of the most important points discussed in this chapter include the following:

1. At the corporate level, management responsibilities include direction setting, development of a corporate strategy, selection of businesses and management of the portfolio of businesses, selection of tactics for diversification and growth, and management of corporate-level resources.
2. The three broad approaches to corporate strategy are single business/concentration, vertical integration, and diversification, which is divided into two broad categories, related and unrelated diversification.
3. Single business/concentration strategies allow an organization to focus on doing one business very well; however, a key disadvantage is that the organization is dependent on that one business for survival.
4. Vertical integration allows an organization to become its own supplier or customer. However, according to the theory of transaction cost economics, if an organization can obtain required resources from a competitive open market without allocating an undue amount of time or other resources to the contracting process or contract enforcement, it is probably in the organization's best interests to buy from the market instead of vertically integrating.
5. Unrelated diversification was very popular during the 1950s, 1960s, and the early 1970s. However, research results indicate that it did not lead to the high performance or reduced risks that many executives had expected. Many organizations are now restructuring to reduce unrelated diversification.
6. Related diversification, on the other hand, is still a very popular strategy. Businesses are related if they share a common market, technology, raw material, or any one of many other factors. However, for a related diversification strategy to have its full positive impact, strategic and organizational fit is required.
7. Diversification can be accomplished through internal venturing, acquisition of existing businesses, or strategic alliances/joint ventures. Each of these tactics have both advantages and disadvantages.

APPENDIX 5

Portfolio Management

Portfolio management refers to managing the mix of businesses in the corporate portfolio. CEOs of large diversified organizations like GE continually face decisions concerning how to divide organizational resources among diversified units and where to invest new capital. Portfolio models are designed to help managers make these types of decisions.

In spite of their adoption in many organizations, portfolio management techniques are the subject of considerable criticism.[60] However, because they are still in wide use, this book would be incomplete without discussing them. Keep in mind that these techniques are not a panacea and should not replace other types of sound strategic analysis.

We will begin by describing the simplest and first widely used portfolio model, the Boston Consulting Group matrix. The model has many shortcomings, stemming mostly from its simplicity. However, most of the other portfolio techniques are adaptations of it, and its simplicity makes it a good starting point. We will then describe a more complete model.

Boston Consulting Group Matrix

The Boston Consulting Group (BCG) matrix, which is displayed in Figure 5A.1, is based on two factors: industry growth rate and relative market share. Industry growth rate is the growth rate of the industry in which a particular business unit is involved. Relative market share is calculated as the ratio of the business unit's size to the size of its largest competitor. The two factors are used to plot all of the businesses in which the organization is involved, represented as stars, question marks (also called Problem Children), cash cows, and dogs. The size of the circles in Figure 5A.1 represents the size of an organization's various businesses. Remember that only one organization, made up of many different business units, is plotted on each matrix.

The BCG matrix is sometimes useful in planning cash flows. Cash cows tend to generate more cash than they can effectively reinvest, whereas question marks require additional cash to sustain rapid growth and stars generate about as much cash as they use, on average.[61] According to the Boston Consulting Group, stars and cash cows, with their superior market share positions, tend to be the most profitable businesses.[62]

Consequently, the optimal BCG portfolio contains a balance of stars, cash cows, and question marks. Stars have the greatest potential for growth and tend to be highly profitable. However, as the industries in which stars are involved mature and their growth slows, they should naturally become cash cows. Therefore, question marks are important because of their potential role as future

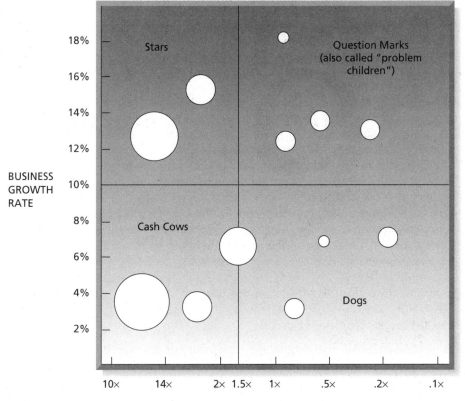

Source: B. Hedley, "Strategy and the Business Portfolio," *Long Range Planning* 10 (February 1977): 12. Copyright © 1977. Reprinted with permission from Pergamon Press Ltd., Headington Hill Hall, Oxford OX3 OBW, United Kingdom.

Figure 5A.1 *The Boston Consulting Group Matrix*

stars in the organization. Dogs are the least attractive types of business. The original prescription was to divest them.[63] However, even dogs can be maintained in the portfolio as long as they do not become a drain on corporate resources. Also, some organizations are successful at positioning their dogs in an attractive niche in their industries.

One of the shortcomings of the BCG matrix is that it does not allow for changes in strategy due to differing environments. The standard BCG prescription is this: achieve high market share leadership and become a star or a cash cow. The problem is that this prescription may only be valid for firms pursuing a low-cost leadership strategy. The use of market share as a measure of competitive strategy carries with it the implicit assumption that size has led to economies of scale and learning effects and that these effects have resulted in competitive success through the creation of a low-cost position. Differentiation and focus competitive strategies are not incorporated into the model. Also, companies that are successful in pursuing focus strategies (through low cost or differentiation) in low-growth industries may be classified as dogs even though their profit streams are strong. For example, Rolex would qualify as a dog.

Other problems with the BCG matrix relate to its simplicity. Only two factors are considered and only two divisions, high and low, are used for each factor. Also, growth rate is inadequate as the only indicator of the attractiveness of an industry. For example, some fast-growing industries have never been particularly profitable.[64] Market share, for all of the reasons stated, is also an insufficient indicator of competitive position. Other variables, such as corporate image, cost position, or R&D advantages, are likely to be equally or more important to the competitiveness of a business.

A common criticism that applies to many portfolio models, especially the BGG matrix, is that they are based on the past instead of the future.[65] Given the rate of change in the current economic and political environments, this criticism is probably valid. Finally, another problem inherent in all matrix approaches is that industries are hard to define.

In conclusion, the BCG matrix is only applicable to firms in particular operating environments that are pursuing low-cost leadership strategies based on the experience curve. Nevertheless, the matrix may help firms anticipate cash needs and flows. Numerous organizational managers and business writers have developed portfolio matrices that overcome some of the limitations of the BCG matrix. We will now describe one of these approaches.

General Electric Business Screen

Virtually any variables or combination of variables of strategic importance can be plotted along the axes of a portfolio matrix. The selection of variables depends on what the organization considers important. Many matrices contain factors that are composites of several variables. One of the most famous of these, developed at General Electric, is illustrated in Figure 5A.2. The GE model is referred to as the GE portfolio matrix, the nine-cell grid, or the GE business screen.

In the GE business screen, the area in the circles represents the size of the industries in which each business competes. The slice out of the circle is the market share of the business unit in each of these industries. The variables that are used to assess industry attractiveness are typically derived from the objectives and characteristics of the organization (i.e., its attitude toward growth, profitability, or social responsibility) and the industries themselves. Assessment of competitive position is based on a firm's position with respect to the key success factors in an industry.[66]

An organization would like to have all of its businesses in the top-left cell. These businesses are called winners. However, some of these winners should be established businesses that are not growing rapidly so that a portion of their cash flow can be used to support developing winners.

The way an organization allocates its internal resources reconfirms its selection of businesses. For example, business units that are considered critical to the future success of an organization should receive high priority in resource allocation decisions, whereas unimportant businesses may receive only maintenance levels of support. From a portfolio management perspective, businesses that are in a strong competitive position in attractive industries should be given the highest priority.

In conclusion, although all portfolio management models have weaknesses and limitations, they provide an additional tool to assist managers in anticipating cash flows and making resource allocation decisions. The GE business screen, in

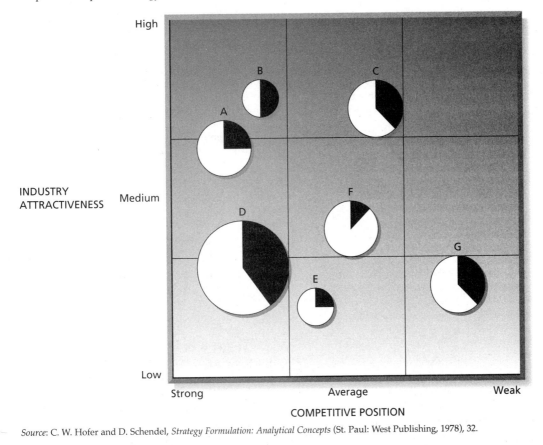

Source: C. W. Hofer and D. Schendel, *Strategy Formulation: Analytical Concepts* (St. Paul: West Publishing, 1978), 32.

Figure 5A.2 *The General Electric Business Screen*

particular, is flexible enough to accommodate a wide variety of indicators of industry attractiveness and competitive strength.

REFERENCES

1. C. Rapoport, "A Tough Swede Invades the U.S.," *Fortune* (June 29, 1992): 76–77. Used with permission.

2. R. P. Rumelt, *Strategy, Structure and Economic Performance* (Boston: Harvard Business School, 1974); R. P. Rumelt, "Diversification Strategy and Profitability," *Strategic Management Journal* 3, (1982): 359–369.

3. H. I. Ansoff, *Corporate Strategy: An Analytical Approach to Business Policy for Growth and Expansion* (New York: McGraw-Hill, 1965): 129–130.

4. A. D. Chandler, Jr., *Strategy and Structure: Chapters in the History of the Industrial Enterprise* (Cambridge, Mass.: MIT Press, 1962).

5. J. R. Galbraith and R. K. Kazanjian, *Strategy Implementation: Structure, Systems and Process*, 2nd ed. (St. Paul: West Publishing, 1986), Chapter 4.

6. K. R. Harrigan, "Formulating Vertical Integration Strategies," *Academy of Management Review* 9 (1984): 639.

7. O. E. Williamson, *Markets and Hierarchies: Analysis and Antitrust Implications* (New York: The Free Press, 1975) and *The Economic Institutions of Capitalism* (New York: The Free Press, 1985).

8. Rumelt, *Strategy, Structure and Economic Performance*; Rumelt, "Diversification Strategy and Profitability."

9. Harrigan, "Formulating Vertical Integration Strategies."

10. R. A. D'Aveni and D. J. Ravenscraft, "Economies of Integration versus Bureaucracy Costs: Does Vertical Integration Improve Performance?" *Academy of Management Journal* 37 (1994): 1167–1206.

11. R. E. Hoskisson, J. S. Harrison, and D. A. Dubofsky, "Capital Market Implementation of M-Form Implementation and Diversification Strategy," *Strategic Management Journal* 12 (1991): 271–279.

12. Citations for the diversification arguments contained in this section are not broken down by author because many of the arguments are repeated by many or most authors. Information on strategic arguments can be found in H. I. Ansoff, *Corporate Strategy: An Analytical Approach to Business Policy for Growth and Expansion* (New York: McGraw-Hill, 1965): 130–132; J. S. Harrison, "Alternatives to Merger—Joint Ventures and Other Strategies," *Long Range Planning* (December 1987): 78–83; C. W. L. Hill and G. S. Hansen, "A Longitudinal Study of the Cause and Consequence of Changes in Diversification in the U.S. Pharmaceutical Industry," *Strategic Management Journal* 12 (1991): 187–199; W. G. Lewellen, "A Pure Financial Rationale for the Conglomerate Merger," *Journal of Finance* 26 (1971): 521–537; F. M. McDougall and D. K. Round, "A Comparison of Diversifying and Nondiversifying Australian Industrial Firms," *Academy of Management Journal* 27 (1984): 384–398; R. Reed and G. A. Luffman, "Diversification: The Growing Confusion," *Strategic Management Journal* 7 (1986): 29–35. The personal arguments are outlined in W. Baumol, *Business Behavior, Value and Growth* (New York: Harcourt, 1967); D. C. Mueller, "A Theory of Conglomerate Mergers," *Quarterly Review of Economics* 83 (1969): 644–660; N. Rajagopalan and J. E. Prescott, "Determinants of Top Management Compensation: Explaining the Impact of Economic, Behavioral, and Strategic Constructs and the Moderating Effects of Industry," *Journal of Management* 16 (1990): 515–538.

13. This section and portions of other sections in this chapter were strongly influenced by the ideas of Michael Goold and Kathleen Luchs of the Ashridge Strategic Management Centre, London, England.

14. Rumelt, "Diversification Strategy and Profitability," 361.

15. T. H. Naylor and F. Tapon, "The Capital Asset Pricing Model: An Evaluation of Its Potential as a Strategic Planning Tool," *Management Science* 10 (1982): 1166–1173.

16. A few examples of the many studies that demonstrate low performance associated with unrelated diversification are R. Amit and J. Livnat, "Diversification Strategies, Business Cycles, and Economic Performance," *Strategic Management Journal* 9 (1988): 99–110.; R. A. Bettis and V. Mahajan, "Risk/Return Performance of Diversified Firms," *Management Science* 31 (1985): 785–799; D. Ravenscraft and F. M. Scherer, *Mergers, Selloffs, and Economic Efficiency* (Washington, D.C.: Brookings Institution, 1987); P. G. Simmonds, "The Combined Diversification Breadth and Mode Dimensions and the Performance of Large Diversified Firms," *Strategic Management Journal* 11 (1990): 399–410; P. Varadarajan and V. Ramanujam, "Diversification and Performance: A Reexamination Using a New Two-Dimensional Conceptualization of Diversity in Firms," *Academy of Management Journal* 30 (1982): 380–393. On the other hand, the following studies are among those that support the superiority of unrelated diversification: R. M. Grant and A. P. Jammine, "Performance Differences between the Wrigley/Rumelt Strategic Categories," *Strategic Management Journal* 9 (1988): 333–346; A. Michel and I. Shaked, "Does Business Diversification Affect Performance?" *Financial Management* (Winter 1984): 18–25.

17. M. C. Lauenstein, "Diversification—The Hidden Explanation of Success," *Sloan Management Review* (Fall 1985): 49–55; M. Lubatkin and R. C. Rogers, "Diversification, Systematic Risk and Shareholder Return: A Capital Market Extension of Rumelt's 1974 Study," *Academy of Management Journal* 32 (1989): 454–465; M. Lubatkin and H. G. O'Neill, "Merger Strategies and Capital Market Risk," *Academy of Management Journal* 30 (1987): 665–684; M. Lubatkin, "Value Creating Mergers: Fact or Folklore," *Academy of Management Executive* (November 1988): 295–302; C. A. Montgomery and H. Singh, "Diversification Strategy and Systematic Risk," *Strategic Management Journal* 5 (1984): 181–191.

18. A. B. Fisher, "Ford Rolls Out a Money Machine," *Fortune* (April 15, 1996): 48.

19 "A Conversation with Roberto Goizueta and Jack Welch," *Fortune* (December 11, 1995): 98–99.

20. R. E. Hoskisson and M. A. Hitt, "Antecedents and Performance Outcomes of Diversification: A Review and Critique of Theoretical Perspectives," *Journal of Management* 16 (1990): 461–509; A. Shleifer and R. W. Vishny, "Takeovers in the '60s and the '80s: Evidence and Implications," *Strategic Management Journal* 12 (Special Issue, 1991): 51–59.

21. Hoskisson and Hitt, "Antecedents and Performance Outcomes," 461.

22. A detailed review of this literature is found in R. E. Hoskisson and M. A. Hitt, "Antecedents and Performance Outcomes" 468. More recent evidence is found in P. S. Davis, R. B. Robinson, Jr., J. A. Pearce, and S. H. Park, "Business Unit Relatedness and Performance: A Look at the Pulp and Paper Industry," *Strategic Management Journal* 13 (1992): 349–361 and in J. S. Harrison, E. H. Hall, Jr., and R. Nargundkar, "Resource Allocation as an Outcropping of Strategic Consistency: Performance Implications," *Academy of Management Journal* 36 (1993): 1026–1051.

23. M. Lubatkin and S. Chatterjee, "Extending Modern Portfolio Theory into the Domain of Corporate Diversification: Does It Apply?" *Academy of Management Journal* 37 (1994): 109–136.

24. M. E. Porter, *Competitive Advantage: Creating and Sustaining Superior Performance* (New York: The Free Press, 1985): 317–363.

25. D. J. Teece, "Economies of Scope and the Scope of the Enterprise," *Journal of Economic Behavior and Organization* 1 (1980): 223–247.

26. B. Gold, "Changing Perspectives on Size, Scale and Returns: An Integrative Survey," *Journal of Economic Literature,* 19 (1981): 5–33

27. H. I. Ansoff, *Corporate Strategy* (New York: McGraw-Hill, 1965).

28. H. Itami, *Mobilizing Invisible Assets* (Cambridge, Mass.: Harvard University Press, 1987).

29. P. R. Nayyar, "On the Measurement of Corporate Diversification.Strategy: Evidence from Large U.S. Service Firms," *Strategic Management Journal,* 13 (1992): 219–235; R. Reed and G. A. Luffman, "Diversification: The Growing Confusion," *Strategic Management Journal* 7 (1986): 29–36.

30. D. B. Jemison and S. B. Sitkin, "Corporate Acquisitions: A Process Perspective," *Academy of Management Review* 11 (1986): 145–163.

31. C. K. Prahalad and R. A. Bettis, "The Dominant Logic: A New Linkage between Diversity and Performance," *Strategic Management Journal* 7 (1986): 491.

32. P. Haspeslagh and D. B. Jemison, *Managing Acquisitions* (New York: The Free Press, 1991), 23.

33. O. Port, "Beg, Borrow and Benchmark," *Business Week* (November 30, 1993): 74–75.

34. M. E. Porter, "From Competitive Advantage to Corporate Strategy," *Harvard Business Review* (May/June 1987): 43–59.

35. R. Normann, "Organizational Innovativeness: Product Variation and Reorientation," *Administrative Science Quarterly* 16 (1971): 203–215.

36. R. A. Burgelman, "Designs for Corporate Entrepreneurship in Established Firms," *California Management Review* (Spring 1984): 154–166.

37. "Lessons from a Successful Entrepreneur," *Journal of Business Strategy* (March/April 1988): 20–24.

38. R. K. Kazanjian and R. Drazin, "Implementing Internal Diversification: Contingency Factors for Organization Design Choices," *Academy of Management Review* 12 (1987): 342–354.

39. R. A. Pitts, "Strategies and Structures for Diversification," *Academy of Management Journal* 20 (1977): 197–208.

40. C. A. Lengnick-Hall, "Innovation and Competitive Advantage: What We Know and What We Need to Learn," *Journal of Management* 18 (1992): 399–429.

41. E. R. Biggadike, "The Risky Business of Diversification," *Harvard Business Review,* (May/June 1979): 103–111;

42. E. Mansfield, "How Economists See R&D," *Harvard Business Review* (November/December 1981): 98–106. See also B. T. Lamont and Carl R. Anderson, "Mode of Corporate Diversification and Economic Performance," *Academy of Management Journal* 28 (1985): 926–934.

43. This discussion of corporate entrepreneurship draws heavily from Burgelman, "Designs for Corporate Entrepreneurship."

44. M. Lubatkin, "Value Creating Mergers: Fact or Folklore?" *Academy of Management Executive* (May 1988): 295–302; J. Pfeffer, "Merger as a Response to Organizational Interdependence," *Administrative Science Quarterly* 17 (1972): 382–394.; J. H. Song, "Diversifying Acquisitions and Financial Relationships: Testing 1974-1976 Behaviour," *Strategic Management Journal* 4 (1983): 97–108; F. Trautwein, "Merger Motives and Merger Prescriptions," *Strategic Management Journal* 11 (1990): 283–295.

45. One of the most active proponents of the view that mergers and acquisitions create value for acquiring-firm shareholders is Michael Lubatkin (see M. Lubatkin, "Value-Creating Mergers: Fact or Folklore?" *Academy of Management Executive* [November 1988]: 295–302). However, he recently reported strong evidence that contradicts his earlier conclusions in S. Chatterjee, M. H. Lubatkin, D. M. Schweiger, and Y. Weber, "Cultural Differences and Shareholder Value in Related Mergers: Linking Equity and Human Capital," *Strategic Management Journal* 13 (1992): 319–334. Other strong summary evidence that mergers and acquisitions do not create value is found in W. B. Carper, "Corporate Acquisitions and Shareholder Wealth," *Journal of Management* 16 (1990): 807–823; D. K. Datta, G. E. Pinches and V. K. Narayanan, "Factors Influencing Wealth Creation from Mergers and Acquisitions: A Meta-Analysis," *Strategic Management Journal* 13 (1992): 67–84; K. M. Davidson, "Do Megamergers Make Sense," *Journal of Business Strategies,* (Winter 1987): 40–48; T. F. Hogarty, "Profits From Merger: The Evidence of Fifty Years," *St. John's Law Review* 44 (Special Edition, 1970): 378–391; S. R. Reid, *Mergers, Managers and the Economy* (New York: McGraw-Hill, 1968).

46. M. A. Hitt, R. E. Hoskisson, R. D. Ireland, and J.S. Harrison, "Are Acquisitions a Poison Pill for Innovation?" *Academy of Management Executive* (November 1991): 20–35.

47. M. E. Porter, "From Competitive Advantage to Corporate Strategy,", 59.

48. These findings are based on original research by the authors, soon to be published in a book by Oxford University Press. See also J. B. Kusewitt, Jr., "An Exploratory Study of Strategic Acquisition Factors Relating to Success," *Strategic Management Journal* 6 (1985): 151–169; L. M. Shelton, "Strategic Business Fits and Corporate Acquisition: Empirical Evidence," *Strategic Management Journal* 9 (1988): 279–287

49. S. Chatterjee, M. H. Lubatkin, D. M. Schweiger, and Y. Weber, "Cultural Differences and Shareholder Value in

Related Mergers: Linking Equity and Human Capital," *Strategic Management Journal* 13 (1992): 319–334; D. K. Datta, "Organizational Fit and Acquisition Performance: Effects of Post-Acquisition Integration," *Strategic Management Journal* 12 (1991): 281–297; D. B. Jemison and S. B. Sitkin, "Corporate Acquisitions: A Process Perspective," *Academy of Management Review* 11 (1986): 145–163.

50. T. H. Brush, "Predicted Change In Operational Synergy and Post-Acquisition Performance of Acquired Businesses," *Strategic Management Journal* 17 (1996): 1–24.

51. F. T. Paine and D. J. Power, "Merger Strategy: An Examination of Drucker's Five Rules for Successful Acquisition," *Strategic Management Journal* 5 (1984): 99–110.

52. B. Boyrs and D. B. Jemison, "Hybrid Arrangements as Strategic Alliances: Theoretical Issues in Organizational Combinations," *Academy of Management Review* 14 (1989): 234–249; K. R. Harrigan, "Joint Ventures and Competitive Strategy," *Strategic Management Journal* 9 (1988): 141–158.

53. J. E. Olson and T. A. Cooper, "CEOs on Strategy: Two Companies, Two Strategies," *Journal of Business Strategy* (Summer 1987): 53.

54. J. S. Harrison, "Alternatives to Merger—Joint Ventures and Other Strategies," *Long Range Planning* (December 1987): 78–83.

55. C. E. Schillaci, "Designing Successful Joint Ventures," *Journal of Business Strategies* (Fall 1987): 59–63.

56. Ibid, 60. See also J. Hennart, "A Transactions Costs Theory of Equity Joint Ventures," *Strategic Management Journal* 9 (1988): 361–374.

57. Harrigan, "Joint Ventures and Competitive Strategy"; R. N. Osborn and C. C. Baughn, "Forms of Interorganizational Governance for Multinational

Alliances," *Academy of Management Journal* 33 (1990): 503–519.

58. P. Lorange and J. Roos, "Why Some Strategic Alliances Succeed and Others Fail," *Journal of Business Strategy*, (January/February 1991): 25–30.

59. Adapted from various sources including Burrows, "How a Good Partnership Goes Bad"; G. Develin and M. Bleackley, "Strategic Alliances—Guidelines for Success," *Long Range Planning*, 21, no. 5 (1988): 18–23; Lorange and Roos, "Why Some Strategic Alliances Succeed and Others Fail"; Treece, Miller, and Melcher, "The Partners."

60. R. A. Kerin, V. Mahajan and P. R. Varadarajan, *Strategic Market Planning* (Needham Heights, Mass.: Allyn & Bacon, 1990), 94; J. A. Seeger, "Reversing the Images of BCG's Growth Share Matrix," *Strategic Management Journal* 5 (1984): 93–97; S. F. Slater and T. J. Zwirlein, "Shareholder Value and Investment Strategy Using the General Portfolio Model," *Journal of Management* 18 (1992): 717–732; R. Wensley, "PIMS and BCG: New Horizons or False Dawn," *Strategic Management Journal* 3 (1982): 147–158.

61. D. C. Hambrick, I. C. MacMillan and D. L. Day, "Strategic Attributes and Performance in the BCG Matrix—A PIMS-Based Analysis of Industrial Product Businesses," *Academy of Management Journal* 25 (1982), 518.

62. Ibid.

63. B. D. Henderson, *Henderson on Corporate Strategy* (Cambridge, Mass.: Abt Books, 1979): 164.

64. C. W. Hofer and D. Schendel, *Strategy Formulation: Analytical Concepts* (St. Paul: West Publishing, 1978), 31.

65. Slater and Zwirlein, "Shareholder Value"; Seeger, "Reversing the Images."

66. Hofer and Schendel, *Strategy Formulation*, 73–76.

6

Strategy Implementation

Lockheed Martin Aircraft and Logistic Centers (LMALC)

A merger between companies in the same industry only leads to enhanced performance to the extent that similar or complementary business operations are consolidated to facilitate efficiency and the exchange of ideas and management. Such was the case for the massive merger of Lockheed and Martin Marietta to form Lockheed Martin. In late 1996, Lockheed Martin announced that it would combine several existing operating companies in its aircraft maintenance, modification, aerostructure, and logistics lines of business into a group called Lockheed Martin Aircraft and Logistics Centers (LMALC), a worldwide operation with 8,000 employees and operations in Saudi Arabia, China, Argentina, Hungary, New Zealand, California, Texas, Maryland, Florida, and South Carolina. Daniel W. Patterson, a seasoned veteran of Lockheed, was appointed president. LMALC would be headquartered in Greenville, South Carolina.

Patterson immediately assigned one of his senior executives to help oversee the integration effort. He then called together the key managers from each operation for a three-day coordination and transition meeting. A mission, vision, and guiding principles were jointly developed at the meeting. Also, individual managers were assigned to oversee the consolidation for each of the major functional areas (e.g., finance, legal, or marketing). They were instructed to report back on their progress based on a time line established at the meeting.

In February 1997, Patterson announced a new organizational structure for LMALC. The structure would be organized around Common Support Services and three major lines of business, which focused on organizational strengths. Common Support Services, to be located in Greenville, included business development (marketing), business management (financial control), human resources, and legal. The three lines of business included aircraft centers, composed of domestic and overseas aircraft modification and maintenance; aerostructures, involved in the development and repair of aerostructures for commercial and military applications; and logistics management, composed of field aircraft and vehicle maintenance and logistics support operations for military and commercial customers.[1]

Organizations employ a wide variety of tactics to implement their strategies. In this example, Lockheed Martin focused on both functional strategies and organizational structure to enhance efficiency and improve the competitiveness of its aircraft and logistics operations.

Strategy implementation typically goes hand in hand with strategy formulation, and we have made no attempt to create an artificial barrier between the two activities. However, two important implementation tools remain to be discussed. Discussing these tools during earlier chapters would have made those chapters too long. The first of these tools is functional-level strategy. The competitive advantages and distinctive competencies that firms seek are often embedded in the skills, resources, and capabilities at the functional level.[2] Functional strategies are the plans for matching those skills, resources, and capabilities to the organization's business and corporate strategies. The second topic is organizational structure.

MANAGING FUNCTIONAL STRATEGIES

Some of the most successful companies of our time are operating in low-growth, moderately profitable industries and are pursuing strategies that are not unique. The reason for their extraordinary success is their attention to the details associated with strategy implementation. For example, one reason McDonald's continues to grow and profit at a time when other hamburger chains are suffering is its fast, reliable service, clean restrooms and dining areas, and attentive, polite employees. Also, although two warehouse-style toy chains, Lionel and Child World, filed for Chapter 11 protection under federal bankruptcy law some years ago, Toys 'R' Us continues to grow and prosper because of its attention to product line and inventory management, store location and appearance, and technological improvements that reduce operating costs.

The collective pattern of day-to-day decisions made and actions taken by employees responsible for value activities create **functional strategies,** which implement the growth and competitive strategies of the business. In the following sections, we will discuss the responsibilities and patterns of decisions made by marketing, operations, R&D, information systems, human resources, and finance functions in organizations.

Marketing Strategy

One of the most critical responsibilities of marketing employees is to span the boundary of the organization and interact with external stakeholders such as customers and competitors. Marketing is responsible for bringing essential information about new customer needs, projected future demand, competitor actions, and new business opportunities into the organization as an input to plans for continuous improvements, capacity and workforce expansions, new technologies, and new products and services. In describing how Motorola makes the most of its technology, CEO George Fisher described the essential boundary-spanning role of marketing:

Members of our sales force are surrogates for customers. They should be able to reach back into Motorola and pull out technologists and other people they need to solve problems and anticipate customer needs. We want to put the salesperson at the top of the organization. The rest of us then serve the salesperson.[3]

Marketing strategy evolves from the cumulative pattern of decisions made by the employees who interact with customers and perform marketing activities. To support growth strategies, the organization's marketing function identifies new customer opportunities, suggests product opportunities, creates advertising and promotional programs, arranges distribution channels, and creates pricing and customer service policies that help position the company's products for the proper customer groups. If a company pursues a stability or retrenchment strategy within one of its businesses, the demands placed on marketing will change. Instead of pursuing growth, the marketing function may manage a reduction in the number of customer groups, distribution channels, and products in the product line—all in an attempt to focus on the more profitable and promising aspects of the business. Such was the case with Sturm Ruger & Co., a maker of guns for hunters, target shooters, and collectors. Facing a decline in the gun industry, the company decided it could no longer support wholesalers who also sold Smith & Wesson weapons. As a result, 50% of its distributors agreed to supply Ruger guns only, which reduced the company's marketing costs and helped create a prestigious, hard-to-find image for its products.[4]

A firm's competitive strategy also influences marketing decisions. Low-cost competitive strategies require low-cost channels of distribution and low-risk product and market development activities. If demand can be influenced by advertising or price discounts, then marketing managers may pursue aggressive advertising and promotion programs or deep price discounts to get demand to a level that will support full capacity utilization and economies of scale within operations, as when soft drink companies advertise and discount their products. Differentiation strategies require that marketing identify the attributes of products and services that customers will value, price and distribute the product or service in ways that capitalize on the differentiation, and advertise and promote the image of difference.

Operations Strategy

Operations strategy emerges from the pattern of decisions made within the firm about production or service operations. The task of operations managers is to design and manage an operations organization that can create the products and services the firm must have to compete in the marketplace. An effective operations unit "is not necessarily one that promises maximum efficiency or engineering perfection, but rather one that fits the needs of the business—that strives for consistency between its capabilities and policies and the competitive advantage being sought."[5]

Operations managers, like marketing managers, must manage multiple stakeholder interests as part of their daily decision making. The total quality management (TQM) movement is a direct result of operations managers' neglect of their most critical stakeholders—customers. In the 1970s, many operations managers took the position that, "We made it, now it is up to marketing to sell it." This cavalier attitude for the concerns of customers led to systemic quality problems that undermined entire industries. Faced with fundamental change in their industries, many operations organizations implemented extensive total quality management and continuous improvement programs to help focus operations decisions on the needs of customers.

Growth strategies put pressure on the systems and procedures used to schedule customer orders, plan employee work arrangements, order raw materials, and manage inventories. Retrenchment strategies often target the operations activities first: line employees are laid off, equipment is idled, plants (offices and stores) are closed. In implementing an improvement program, an organization may move to sole-source arrangements, which will increase dependency on one supplier and sever relationships with others. Differentiation strategies based on flexibility and high-quality service may require a flexible or temporary workforce, special arrangements with suppliers, and very high levels of training for employees. Major capital investments in new equipment depress earnings in the short run, which lowers the earnings per share reported to stockholders. How operations handles these types of trade-off decisions can have a substantial influence on the firm's performance.

Research and Development Strategy

In many organizations, R&D efforts are essential for effective strategy implementation. The strategy that emerges from the decisions and actions within R&D, engineering, and technical support activities is the **research and development strategy**. For example, a firm that is pursuing a market development growth strategy will invest in applications development so that its products can be tested and qualified for more uses. Fabric manufacturers, for example, put their industrial fabrics through extensive wear-testing to qualify them for everything from conveyor belts to tents to bandages. If the firm is seeking growth through product line development, the engineers and scientists within R&D will modify the product to improve its performance or extend its application to different markets. The widespread use of DuPont's Teflon fibers, coating, films, and membranes in everything from pots and pans to industrial equipment results from aggressive product development activities within the company.

Once products and entire product lines begin to mature, the focus of much of the R&D effort often shifts to process development.[6] Although some product changes may still be required, the firm is primarily concerned with reducing its costs of production. Engineers and scientists work to improve processing methods and conditions and to design special-purpose equipment that can efficiently produce the company's products. For example, some of the R&D efforts within many computer and electronics firms have been redirected toward process development as product lines have matured and foreign competitors have achieved lower processing costs.

Information Systems Strategy

Since the early 1980s, the role of information systems in organizations has changed fundamentally. Before microcomputers, computer information systems were used primarily for accounting transactions and information record keeping. In the 1980s, computer technology revolutionized the way organizations do business. In some organizations, an information systems department plans computer use organization-wide so that computer resources are compatible and integrated. However, as systems become more user-friendly and decentralized, many information system activities are being managed within other departments. The pattern of information systems decisions creates an **information systems** strategy, which provides the organization with the technology and systems that, at a minimum, are necessary for operating, planning, and controlling the business. In some instances, well-designed integrated information systems serve as the foundation for a competitive advantage by allowing more aggressive cost management than competitors or by providing more effective use of timely market information.

In many organizations, computer information systems affect every aspect of business operations and serve a major role in linking stakeholders. Local area networks (LAN) and internal webs sometimes called "Intranets" link employees and improve communications and decision making.[7] With spreadsheet packages, expert systems, and other decision-support software, employees at the lowest levels of the organization have the information and the tools necessary to make decisions that were once reserved for middle managers. Computer-aided design (CAD) systems help employees in marketing, manufacturing, and R&D to develop designs faster and with fewer errors. In computer-integrated manufacturing (CIM) environments, product designs and production schedules are linked directly to manufacturing equipment, which increases accuracy, flexibility, and speed in meeting customer orders. Direct linkages with suppliers help organizations to manage just-in-time delivery arrangements. Real-time inventory systems linked to order-taking systems provide valuable information, which improves customer service. Direct computer linkages with customers provide real-time sales data, which the organization may use to plan for the future.

Some organizations have built their entire competitive strategy on the effective use of information systems. Toys 'R' Us uses scanners to record sales data by product and by store. Store managers use the data to update inventory records and reorder products so that their in-stock position will be assured. The sales data from the hundreds of stores are transmitted daily to the corporate office where they are studied by product and by store to determine patterns and trends in customer buying behavior. Toys 'R' Us has made such effective use of its customer buying information that toy manufacturers regularly consult the company before scaling up to manufacture a new product.

Human Resources Strategy

The pattern of decisions about selection, training, rewards, and benefits creates a **human resources (HR) strategy**. Human resources managers serve a coordinating role between the organization's management and employees, and between the organization and external stakeholder groups including labor unions and government regulators of labor and safety practices such as the Equal Employment Opportunity Commission and the Occupational Safety and Health Administration.

Different industry environments and organizational strategies tend to reinforce different HR practices. In high technology and growth organizations, employees are usually hired from outside the organization to fill positions at all levels, and entry positions through top-level management. Compensation systems emphasize long-range performance goals, with frequent use of bonus and profit-sharing plans.[8] Therefore, in organizations pursuing growth strategies, like Microsoft in software and Merck in pharmaceuticals, the HR strategy focuses on hiring, training, and placing employees at all levels in the organization, as well as on developing performance-based compensation strategies.

Mature or cost-oriented businesses usually hire employees at the entry level and promote from within to fill higher-level positions. They are more likely to focus rewards on short-range performance goals and to include seniority issues in compensation systems.[9] Firms following retrenchment strategies, such as General

Motors, IBM, and Delta Airlines, have to focus their HR priorities on programs for early retirements, structured layoffs, skills retraining, and outplacement services.

As companies become more global, the challenges for the HR staff mount. The HR staff must determine what skills are needed to manage people of different cultures, recruit top candidates worldwide, create training programs and experiences that help employees appreciate other cultures, and conduct global relocations.[10] Furthermore, the HR staff may need to create compensation strategies for employees who, because of their national culture, value different reward and benefit packages. For example, in cultures that value personal accomplishment, control of one's destiny and independence, such as the United States and Britain, compensation strategies may focus on individual performance. In cultures that value team accomplishment, sacrifice for others, and external control or fate, the rewards may focus on group measures and seniority.[11]

Financial Strategy

The finance and accounting functions play a strategic role within organizations because they control one of the most important resources needed to implement strategies: money. In implementing strategy, two sources of funds are needed: (1) large amounts of capital for growth and maintenance-related objectives and strategies and (2) expense budgets to support the ongoing, daily activities of the business. The primary purpose of a **financial strategy** is to provide the organization with the capital structure and funds that are appropriate for implementing growth and competitive strategies.

The finance group decides the appropriate levels of debt, equity, and internal financing needed to support strategies by weighing the costs of each alternative, the plans for the funds, and the financial interests of various internal and external stakeholder groups. Finance also determines dividend policies and, by preparing financial reports, influences how financial performance will be interpreted and presented to stockholders. In fact, financial reports may be the only contact some members of the investment community and most stockholders have with the organization.

Capital and expense budgets are an extremely important means for allocating funds to those departments, projects, and activities that need them to support strategies. All expenditures in capital and expense budgets should link back to the strategies of the firm.

The structure that a mature enterprise takes on at any point in time essentially represents the accumulation of a long series of prior resource allocation decisions. If a company wants to develop in a specific direction, it must make these resource allocation decisions in an organized fashion.[12]

The trade-offs that are embedded in financial decisions carry significant implications for strategy implementation. Should the firm pay earnings out in dividends to satisfy stockholders who want a fast return on their investment, or should the firm invest earnings back into the company to benefit employees, communities, and stockholders who want a longer-term increase in share price? In assessing expenses, investments, and earnings, should long-run or short-run performance be given more emphasis and how should that information be presented to stockholders and the investment community? Which internal stakeholder groups—marketing, operations, R&D, employees—should be most influential in capital allocation decisions?

Integrating Functional Strategies

Some researchers have found that in those firms where strategies were implemented effectively, employees worked as a coordinated system with all of their separate but interdependent efforts directed toward the goals of the firm.[13] Consequently, each functional area is one piece of a larger system and coordination among the pieces is essential to successful strategy execution. Therefore, well-developed functional strategies should have the following characteristics:

1. *Decisions made within each function will be consistent with each other.* For example, if marketing chooses to spend a great deal of money creating a premium brand name for a new product, it should take advantage of distribution channels that allow the product to reach customers who will pay a premium price. If the wrong distribution channels are chosen, then the efforts spent on advertising, promotion, and product placement will be lost. Several years ago, one of the synthetic fiber producers allowed one of its best branded products to become associated with discount, low-quality garments and its investment in the trademark was lost.

2. *Decisions made within one function will be consistent with those made in other functions.* Unfortunately, it is common for the decisions made by one department to be inconsistent with those of another department. Marketing and operations frequently advocate very different approaches to the many interdependent decisions that exist between them. Left to their own devices, with no guidance from the organization, it is likely that marketing, over time, will make decisions that implement a differentiation strategy while manufacturing, over time, implements a low-cost strategy.

3. *Decisions made within functions will be consistent with the strategies of the business.* In a healthy business environment, marketing may pursue market share increases and revenue growth as its top priority. If the business environment changes—demand slows down and profits are squeezed—then the focus of marketing may have to change to stability and profit improvement over sales volume increases. Unless prodded by the organization, marketing may be very reluctant to change from its traditional way of doing business.[14]

The rapid success and subsequent decline of People Express Airlines is a good demonstration of what can happen when there is inconsistency in tactical decisions across departments or between a business strategy and functional strategies.

Following the deregulation of the airlines, Donald Burr started People Express as a low-cost commuter airline. In the beginning, every management decision supported low costs: aircraft were bought second hand, pilots kept planes in the air more hours per day than any other airline, terminal leases were inexpensive, and human resource policies required cross-training, encouraged high productivity, and rewarded employees with profit-sharing plans. In line with its no-frills commuter approach, the company did not book reservations or provide in-flight meals. The airline was extraordinarily successful with its strategy, and achieved the lowest cost position in the industry. However, with success, People Express began to alter its pattern of decisions and, over time, drifted from its low-cost strategy. It pursued longer routes which pulled it into direct competition with the full-service airlines, even though it did not have the elaborate reservation systems and customer services. It contracted more expensive terminal arrangements and purchased new aircraft at market prices. The close-knit, high-performance culture which encouraged an extraordinary work pace in exchange for profit-sharing was undermined by rapid growth and too many new faces. Just a few years after its start-up, People Express was in serious financial trouble and was forced to sell out to another airline.

Value chain analysis, which we introduced in Chapter 3, is useful for planning the coordination of functional activities during strategy implementation. For managers, the key task of strategy implementation is to align or fit the activities and capabilities of the firm with its chosen strategy. An understanding of the linkages and interdependencies among the value-adding activities becomes critical. For example, in a firm pursuing a low-cost strategy, systemwide low costs are the goal. If the firm manages each activity independently, then what may appear to be a proper low-cost decision may, in fact, work to create higher systemwide costs. For example, if the firm purchases raw materials at the lowest possible price, it may actually be creating higher production costs because of the rework and extra handling required to accommodate lower-quality materials. In such a case, the decisions within each activity seem to fit the firm's strategy but collectively they do not. Table 6.1 summarizes the functional strategy decision areas. It may be used as a tool for determining functional strategy needs and critiquing consistency among value-adding activities.

STRUCTURING TO SUPPORT STRATEGY

The **formal structure** specifies the number and types of departments or groups and provides the formal reporting relationships and lines of communication among internal stakeholders. An organization's structure should be designed to support the firm's intended strategy.[15] The underlying assumption is that a strategy-structure fit will lead to superior organization performance. When making decisions about how to structure an organization, it is important for managers to remember the following:

1. Structure is not an end, but a means to an end. The end is successful organizational performance.
2. There is no one best structure. A change in organizational strategy may require a corresponding change in structure to avoid administrative inefficiencies, but the organization's size, strategies, external environment, stakeholder relationships, and management style all influence the appropriateness of a given structure. All structures embody trade-offs.[16]
3. Once in place, the new structure becomes a characteristic of the organization that will serve as a constraint on future strategic choices.
4. Administrative inefficiencies, poor service to customers, communication problems, or employee frustrations may indicate a strategy-structure mismatch.

Business-Level Structures

In Chapter 5, we discussed the types of growth and competitive strategies available to businesses. When managers organize the activities of a business, they usually seek a structure that will support those growth and competitive strategies. Managers typically use one of four organizational structures when grouping the activities of a single business or division: functional, product or market group, project matrix, or network. Each of the four structures, illustrated in Figure 6.1, has important strengths and weaknesses, which the organization's managers must consider when making organizational design decisions. The attributes of the four structures are summarized in Table 6.2.

Functional Structure. A **functional structure,** illustrated in Figure 6.1, is organized around the inputs or activities that are required to produce products and services, such as marketing, operations, finance, and R&D.[17] Organizations that are functionally structured usually have marketing, operations, finance, and R&D departments. The structure is centralized, highly specialized, and most appropriate when a company is offering a limited product line to a particular market seg-

Table 6.1 *Conducting a Functional Strategy Audit*

The functional strategy audit is a procedure for systematically reviewing the decisions in each of the functional areas to determine which ones should be changed to support the new strategy and needs of stakeholders. The format for the audit is shown.

	Current	Change Needed

Marketing Strategy Decisions

Target customers
  (few versus many, what groups, what regions)

Product positioning
  (premium, commodity, multiuse, specialty use)

Product line mix
  (a mix of complementary products)

Product line breadth
  (a full line offering of products)

Pricing strategies
  (discount, moderate, premium prices)

Promotion practices
  (direct sales, advertising, direct mail)

Distribution channels
  (few or many, sole contract relationships)

Customer service policies
  (flexibility, responsiveness, quality)

Product/service image
  (premium quality, good price, reliable)

Market research
  (accuracy and frequency of information
  on customers and competitors)

Operations Strategy Decision Areas

Capacity planning
  (lead demand to ensure availability or lag demand
  to achieve capacity utilization)

Facility location
  (locate near suppliers, customers, labor, natural
  resources, transportation)

Facility layout
  (continuous or intermittent flow)

Technology and equipment choices
  (degree of automation, computerization)

Sourcing arrangements
  (cooperative relationships with a few versus competitive bid)

Planning and scheduling
  (make to stock, make to order, flexibility to
  customer requests)

(continued on next page)

Table 6.1 *Conducting a Functional Strategy Audit (continued)*

	Current	Change Needed
Quality assurance (acceptance sampling, process control, standards)		
Workforce policies (training levels, cross-training, reward systems)		
R&D/Technology Strategy Decision Areas Research focus (product, process, applications)		
Orientation (leader versus follower)		
Project priorities (budget, quality, creativity, time)		
Linkages with external research organizations		
Information Systems Strategy Decision Areas Hardware capability and integration across the organization (mainframe, network, hardwire linkages, dial-up)		
Software capability and integration across the organization (user support, compatibility, security, standardization)		
Linkages with customers and suppliers (direct links, shared systems)		
Investments in new technologies (Internet, bar-code scanners, satellite technology)		
Strategic use of internal and external information (Decision support, operations support, marketing support, forcasting)		
Human Resources Strategy Decision Areas Recruitment (entry-level versus experienced employees)		
Selection (selection criteria and methods)		
Performance appraisal (appraisal methods, frequency)		
Salary and wages (relationship to performance, competitiveness)		
Benefits (bonuses, stock-ownership programs, other benefits)		
Personnel actions (disciplinary plans, outplacement, early retirements)		
Training (types of training, availability to all employees)		

(continued)

Table 6.1 *Conducting a Functional Strategy Audit (continued)*

	Current	Change Needed

Financial Strategy Decision Areas
Capital
  (debt versus equity versus internal financing)

Financial reporting to stockholders

Minimum return on investment levels
  (relationship to cost of capital)

Basis for allocating overhead costs
  (direct labor, machine use, sales volume, activity)

Evaluation of Consistency
Are all of the marketing decisions internally consistent?

Operations decisions? R&D decisions? Human
resource decisions?

Financial decisions? Information system decisions?

Are the decisions in each function consistent with decisions in other functions?

Are the functional decisions consistent with the
planned strategy of the firm and the expectations of
stakeholders?

ment and the needs of external stakeholders are relatively stable. The functional structure is oriented toward internal efficiency and encourages functional expertise. It is particularly appropriate in organizations that want to exploit economies of scale and learning effects from focused activities. Small and start-up businesses often employ functional structures very effectively. A functional structure can also be effective for a firm pursuing a market penetration strategy because the organizational scope (i.e., the number of products and markets) and stakeholder requirements will be relatively stable over time.

Product/Market Structure. A **product or market group** structure organizes activities around the outputs of the organization system, such as products, customers, or geographical regions.[18] Figure 6.1(b) is an example of a product/market structure organized around product groups, but the other varieties of this structure are just as common. When a business pursues a product development strategy, it adds products to its product line and interacts with more customers, distributors, and suppliers. If the growth and complexity leads to administrative inefficiencies and confusion, then the business may need to shift from a functional structure to product divisions or groups. The more decentralized groups can handle the broader scope of activities and be more responsive to the diverse needs of customers.

Firms that pursue market development growth strategies also add complexity that may require a new structure. A firm that expands its business from a

Figure 6.1 *Types of Business-Level Structures*

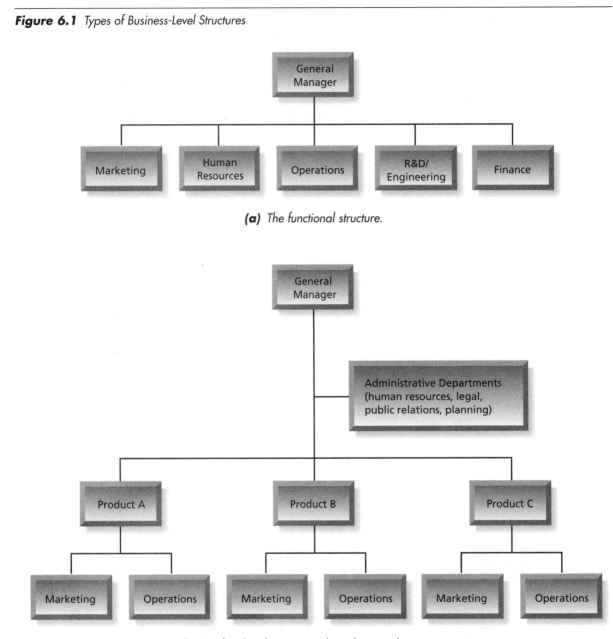

(a) The functional structure.

(b) Product/market structure based on product groups.

(continued on next page)

regional market base to a national market base may form new units around geographical market segments. For example, a restaurant chain or retail toy chain may be divided into units responsible for eastern and western regions. A firm that seeks out new customer groups and new product applications may reorganize around customer groups. For example, a soft drink company may divide its business into "fountain" and "retail" segments, with the fountain unit targeting its marketing and sales efforts to restaurants and theaters and the retail unit focusing

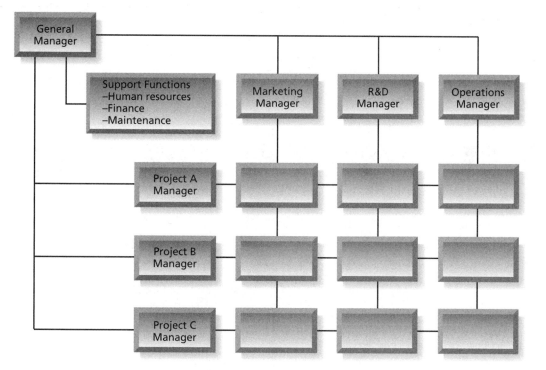

(c) The project matrix structure.

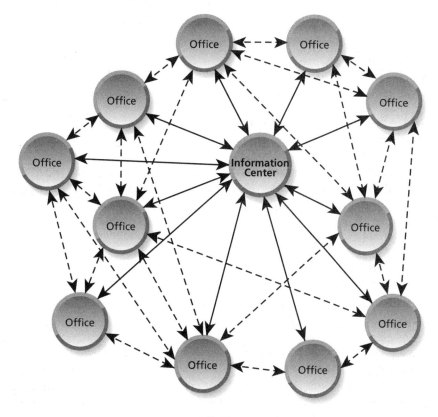

(d) The network structure.

	Functional	Product/Market	Project Matrix	Network
Organizing Framework	Inputs	Outputs	Inputs and outputs	Outputs
Degree of Centralization	Centralized	Decentralized	Decentralized with sharing	Very decentralized
Competitive Environment	Stable	Dynamic with external market pressures	Dynamic with external market pressures and internal technical pressures	Competitive conditions differ from region to region
Growth Strategy	Market penetration	Market or product development	Frequent new product/market development managed as project teams	Market penetration and market development

Table 6.2 Attributes of Business-Level Structures

on grocery and convenience stores. An architectural firm might organize around commercial, military, and residential projects.

Project Matrix Structure. A hybrid structure that combines some elements of both functional and product/market forms is called a **project matrix structure**. The project matrix structure is viewed by some as a transition stage between a functional form and a product/market group structure and by others as a complex form necessary for complex environments.[19] Either way, the many influences that simultaneously pull an organization toward functional forms and the more diverse market/product forms reach an equilibrium in the matrix structure. Project matrix structures are most common in turbulent or uncertain competitive environments where coordination between different functional departments is extremely important and external stakeholder demands are diverse and changing.[20] Matrix structures can improve communications between groups, increase the amount of information the organization can handle, and allow more flexible use of people and equipment.[21]

In a matrix structure, the organization is simultaneously functional and either product, market, or project oriented, as shown in Figure 6.1(c). Fluor Daniel, one of the world's largest engineering design and construction companies, employs a matrix structure.

At Fluor Daniel, it is very common for design engineers to report to two or more managers: the project manager on a particular contract and the functional manager of their particular design area, such as electrical or mechanical systems. The dual reporting relationships of the matrix structure emphasize the equal importance of functional design performance and service on the particular project. The functional dimension encourages employees to share technical information from one project to the next (learning) and helps avoid unnecessary duplication of skills. The project dimension allows the organization to focus on serving the needs of the customer while simultaneously encouraging cooperation and coordination among the different interdependent functions.

Unfortunately, matrix structures can be disconcerting for employees because of the "too many bosses" problem. Not only is it difficult to balance the needs of the different lines of authority and coordinate among the many people and schedules, the sheer number of people that must be involved in decision making can slow decision processes and add administrative costs.[22] The overall complexity of the structure can create ambiguity and conflict between functional and product managers and between individuals.

Network Structure. Some organizations, particularly large integrated service organizations, use the network, or spider's web, structure.[23] The **network structure** is very decentralized and is organized around customer groups or geographical regions. As shown in Figure 6.1(d), a network structure represents a web of independent units, with little or no formal hierarchy to organize and control their relationships. The independent units are loosely organized to capture and share useful information. Other than information sharing, however, little formal contact exists among operating units. When formal contact is needed, committees and task forces are created on an ad hoc basis. The network structure is particularly appropriate in knowledge intensive industries where decentralization and duplication of resources are required to service the market, yet there are no manufacturing or technology economies of scale to drive centralization, such as large medical and legal practices, investment banking firms, and charitable institutions like United Way and Girl Scouts of America.

Arthur Anderson & Co. is an accounting firm with 243 offices managed by over 2,000 partners in 54 countries. Using a CD-ROM system, the company links its highly independent offices so they can share information. It maintains worldwide customer reference files and up-to-date resource information on tax rules, customers, court rulings, and professional standards. The files are updated regularly and distributed to each office.[24]

A network structure may not be appropriate when high levels of coordination and resource sharing are required because it represents an extreme form of decentralization, with executive level management serving primarily an advisory function and lower level managers controlling most decisions. The weaknesses of the network structure include the potential for lost control of the autonomous units and high costs from the extensive duplication of resources.

CORPORATE-LEVEL STRUCTURES

As organizations grow and pursue different business opportunities, administrative problems and complexity create pressures to break the organization into more manageable units. As part of the process of corporate strategy implementation, managers must structure and align the different business units. Earlier we discussed structuring *within* a business unit. In this section we are concerned with structuring relationships *among* an organization's businesses.

Depending on the strategies that are being pursued, management may be interested in cultivating independence or interdependence among business units. **Independence** among units requires an organizational structure that encourages separation and autonomy, as well as coordinating mechanisms that achieve hierarchical (between business units and top management) rather than lateral (among business units) coordination. An independent structure is appropriate when businesses are unrelated and managers only seek financial synergies.

When pursuing a related diversification strategy, managers try to convert the theoretical relatedness and fit of multibusiness strategies and strategic alliances into true synergistic relationships that benefit the organization as a whole. To exploit operational synergies, managers must structure relationships among businesses and partners in ways that encourage **interdependence** and manage them over time with shared goals, shared information, shared resources, and cooperative program development.[25]

Multibusiness organizations use four general types of structures: multidivisional, strategic business unit, corporate matrix, and transnational. Table 6.3 shows the issues that are raised when deciding among corporate-level structures.

Multidivisional Structure. If an organization has a few businesses in its portfolio, management may choose a line-of-business, or **multidivisional** structure, with each business existing as an autonomous unit. For example, a multidivisional organization may have an agricultural chemicals division, an industrial chemicals division, and a pharmaceuticals division. In this type of structure, a general manager—usually referred to as a divisional vice president—heads up each of the three divisions. Each division has its own support activities, including sales, accounting and finance, personnel, and research and development. Services that are common to all three businesses, such as legal services, public relations, and

	Number of Businesses	Relatedness	Need for Coordination	Expected Synergy
Divisional	Few	Moderate/low	Moderate/low	Financial Limited operational
SBU	Many	Groups of related businesses	Moderate within SBU Low between SBUs	Limited operational within SBU Financial among SBUs
Corporate Matrix	Few or many	High	Very high	High operational synergies: cost, access, or innovation
Transnational	Many, in different nations	High	Very high	High operational synergies: cost, access, or innovation

***Table 6.3** Making the Corporate Structure Choice*

corporate research are housed at the corporate level. The multidivisional structure is appropriate when management of the different businesses does not require sharing of employees, marketing resources, or operations facilities.

The multidivisional structure, shown in Figure 6.2, has several advantages. By existing as a separate unit, each business is better able to focus its efforts on the needs of its particular stakeholders, without being distracted by the problems of other businesses. Corporate-level management is freed from day-to-day issues and is able to take a long-term, integrative view of the collection of businesses. Corporate executives may monitor the performance of each division separately and allocate corporate resources for specific activities that show promise.

With the multidivisional structure, it is often difficult to decide which activities will be performed at the corporate level and which will be held within each division. Competition for corporate resources (e.g., R&D, legal, and investment funds) may create coordination difficulties among divisions. Also, organizational efforts may be duplicated, particularly when the different businesses within the corporate portfolio are highly related. Shared distribution channels or common process development may save costs for the two businesses, yet separation in the organizational structure discourages cooperation. Although many firms use multidivisional structures when configuring the relationships between related businesses, the structure makes resource sharing and cooperation difficult. Unfortunately, resource sharing and cooperation are necessary for synergy. Therefore, multidivisional corporate structures may interfere with the creation of synergies within organizations.

Strategic Business Unit Structure. When an organization is broadly diversified with several businesses in its portfolio, it becomes difficult for top management to keep track of and understand the many different industry environments and busi-

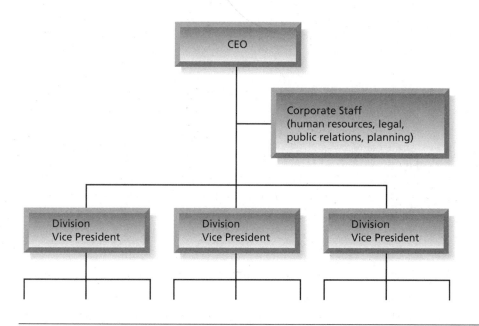

Figure 6.2 The Multidivisional Structure

ness conditions. Management may choose to form **strategic business units** (SBUs) with each SBU incorporating a few closely related businesses. Each SBU is composed of related divisions, with divisional vice presidents reporting to an SBU or group vice president. If an organization becomes very large, it may combine strategic business units into groups or sectors, thus adding another level of management. An example of an SBU structure is shown in Figure 6.3.

advantage

The SBU structure makes it possible for top management to keep track of many businesses at one time. It allows decentralization around dimensions that are meaningful to the business, such as markets or technologies, so that the complexity will not overload top managers. The intent of the structure is to provide top management with a manageable number of units to keep track of and to force responsibility for decision making lower in the organization, near the important internal and external stakeholders. The difficulty of the SBU structure is that operating units, and therefore the customer, are even further removed from top management than in the multidivisional form. As with the multidivisional form, there

disadvantage

is competition for corporate financial and staff resources, which may create conflicts and coordination problems.

Corporate Matrix Structure. The **corporate matrix** is the corporate-level counterpart to the project matrix structure described earlier. It is a way to achieve a high degree of coordination among several related businesses. Corporate matrix structures are used when the individual businesses within a corporation's portfolio need to take advantage of resource, information, or technology sharing in order to succeed in their industries. The corporate matrix structure tries to reach a balance between pressures to decentralize units closer to market and technological trends, and pressures to maintain centralized control to bring about economies of scope and shared learning.

3M is a global company with 23 business units producing 60,000 products in 55 countries. Harry Hammerly, executive vice president of international operations, has described the 3M structure this way:

When people ask how we structure a corporation with such a disparate lot of variables, I begin by discussing 3M's matrix management structure. One side of the matrix represents the company's product divisions. Along the other axis are the international subsidiaries. For any business in an international subsidiary, responsibility is shared by the managing director of the subsidiary (who reports through area or regional vice-presidents to me as head of International Operations) and the product manager (who reports to the vice-president of his or her division).[26]

The corporate matrix structure is particularly appropriate for related diversification strategies and global strategies. For example, a consumer products firm that has businesses in beverages, snack foods, and packaged foods may use a matrix structure to capitalize on economies of scale and capture synergies in marketing and distribution, as shown in Figure 6.4. When properly managed, the corporate matrix structure improves coordination among different internal stakeholders by forcing managers within related businesses to maintain close contact with each other. It can help the organization become more flexible and responsive to changes in the business environment and can encourage teamwork and participation.[27]

The corporate matrix form may also be effective in structuring an organization that produces several products that are all sold in several nations. A multinational organization may create a matrix structure, which groups all products under each national manager and simultaneously groups all nations under each

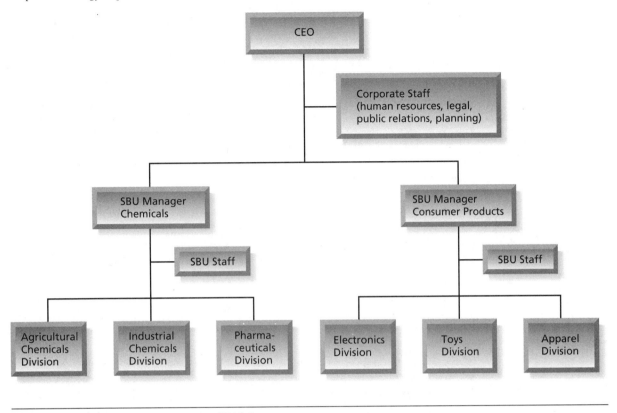

Figure 6.3 *The Strategic Business Unit (SBU) Structure*

product manager. This type of matrix structure allows the firm to achieve a national focus in its marketing and distribution practices and encourages synergies through economies of scale and shared information within each product category. The corporate matrix structure applied to a multinational organization is also shown in Figure 6.4.

Transnational Structure. A more complex version of the corporate matrix structure is the **transnational** form.[28] Whereas the global matrix structure organizes businesses along two dimensions, the transnational structure organizes businesses along three dimensions: nation or region, product, and function. The transnational form is an attempt to achieve integration within product categories, within nations, and within functions while simultaneously achieving coordination across all of those activities. Organizations that employ transnational structures can build three capabilities: responsiveness and flexibility at the national level, global scale economies, and learning, which transcends national, functional, and product boundaries.[29] Many large multiproduct global organizations, in industries ranging from computers to consumer products, are making the transition to a transnational structure. Xerox uses a transnational structure, as described by chairman and CEO Paul Allaire:

We have created an organization that by its very design forces managers to confront—and manage—the necessary tensions between autonomy and integration . . . In a sense, we have turned the traditional vertically organized company on its side. At one end is technology, and

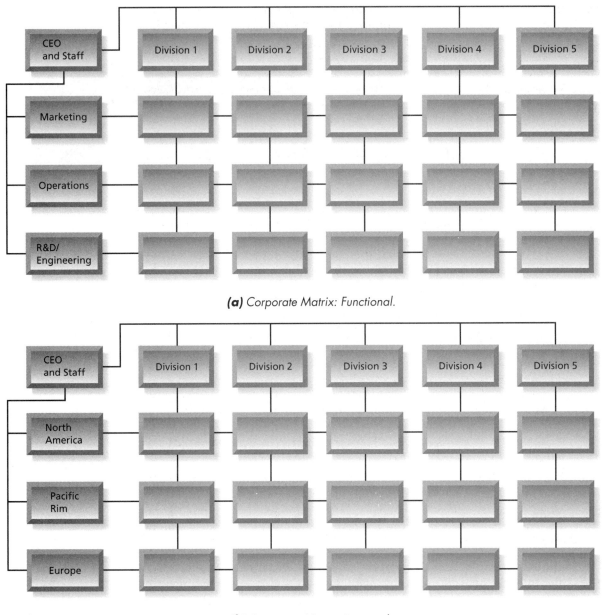

(a) Corporate Matrix: Functional.

(b) Corporate Matrix: Regional.

Figure 6.4 Types of Corporate Matrix Structures

we have retained an integrated corporate research and technology organization. At the other end is the customer. We have organized our sales and service people into three geographic customer-operations divisions, so that we can keep a common face to the customer. Between these two poles are the new business divisions. Their purpose is to create some suction on technology and pull it into the marketplace.[30]

The corporate matrix and transnational structures are plagued by one serious difficulty: sheer complexity may interfere with what they are designed to accomplish. It is difficult to balance the needs of the different functional, national, and product stakeholders. The unusual command structure can create an atmosphere of ambiguity, conflict, and mixed loyalties. The overall complexity and bureaucracy of the structure may stifle creativity and slow decision making because of the sheer number of people that must be involved. Furthermore, the administrative costs associated with decision delays and extra management may overwhelm the benefits of coordination.[31] To derive the benefits of any of the corporate-level or business-level structures, but especially those that are more complex, managers must take extra steps to ensure coordination.

KEY POINTS SUMMARY

In this chapter, we described the functional strategies and organizational structures that are used in implementing strategies. The following points were discussed:

1. Strategies are implemented through the day-to-day decisions and actions of employees throughout the organization.
2. Management's challenge is to create a pattern of integrated, coordinated decisions that meets the needs of stakeholders and fulfills the planned strategy of the organization.
3. Functional strategies are represented by the pattern of decisions made by employees in marketing, operations, research and development, information systems, human resources, and finance. Managers must ensure that decisions within each area are consistent with each other, with other functions, and with the stated strategies of the firm.
4. In configuring the relationships among departments in a single business, organizations usually employ one of the following structures: functional, product/market group, project matrix, or network.
5. The functional structure encourages functional specialization and focus but discourages coordination between functions or departments.
6. The product/market group segments products and markets into smaller, more manageable subunits that may improve service to customers or economies of scale but result in resource duplication.
7. The project matrix structure employs a dual-reporting relationship that is intended to balance functional focus and expertise required for learning with responsiveness to customer needs. However, it may create ambiguity and slow decision making if managed improperly.
8. The network structure is a very decentralized form that is particularly well suited to geographically dispersed offices, stores, or units that, except for some sharing of information and operating policies, operate independently.
9. At the corporate level, multidivisional and strategic business unit structures divide businesses into divisions. Although these structures focus the organization on the needs of its stakeholders, they make coordination and resource sharing among businesses, which are necessary to exploit operating synergies, very difficult.
10. Corporate matrix and transnational structures are intended to exploit economies, learning, and resource sharing across businesses; however, they require extra measures of coordination to avoid divided loyalties, slow decision making, and management conflicts.

REFERENCES

1. Based on news releases, internal company documents, and personal knowledge.
2. L. G. Hrebiniak and W. F. Joyce, *Implementing Strategy* (New York: Macmillan, 1984).
3. B. Avishai and W. Taylor, "Customers Drive a Technology-Driven Company: An Interview with George Fisher," *Harvard Business Review* 67, no. 6 (November-December 1989): 107–108.
4. J. Millman, "Steady Finger on the Trigger," *Forbes*, (November 9, 1992): 188–189.
5. R. Hayes and S. Wheelwright, *Restoring Our Competitive Edge: Competing through Manufacturing* (New York: John Wiley & Sons, 1984): 30.
6. W. J. Abernathy and P. L. Townsend, "Technology, Productivity, and Process Change," *Technological Forecasting and Social Change* 7, no. 4 (1975): 379–396.
7. A. Cortese, "Here Comes the Intranet," *Business Week* (February 26, 1996): 76–80; A. L. Sprout, "The Internet Inside Your Company," *Fortune* (November 27, 1995): 161–168.
8. C. Fisher, "Current and Recurrent Challenges in HRM," *Journal of Management* 15, no. 2 (1989): 157–180.
9. C. Fisher, "Current and Recurrent Challenges in HRM."
10. N. M. Tichy, "Setting the Global Human Resource Management Agenda for the 1990s," *Human Resource Management* 27, no. 1 (Spring 1988): 1–18.
11. L. R. Gomez-Mejia and T. Welbourne, "Compensation Strategies in a Global Context," *Human Resource Planning*, 14, no. 1, (Spring 1992): 29–41.
12. R. H. Hayes, S. C. Wheelwright, and K. B. Clark, *Dynamic Manufacturing* (New York: The Free Press, 1988), 61.
13. F. W. Gluck, S. D. Kaufman, and A. S. Walleck, "Strategic Management for Competitive Advantage," *Harvard Business Review* (July/August 1980):154–161.
14. Hayes and Wheelwright, *Restoring our Competitive Edge: Competing Through Manufacturing.*
15. A. D. Chandler, *Strategy and Structure: Chapters in the History of the American Industrial Enterprise* (Cambridge, Mass.: The MIT Press, 1962).
16. P. R. Lawrence and J. W. Lorsch, *Organization and Environment* (Homewood, Ill.: Irwin, 1969): 23–39.
17. A. C. Hax and N. S. Majluf, *The Strategy Concept and Process: A Pragmatic Approach* (Englewood Cliffs, N.J.: Prentice Hall, 1991).
18. Hax and Majluf, *The Strategy Concept and Process: A Pragmatic Approach.*
19. J. R. Galbraith and R. K. Kazanjian, *Strategy Implementation: Structure, Systems, and Processes,* 2nd ed. (St. Paul: West Publishing, 1986).
20. R. L. Daft, *Organization Theory and Design*, 3rd ed. (St. Paul: West Publishing, 1989): 240.
21. R. C. Ford and W. A. Randolph, "Cross-Functional Structures: A Review and Integration of Matrix Organization and Project Management,"*Journal of Management*, 18, no. 2 (1992): 267–294.
22. Ford and Randolph, "Cross-Functional Structures: A Review and Integration of Matrix Organization and Project Management."
23. J. B. Quinn, *Intelligent Enterprise* (New York: The Free Press, 1992).
24. Quinn, *Intelligent Enterprise.*
25. C. W. L. Hill, M. A. Hitt, and R. E. Hoskisson, "Cooperative versus Competitive Structures in Related and Unrelated Diversified Firms," *Organization Science* 3, no. 4 (November 1992): 501–521.
26. H. Hammerly, "Matching Global Strategies with National Responses," *The Journal of Business Strategy* (March/April 1992): 10.
27. R. C. Ford and W. A. Randolph, "Cross-Functional Structures: A Review and Integration of Matrix Organization and Project Management," *Journal of Management*, 18, no. 2 (1992): 267–294.
28. C. A. Bartlett and S. Ghoshal, *Managing across Borders: The Transnational Solution* (Boston, Mass.: Harvard Business School Press, 1989).
29. C. A. Bartlett and S. Ghoshal, "The New Global Manager," *Harvard Business Review* (September/October 1992): 124–132.
30. R. Howard, "The CEO as Organizational Architect: An Interview with Xerox's Paul Allaire," *Harvard Business Review* (September/October 1992): 112.
31. Ford and Randolph, "Cross Functional Structures: A Review and Integration of Matrix Organization and Project Management."

chapter7

Strategic Control and Restructuring

Pinkerton's Inc.

In 1992, Pinkerton's Inc., one of the world's largest security companies, was out of control. In the first six months, operating expenses rose 36%, accompanied by a drop in earnings of 41%. All the time executives were telling investors that business was booming. As a result, a group of shareholders filed a legal suit charging that executives misled them so that they could sell some of their shares at an inflated price. The stock price fell from $36 at the beginning of 1992 to around $15 in September.

In an effort to increase revenues, Pinkerton's engaged in a major acquisition program in 1991. The company bought a host of small security guard contracting firms with the intention of making the combined businesses more efficient through economies of scale. Instead, costs increased dramatically and the recession hurt profit margins, but no one at Pinkerton's had any idea what was happening. Investment manager James Ruf, president of Ruf Investment Group, explained, "The real fault with the company was not having stronger financial controls."

Thomas Wathen, CEO of Pinkerton's, is tightening those controls, reducing overhead, and cutting costs. In particular, he purchased a new computer system and hired a new financial officer to keep tabs on operations. He also consolidated offices to reduce expenses and canceled a planned expansion into alarm systems. Concerning his too rosy financial forecast, he claimed, "I probably won't ever make another projection in my life."[1]

How can a large security company with experienced managers end up in such an undesirable situation by surprise? The answer is that top executives were not adequately keeping track of organizational progress. Wathen led Pinkerton's in an ambitious external growth strategy without checking to see what effect the acquisitions were having on financial performance. Now he must scramble to recoup his lost credibility as a manager. In responding to the crisis, Wathen is trying to set his organization on a new course by emphasizing a series of restructuring tactics. In the first half of this chapter, we address the development of strategic control systems, which should warn managers when performance is off target. In the second half, we discuss the restructuring methods that may be used to reorient an organization that has slipped out of control.

STRATEGIC CONTROL SYSTEMS

From the perspective of top executives, a **strategic control system** is "a system to support managers in assessing the relevance of the organization's strategy to its progress in the accomplishment of its goals, and when discrepancies exist, to support areas needing attention."[2] Many existing control systems are based almost exclusively on accounting measures such as return on investment (ROI).[3] Because financial reporting requirements included figures for income, assets, and sales, managers can easily calculate ROI or related measures from existing data. In some organizations they are the only important measure of success. In the words of Roger Smith, past CEO of General Motors, "I look at the bottom line. It tells me what to do."[4]

Unfortunately, according to some control experts, accounting-based measures are "too late, too aggregated, and too distorted to be relevant for managers' planning and control decisions."[5] Lateness refers to the long lag times between the organizational transactions themselves and the dates financial reports come out. For example, Pinkerton's management did not know the company was in trouble until so much time had passed that the problem became very large. The aggregation problem simply means that accounting measures do not contain the detail that is necessary to make meaningful improvements to specific organizational processes. Finally, by relying too heavily on accounting information only, managers can develop a distorted view of an organization's performance. Distortion is a particular problem when managers do not understand the effects of the policies that determine the way inventories, plant, and equipment are valued and the way overhead costs are allocated to various departments and divisions.

In addition, accounting-based financial measures can prompt managers to behave in ways that are counterproductive over the long run. For example, financial measures such as ROI, if given too much emphasis in the short run, discourage investments in long-term research and development projects because expenses must be paid out immediately whereas benefits may not accrue until many financial periods later.[6] Also, managers may shut down lines or cancel services that appear to be too costly, placing an emphasis on products and services that are produced most efficiently. These types of decisions are fine as long as customers do not prefer the more costly products and services. However, the end result is often that the overproduced "efficient" goods and services have to be sold at a discount to stimulate customer interest. Consequently, profit margins are eroded and the organization would have been better off keeping the lines or services that were dropped.

In traditional accounting-based control systems, control information tends to be collected at the top of the organization. Consequently, top executives possess all of the power to control organizational processes. These managers analyze the information and instruct subordinates on the expected levels of performance. This type of system assumes that organizational learning occurs at the top of the organization. Unfortunately, most top managers are too distant from the value creating activities of their companies to understand or learn what needs to be done to improve long-run performance. This type of management is known as "management by remote control."[7] As a control expert put it:

> The chief problem with using accounting information to control operations—managing by remote control—is the tendency for businesses to lose sight of the processes by which people and customers make a company competitive and profitable. What I believe has happened in American businesses since the 1950s is that managers and operating personnel at all levels have lost sight of people, customers, and processes as top management has turned everyone's attention to accounting results.[8]

Competitive forces in the global economy have led to the need for a more diverse set of control procedures. In particular, although traditional accounting-based controls do not necessarily need to be eliminated, they should be balanced with other types of controls. For example, "grassroots" or "bottom-up" controls leave as much information as possible as close to the customer as possible. For these types of systems to work, feedback from customers must be available to the workforce so that employees can make the adjustments that are required for continuous improvement to organizational activities. Bottom-up approaches are, by their nature, flexible and adaptable to the peculiarities of particular systems.

The extreme case of grassroots control occurs when customers actually control the activities of the companies from which they buy. For example, Ito-Yokado Co., a company that manages 7-Eleven stores in Japan, controls the product mix, the manufacturing schedule, and the delivery of its most important supplies. "The moment a 7-Eleven customer in Japan buys a soft drink or a can of beer, the information goes directly to the bottler or brewery. It immediately becomes both production schedule and delivery schedule, actually specifying the hour when the new supply has to be delivered and to which of the 4,300 stores."[9] This process eliminates five or six wholesale levels. A little closer to home, Wal-Mart has similar practices with many of its suppliers. According to Peter Drucker, a very well known business writer, these trends result from the availability of better information: "Now that we have real-time information on what goes on in the marketplace, decisions will increasingly be based on what goes on where the ultimate customers, whether housewives or hospitals, take *buying* action."[10]

A basic strategic control model is displayed in Figure 7.1. It illustrates three different types of control: feedback, concurrent, and feedforward. **Feedback control** provides managers with information concerning outcomes from organizational activities. **Concurrent control** provides managers with real-time information about processes and activities so that deviations from the plan can be identified before they affect organizational results. **Feedforward control** helps managers anticipate changes in the external and internal environments, based on analysis of inputs from stakeholders and the remote environment. We now describe several types of feedback, feedforward, and concurrent control methods and some of their uses. We then describe the processes associated with developing a comprehensive strategic control system.

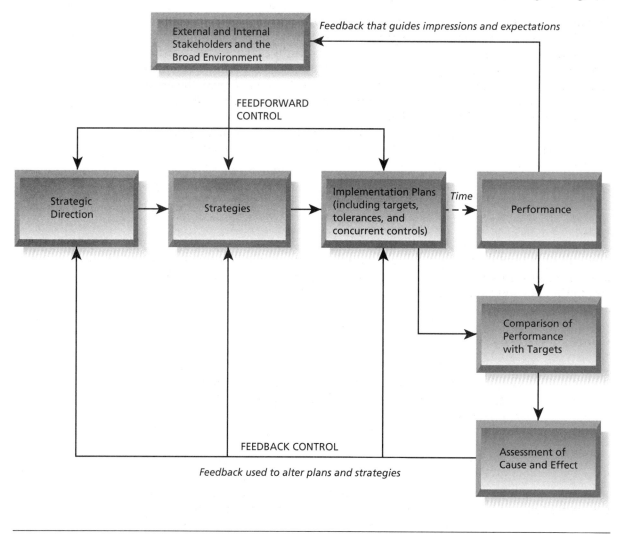

Figure 7.1 *The Strategic Control Process*

Feedback Controls

Feedback control systems share several elements in common. As a part of the implementation process, managers establish targets (e.g., specific objectives or goals) and tolerances (e.g., acceptable variations from the targets) for activities and in areas that are critical to the success of a strategy and the attainment of organizational goals. A time frame for measuring performance is also established. When the appropriate amount of time has elapsed, performance is measured against targets. If performance is within established tolerances for a certain factor, managers have learned that their expectations concerning performance for that factor are possible, given current organizational and environmental conditions. However, if performance is out of the tolerance limits, managers should assess cause and effect in an effort to learn why.

As an example of assessing cause and effect, assume that a passenger airline has established as an operating target that its planes should be 80% full over the next three months, plus or minus 5%. At the end of the three-month period, performance is at 70%. Because performance is not within tolerance limits, managers investigate. They discover that customer complaints and lost baggage both increased during the period. Now they have the information that they need to correct the problem. If critical customer satisfaction data such as number of customer complaints and amount of lost baggage had not been collected in a timely fashion, managers would not have been in a position to identify the problem fast enough to make corrections for the next period.

Feedback control systems perform several important functions in organizations.[11] First, creating specific objectives or targets ensures that managers at various levels and areas in the organization understand the plans and strategies that guide organizational decisions. Second, feedback control systems motivate managers to pursue organizational interests as opposed to purely personal interests, because they know they will be held accountable for the results of their actions. Finally, feedback control systems help managers decide when and how to intervene in organizational processes by identifying areas that require further attention. Without good control systems, managers can fall into the trap of spending too much time dealing with issues and problems that are not particularly important to the future of the organization. Table 7.1 describes some common feedback controls.

Concurrent Controls

Concurrent controls are also established during the implementation process. Concurrent controls are very similar to feedback controls, except that the time horizon is shortened to "real time." For example, the warning systems that are built into navigational equipment on an aircraft tell the pilot immediately if the aircraft has fallen below an acceptable altitude. They do not just feed back an aggregate report at the end of the flight telling the pilot how many times the aircraft fell below acceptable standards. That aggregate feedback information might be important for some uses, such as designing new navigational systems, but it would not be useful for the pilot. Within a business environment, real-time feedback is also useful in some instances but would be a disadvantage in others. Real-time financial feedback, for example, would make managing a business much like operating on the floor of the stock market—frenetic. On the other hand, real-time controls in service delivery environments and in production environments can be very useful.

Some of the most common types of concurrent controls are those associated with production and service processes and with quality standards. Statistical process control involves setting performance standards for specific work activities. The employees performing the activities monitor their own performance and the "outputs" of their efforts. If their work is out of specification, they fix it before handing it off to someone else, as when an automotive worker "stops the line" to prevent a defective automobile from continuing to the next work station. In those cases, real-time controls encourage autonomy and improve quality and efficiency. Other kinds of concurrent controls are those associated with inventory levels and order taking. For example, the more successful mail-order firms have real-time inventory systems that allow managers to know when stock is low for a particular item so that a new order can be sent to manufacturers as soon as needed. They also use the real-time inventory controls to give customers specific information about what items will be shipped, on what day, and when the customer will receive them.

1. **Budgets**: The targets in a budget are the revenue and expense accounts, and managers and employees are held responsible for variations that are greater than established tolerances. Sometimes tolerances are not stated, but are implied or are understood due to past budgeting processes. Budgets may also be used to evaluate the performance of managers; however, this procedure can be problematic because it may discourage investments in training, R&D, or new capital equipment due to their short-term impact on expense accounts. If a budget is used to evaluate managerial performance, organizations should consider adding back these types of investments before evaluation. Another alternative is to create separate accounts for longer-term investment programs that are independent of the rest of the budget.

2. **Ratio analysis**: Financial ratios such as return on investment (ROI) or a current ratio are measured against targets that are established on the basis of past performance or in comparison with competing firms. Although overdependence on this type of control can be dangerous to the long-term performance of firms, in some situations ratio analysis provides good control information. For example, a financial ratio such as the current ratio is important to managing working capital, and a debt-to-equity ratio can tell an organization whether it is assuming too much financial risk.

   Sometimes corporate-level managers use ratios such as ROI to evaluate the performance of managers of individual business units. In those cases, top managers should consider adding back long-term investments before calculating ROI to discourage a short-term orientation in decision making. In related diversified firms, ROI-based rewards systems (financial controls) may be inappropriate because they encourage competition among business units instead of the cooperation that is necessary to achieve synergy. Also, because the operations of the various business units should be highly interconnected, it is hard to determine which unit is really most responsible for success. Therefore, in the case of a related diversified firm, ROI is probably an ineffective control measure as it relates to the rewards system.

   However, in an unrelated diversified firm, financial performance ratios may be appropriate for determining the performance of business unit managers. In this situation, organizational managers should only be held accountable for their own financial performance because linkages with other firms in the portfolio are uncommon. Consequently, ROI (after adjustments) may be an appropriate gauge of the performance of business unit managers in unrelated diversified organizations.

3. **Audits**: An audit measures firm conduct and outcomes against established guidelines. Financial audits control accuracy within accounting systems, based on generally accepted accounting principles (GAAP). Social audits control ethical behavior, based on criteria that are established either totally in-house or in conjunction with activist groups, regulatory agencies, or editors of magazines that compile this sort of information (e.g., Business and Society Review). Customer surveys may also be used to generate feedback for control as part of a customer service audit.

4. **Goals and objectives**: Goals and objectives provide performance targets for individuals, departments, and divisions. Specific operating goals are established to bring the concepts found in the mission statement to life—to a level that managers and employees can influence and control. One of the keys to effective goal setting is that the goals must be well integrated from level to level.

Table 7.1 Types of Feedback Controls

Another category of concurrent controls is associated with the control of behavior. Within an organization, managers must depend on employees to perform their duties properly, even when management is not around. Behavioral controls encourage employees to comply with organizational norms and procedures. They are "real time" in that they influence the employee as the job is being performed. Table 7.2 describes two types of behavioral controls.

Bureaucratic controls and **clan controls** are two common types of behavioral controls.

Bureaucratic controls: *Rules, procedures, and policies that guide the behavior of organizational members.* Rules provide standards or outline a specific way of doing something, such as check approval. A policy is a more general guide to action, and it provides a framework for decisions that are made routinely. One of the ways McDonald's achieves such a high level of control over its business is by establishing rules and policies that guide the daily decisions and actions of employees. Unfortunately, many companies do not see everyday rules, procedures, and policies as "strategic." However, because bureaucratic controls guide the decisions and actions of employees, they are a major determinant of how well strategies are implemented.

Clan controls: *Socialization processes through which an individual comes to appreciate the values, abilities, and expected behaviors of an organization.* Socialization also makes organizational members more inclined to see things the same way, by espousing common beliefs and assumptions that, in turn, shape their perceptions. Socialization processes for existing employees take the form of intensive training, mentoring relationships and role models, and formal organizational communications including the vision, mission, and values statements.

Table 7.2 *Behavioral Controls*

Feedforward Controls

Good feedforward control systems are important because of **environmental discontinuities**, which are major, unexpected changes in the social, economic, technological, and political environments that necessitate change within organizations.[12] In other words, environmental change increases the need for organizational change and learning. However, even in stable environments, where environmental discontinuities play a minor role (e.g., production of commodities), feedforward control systems are essential to learning processes that allow organizations to move toward the accomplishment of their goals. Feedforward controls are an integral part of the strategic management process advanced in this book. The distinction between the "strategic planning" of the 1960s and 1970s and the "strategic management" of today is the recognition of the importance of implementation and control.

Strategic direction and strategies are established based on premises about the organization and its external environment, including the interests of stakeholders. These premises are assumptions about what will happen in the future. For example, an organization may plan to expand its manufacturing facilities over a period of five years based on the assumption that interest rates will remain approximately the same. A dramatic change in interest rates could make the planned expansion unprofitable. Also, as discussed in earlier chapters, stakeholder needs and expectations can change—customers may want quality improvements, suppliers may experience capacity shortages, communities may change their tax and zoning regulations—which will lead managers to evaluate the impact of these changes on existing strategies.

These types of situations demonstrate the need for premise control. **Premise control,** a type of feedforward control, involves periodically assessing the assumptions, or premises, that underlie strategy choices. Premise control helps organizations avoid situations in which their established strategies and goals are no longer appropriate.

Premise control has been designed to check systematically and continuously whether or not the premises set during the planning and implementation process are still valid. Accordingly, premise control is to be organized along these premises. The premises should be listed and then assigned to persons or departments who are qualified sources of information. The sales force, for instance, may be a valuable source for monitoring the expected price policy of the major competitors.[13]

The learning processes associated with *both* feedforward and feedback control form the basis for changes to strategic direction, strategies, implementation plans, or even the targets themselves, if they are found to be unreasonable given current conditions. In addition to the traditional measuring and monitoring functions, a recent study found that top managers use control systems to overcome resistance to change, communicate new strategic agendas, ensure continuing attention to new strategic initiatives, formalize beliefs, set boundaries on acceptable strategic behavior, and motivate discussion and debate about strategic uncertainties.[14] Control systems become one of the "tools of strategy implementation."[15]

So far this chapter has described types of control methods and issues surrounding them. Numerous control methods at multiple levels are necessary to keep an organization and its component parts headed in the right direction. However, they should be integrated in such a way that information can be shared. In other words, information from all parts of the organization should be accessible when and where it is needed to improve organizational processes. The next section discusses the development of an integrated strategic control system within organizations.

DESIGNING A STRATEGIC CONTROL SYSTEM

For our purposes, the previous discussion of feedback, concurrent, and feedforward controls provides a foundation for an overall system of strategic control. The processes associated with developing strategic control systems include determining what factors need to be controlled, identifying appropriate measures of the factors, and integrating information from all levels and all areas of the organization into a system that makes sense.

Determination of Control Factors

The first step in developing a strategic control system is determining what needs to be controlled. The stakeholder view of organizations provides a integrative view of control. By considering organization performance from a variety of stakeholder perspectives, key indicators of success can be derived from activities that lead to the satisfaction of stakeholders such as customers, employees, and shareholders.

Robert Kaplan and David Norton have developed a comprehensive approach to designing a strategic control system that considers organizational performance from four perspectives: financial, customer, internal business, and innovation and learning.[16] Each of these performance perspectives have their own set of feedback controls and are linked to particular stakeholder groups. For example, those stakeholders who evaluate an organization's performance using financial targets will typically look to return on investment, cash flow, stock price, and stability of earnings. Customers, however, evaluate other types of information such as pricing, innovation, quality, value, and customer service.

From an internal stakeholder perspective, another set of "performance" indicators becomes important, such as cost controls, skill levels and capabilities, product line breadth, safety, on-time delivery, quality, and many others. From an innovation and learning perspective, an organization may consider the foundation it is building for the future, such as workforce morale, innovation, and progress in continuous improvement.

According to Kaplan and Norton, an organization should ask itself the following question: "If we achieve our vision, how will we differ?" The "differences" should then be expressed from each of the four perspectives. The specifics of the differences that the firm expects to see are tied to the strategies that it intends to follow. For example, suppose a firm seeks to become the dominant shareholder in its industry (vision) through superior quality and service (strategy). The specifics of that vision can be expressed as future changes in financial performance (e.g., increased ROI), customer perceptions and behavior (e.g., perceived improved quality and reputation), and internal skills and capabilities (e.g., improved sales activity and higher-quality standards and outputs). The next step in the process is to identify those critical success factors that are keys to ensuring that the organization accomplishes its vision. Once identified and linked specifically to financial, customer, internal process, and learning outcomes, the critical success factors become the guiding goals that pace strategy implementation and serve as a critical link between strategic plans and action-oriented objectives and rewards. By specifically linking financial, customer, internal, and learning performance targets to the vision, the firm can structure a control system that is strategically relevant. The process advanced by Kaplan and Norton is summarized in Table 7.3.

The Kaplan and Norton approach focuses on three important stakeholders: owners, customers, and organization members. Some advocates of stakeholder management believe that performance should be evaluated and controlled from an even broader base of perspectives, including that of suppliers, consumer groups, and environmentalists. Table 7.4 provides a comprehensive list of the types of information that might be monitored as part of a broad perspective strategic control system.

Using Strategic Control Information

Rapidly advancing information technologies have made continuous improvements through control systems possible. Information systems can track large volumes of transactions, operating results, and external data efficiently, providing appropriate reports in a timely fashion to the right people. Unfortunately, few organizations currently make optimal use of available information technologies to control strategic processes.[17] However, rapid changes in an increasingly competitive global marketplace will make sophisticated strategic control systems a requirement for success in many industries in the future.

To enhance the quantity and quality of organizational learning, comprehensive organizational control systems should have the following characteristics:

1. Information generated by the control systems should be an important and recurring item to be addressed by the highest levels of management.
2. The control process should also be given frequent and regular attention from operating managers at all levels of the organization.
3. Data from the system should be interpreted and discussed in face-to-face meetings among superiors and subordinates.
4. The success of the control process relies on the continual challenge and debate of underlying data, assumptions, and strategies.[18]

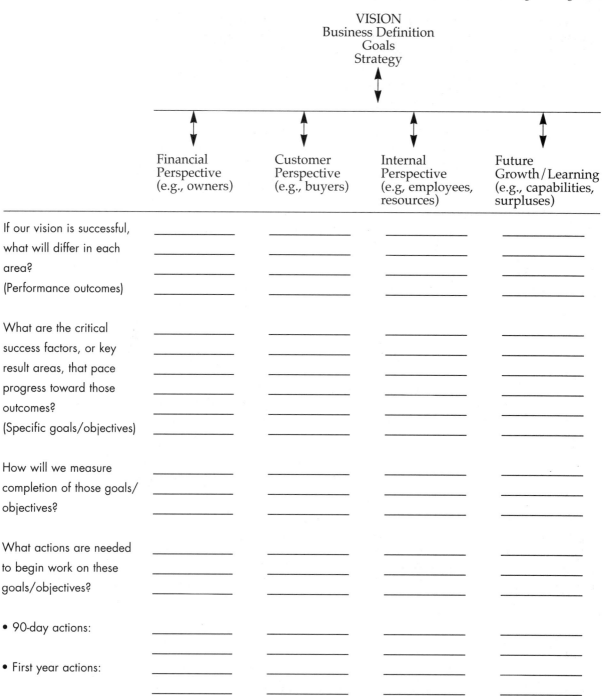

VISION
Business Definition
Goals
Strategy

	Financial Perspective (e.g., owners)	Customer Perspective (e.g., buyers)	Internal Perspective (e.g, employees, resources)	Future Growth/Learning (e.g., capabilities, surpluses)
If our vision is successful, what will differ in each area? (Performance outcomes)				
What are the critical success factors, or key result areas, that pace progress toward those outcomes? (Specific goals/objectives)				
How will we measure completion of those goals/objectives?				
What actions are needed to begin work on these goals/objectives?				
• 90-day actions:				
• First year actions:				

Source: Adapted and reprinted by permission of *Harvard Business Review*. From "Putting the Balanced Scoreboard to Work," by R. S. Kaplan and D. P. Norton (September/October 1993) 139. Copyright 1993 by the President and Fellows of Harvard College; all rights reserved.

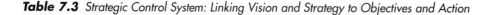

Table 7.3 *Strategic Control System: Linking Vision and Strategy to Objectives and Action*

Stakeholder Category	Possible Near-Term Measures	Possible Long-Term Measures
Customers	Sales (dollars and volume) New customers Number of new customer needs met ("tries")	Growth in sales Turnover of customer base Ability to control price
Suppliers	Cost of raw material Delivery time Inventory Availability of raw material	Growth rates of • Raw material costs • Delivery time • Inventory New ideas from suppliers
Financial Community	EPS Stock price Number of "buy" lists ROE	Ability to convince Wall Street of strategy Growth in ROE
Employees	Number of suggestions Productivity Number of grievances	Number of internal promotions Turnover
Congress	Number of new pieces of legislation that affect the firm Access to key members and staff	Number of new regulations that affect industry Ratio of "cooperative" versus "competitive" encounters
Consumer	Number of meetings Number of "hostile" encounters Number of times coalitions formed Number of legal actions	Number of changes in policy due to consumer advocate Number of consumer advocate initiated "calls for help"
Environmentalists	Number of meetings Number of hostile encounters Number of times coalitions formed Number of EPA complaints Number of legal actions	Number of changes in policy due to environmentalists Number of environmentalist "calls for help"

Source: R. E. Freeman, *Strategic Management: A Stakeholder Approach* (Boston: Pittman, 1984), 179. Reprinted with permission of the author.

Table 7.4 *A Sample Scorecard for Keeping Score with Stakeholders*

A well-designed strategic control system should provide feedback for ongoing, iterative adjustments in direction, resources allocations, and management priorities. When performance suffers, a strategic control system may provide early warnings of performance problems, but it cannot prevent them. Unfortunately some managers find, through their control systems or too late, that their organization's performance does not fit with their expectations or the expectations of their interested stakeholders. To correct an organization that has deviated sharply off course, managers must initiate some sort of restructuring.

STRATEGIC RESTRUCTURING

Many large companies are experiencing performance declines that are causing corporate-level managers to "rethink" their organizations. Apple Computer, once described as the "Magic Kingdom" during the mid-1980s, is now cutting product lines and approaching new markets in an attempt to survive.[19] Even David Glass, CEO of Wal-Mart, is rethinking his company's strategy. The discount retailing giant, after a string of 99 straight quarters of growth in earnings, recently experienced its first decline.[20]

However, some authors suggest that restructuring should be a continuous process that is a natural result of feedback from the strategic control processes.[21] Changes in global markets and technology have created a permanent need for firms to focus on what they do best and divest any parts of their organizations that are no longer contributing to their missions or long-term goals.

Regardless of the reason, restructuring typically involves a renewed emphasis on the things an organization does well, combined with a variety of tactics to revitalize the organization and strengthen its competitive position. Popular restructuring tactics include refocusing corporate assets on distinctive competencies, retrenchment, Chapter 11 reorganization, leveraged buyouts, and organizational changes. Organizations may use any one *or* a combination of these strategies in restructuring efforts.

Refocusing Corporate Assets

Refocusing activities generally are viewed favorably by external stakeholders such as the financial community.[22] Refocusing entails trimming businesses that are not consistent with the strategic direction of the organization. This type of refocusing is often called downscoping. **Downscoping** involves reducing diversification by selling off nonessential businesses that are not related to the organization's core competencies and capabilities.[23]

Researchers have discovered that most restructuring companies are moving in the direction of reducing their diversification as opposed to increasing it.[24] For example, a **divestiture** is a reverse acquisition. One type of divestiture is a sell-off, in which a business unit is sold to another firm or, in the case of a leveraged buyout, to the business unit's managers. For example, Chrysler agreed to sell most of its aerospace and defense holdings to Raytheon, and Mobil is planning to sell its real estate development arm to an investment fund.[25] In another move in the aerospace industry, Rockwell sold its aerospace and defense assets to Boeing.

Another form of divestiture is the spin-off, which occurs when current shareholders are issued a proportional number of shares in the business that was spun off. For example, if a shareholder owns 100 shares of XYZ company and the company spins off business unit J, the shareholder would then own 100 shares of XYZ company and 100 shares of an independently operated company called J. The key advantage of a spin-off relative to other divestiture options is that shareholders still have the option of retaining ownership in the spun-off business. General Motors spun off EDS, but kept a ten-year contract in which EDS will continue to provide GM with computer services. Also, Corning, unable to sell its $1.6 billion laboratory-testing business, spun it off to shareholders.[26]

The businesses that should be divested during a restructuring include those that have little to do with the distinctive competencies of the organization. An obvious example is when Johnson & Johnson, the consumer-oriented drug and toiletry giant, sold its sausage casings company.[27] Also, W. R. Grace, one of the largest chemical companies, refocused its efforts away from basic chemistry and toward chemical conversion processes. Grace has already sold several companies and will have sold off 43% of its business portfolio when restructuring is completed, representing sales of nearly $3 billion.[28]

Refocusing may also involve new acquisitions or new ventures to round out a corporate portfolio or add more strength in an area that is essential to corporate distinctive competencies.[29] For instance, Grand Metropolitan bought Pillsbury and simultaneously sold Bennigans and Steak & Ale restaurants in an effort to redefine its domain in the food processing industry.[30] Also, American Airlines, tired of losses in its airline segment, is headed in the direction of diversifying away from the flying business.[31]

Retrenchment

Retrenchment is a turnaround strategy. It can involve such tactics as reducing the workforce, closing unprofitable plants, outsourcing unprofitable activities, implementing tighter cost or quality controls, or developing new policies that emphasize quality or efficiency. Chrysler Corporation, under the leadership of Lee Iacocca, combined many of these tactics in its amazing recovery more than a decade ago. Chrysler cut its workforce and emphasized quality, which included a five-year, 50,000 mile warranty on its automobiles. Lee Iacocca used a variety of tools, including media releases, television commercials, and speeches, to convince the American public of the "new" Chrysler Corporation.

In the early 1990s, Amoco, one of the largest oil companies in the United States, set out on a retrenchment strategy of major proportions:

Amoco Corp. undertook a restructuring that included cutting 8,500 jobs, or 16% of its work force, and taking an $800 million charge. The charge covered the costs of selling and abandoning oil and gas fields, disposing of various chemical operations at a loss, the write-down of a number of assets, and the expenses associated with the job reductions. "The human impact of our decisions is very real and very painful," said H. Laurance Fuller, Amoco's chairman. Mr. Fuller wrote a letter to all employees in April that Amoco needed to make "an extraordinary effort to identify and eliminate unnecessary costs" and that layoffs were inevitable.[32]

Workforce reductions, sometimes called downsizing, have become commonplace in organizations in the United States as a response to the burgeoning bureaucracies in the post–World War II era. Even the military has a new focus on a "lighter fighter" division that can respond faster to combat situations. The great mystery is that some companies continue to lay off employees in spite of record profits. For example, in 1995 Mobil posted "soaring" first quarter earnings and then announced plans to cut 4,700 jobs.[33]

The evidence is mounting that "downsizing does not reduce expenses as much as desired, and that sometimes expenses may actually increase."[34] Certainly, severance packages are one reason for the increase. Nabisco will take a $300 million charge to cover its restructuring, and ConAgra will spend $505 million. Also, many organizations cut muscle, as well as fat, through layoffs. In addition, a study of white-collar layoffs in the U.S. automobile industry found that most companies experienced problems such as a reduction in quality, a loss in productivity, decreased effectiveness, lost trust, increased conflict, and low morale.[35] Other studies have shown that the "surviving" employees experience feelings of guilt and fear, which may hurt productivity or organizational loyalty.[36] It is not surprising, then, that the stock market often reacts unfavorably to announcements of major layoffs.[37]

Chapter 11 Reorganization

An organization that is in serious financial trouble can voluntarily file for Chapter 11 protection under the Federal Bankruptcy Code:

> Chapter XI provides a proceeding for an organization to work out a plan or arrangement for solving its financial problems under the supervision of a federal court. It is intended primarily for debtors who feel they can solve their financial problems on their own if given sufficient time, and if relieved of some pressure.[38]

One of the major disadvantages of Chapter 11 is that, after filing, all subsequent managerial decisions of substance must be approved by a court. Thus, managerial discretion and flexibility are reduced. Also, in a recent study of firms that had voluntarily filed for Chapter 11 protection, only a little more than half of the firms were "nominally successful in reorganizing," and "two-thirds of those retained less than 50 percent of their assets on completion of the reorganization process."[39]

One organizational response to this problem is the **prepackaged reorganization strategy**. Firms using this strategy negotiate a reorganization plan with creditors *before* filing for Chapter 11. Consequently, the courts stay out of the picture until after a tentative agreement is reached.

Leveraged Buyouts

Leveraged buyouts (LBOs) involve the private purchase of a business unit by managers, employees, unions, or private investors. They are called leveraged because much of the money that is used to purchase the business unit is borrowed from financial intermediaries (often at higher-than-normal interest rates). Because of high leverage, LBOs are often accompanied by the sale of assets to repay debt. Consequently, organizations typically become smaller and more focused after an LBO.

During the late 1970s and early 1980s, LBOs gained a good reputation as a means of turning around failing divisions. For instance, Hart Ski, once a subsidiary of Beatrice, was revived through an LBO led by the son of one of its founders. Also, managers and the union joined forces to turn around American Safety Razor, a failing division of Philip Morris. These LBOs benefited many of these organizations' stakeholders, including employees and local communities.[40]

However, some researchers have discovered that LBOs stifle innovation and research and development, similar to mergers and acquisitions.[41] Others have found that LBO firms have comparatively slower growth in sales and employees and that they tend to divest a larger proportion of both noncore and core businesses, compared to firms that remain public.[42] Also, some executives who initiate LBOs seem to receive an excessive return. For example, John Kluge made a $3 billion profit in two years from dismantling Metromedia following an LBO.[43] Consequently, some business people are starting to wonder if LBOs are really in the best interests of all stakeholders. Plant closings, relocations, and workforce reductions are all common results of LBOs. Not surprisingly, reports of failed LBOs are becoming more common. Successful LBOs require a company be bought at the right price with the right financing, combined with outstanding management and fair treatment of stakeholders.[44]

Structural Reorganization

Organizational structure, which was discussed in detail in Chapter 6, can be a potent force in restructuring efforts. As organizations diversify, top managers have a more difficult time processing the vast amounts of diverse information that are needed to appropriately control each business. Their span of control is too large. Consequently, an organization that is functionally structured may move to a more decentralized product/market or divisional structure. The end result is more managers with smaller spans of control and a greater capacity to understand each of their respective business areas.

In an effort to increase control, some organizations are actually splitting their operations into multiple, public corporations. An extreme case of the spin-off tactic described earlier, this restructuring strategy might be called the "breakup." For example, AT&T is splitting into three independent, publicly traded operating companies. One unit, AT&T's computer business, is what is left from the acquisition of NCR. Another unit is a strong equipment business. The final unit is the communications mainstay for which AT&T is best known. The purpose of the split is to allow AT&T to compete better against the Bell operating companies.[45] Hanson, PLC, the British conglomerate, is also splitting up. The result will be four companies—each one focusing on chemicals, tobacco, energy, and building materials and equipment. All of these units have revenues of more than $3 billion.[46]

On the other hand, some organizations restructure by becoming more centralized. For instance, British Petroleum collapsed its structure from twelve head offices to one head office to save costs. According to Robert Horton, former chairman and CEO of British Petroleum, the savings are enormous.[47] In a similar move, Philip Morris is merging its Kraft and General Foods units into one company.[48]

Restructuring can take time and often involves several restructuring approaches. Navistar's (International Harvester) restructuring reportedly took place over most of a decade and utilized several of the techniques that have been discussed in this chapter.

KEY POINTS SUMMARY

The key points discussed in this chapter include the following:

1. Strategic controls consist of systems to support managers in tracking progress toward organizational goals and ensuring that organizational processes and the behavior of organizational members are consistent with those goals.
2. Organizations should not rely exclusively on accounting-based, top-down controls because, according to some control experts, accounting-based measures are too late, too aggregated, and too distorted to be relevant for managers' planning and control decisions. In addition, too much reliance on accounting-based financial measures can prompt short sightedness among managers.

3. Feedback control provides managers with information concerning outcomes from organizational activities, which is then used as a basis for comparison with the targets that have been established.

4. Concurrent controls provide managers with real-time information for managing performance (e.g., process controls) or serve as a real-time source of influence over the behavior of employees (e.g., bureaucratic and clan controls).

5. Feedforward control helps managers anticipate changes in the external and internal environments, based on analysis of inputs from stakeholders and the remote environment.

6. The learning processes associated with both types of control form the basis for changes to strategic direction, strategies, implementation plans, or even the targets themselves, if they are found to be unreasonable given current conditions.

7. Development of an integrated strategic control system entails determining which factors require control, identifying appropriate measures upon which to determine success or failure, and integrating and interpreting intelligence information.

8. As a result of performance problems or pressure from stakeholders, many firms are now restructuring. The restructuring techniques that were described in this chapter included refocusing assets, retrenchment, Chapter 11 reorganization, leveraged buyouts, and changes to the organizational structure. These methods can also be used in combination.

REFERENCES

1. A. Barrett, "Feeling a Bit Insecure: Overexpansion and Too Rosy Forecast Plague Pinkerton," *Business Week* (September 28, 1992): 69–72; "Bogie's Men: Pinkerton," *The Economist* (October 5, 1991): 73; "Pinkerton's Reports Earnings Pressures, Revises 1992 Earnings Expectations," *Newswire* (June 19, 1992): 0618A1456; "Two Investors Charge Pinkerton's Misled Them to Inflate Stock," *The Wall Street Journal*, June 26, 1992, A7.

2. P. Lorange, M. F. Scott Morton, and S. Ghoshal, *Strategic Control* (St. Paul: West Publishing Company, 1986): 10.

3. J. F. Weston and E. F. Brigham, *Essentials of Managerial Finance*, 7th ed. (Hinsdale, Ill.: The Dryden Press, 1985), 154.

4. A. Lee, *Call Me Roger* (Chicago: Contemporary Books, 1988) 110.

5. H. T. Johnson and R. S. Kaplan, *Relevance Lost: The Rise and Fall of Management Accounting* (Boston, Mass.: Harvard Business School Press, 1987): 1.

6. R. E. Hoskisson and M. A. Hitt, "Strategic Control and Relative R&D Investment in Large Mulitproduct Firm," *Strategic Management Journal* 6 (1988), 605–622.

7. R. H. Hayes and W. J. Abernathy, "Managing Our Way to Economic Decline," *Harvard Business Review* (July/August 1980), 67–77; H. T. Johnson, "Managing By Remote Control: Recent Management Accounting Practice in Historical Perspective," in P. Temin, ed., *Inside the Business Enterprise: Historical Perspectives on the Use of Information* (Chicago: The University of Chicago Press, 1991), 41–66.

8. H. T. Johnson, *Relevance Regained: From Top-Down Control to Bottom-Up Empowerment* (New York: The Free Press, 1992) 30.

9. This entire paragraph is based on P. F. Drucker, "The Economy's Power Shift," *The Wall Street Journal*, September 24, 1992, A16.

10. P. F. Drucker, "The Economy's Power Shift," *The Wall Street Journal*, September 24, 1992, 16.

11. M. Goold and J. J. Quinn, "The Paradox of Strategic Controls," *Strategic Management Journal* 11 (1990), 43–57.

12. Lorange, Scott Morton, and Ghoshal, *Strategic Control*, 2–8.

13. G. Schreyogg and H. Steinmann, "Strategic Control: A New Perspective," *Academy of Management Review* 12 (1987): 96.

14. R. Simons, "How New Top Managers Use Control Systems as Levers of Strategic Renewal," *Strategic Management Journal* 15 (1994), 169–189.

15. R. Simons, "Strategic Orientation and Management Attention to Control Systems," *Strategic Management Journal* 12 (1991), 49–62.

16. Robert S. Kaplan and David P. Norton, "Putting the Balanced Scoreboard to Work," *Harvard Business Review*. (September/October, 1993): 134–147.

17. Goold and Quinn, "The Paradox of Strategic Controls."

18. R. Simons, "Strategic Orientation," 50.

19. J. Carlton, "Apple CEO Outlines Survival Strategy," *The Wall Street Journal*, May 14, 1996, A2, A22; K. Rebello and

P. Burrows, "The Fall of an American Icon," *Business Week* (February 5, 1996): 34–42.

20. P. Sellers, "Can Wal-Mart Get Back the Magic?" *Fortune* (April 29, 1996): 130–136.

21. J. F. Bandnowski, "Restructuring is a Continuous Process," *Long Range Planning* (January 1991): 10–14.

22. C. Markides, "Consequences of Corporate Refocusing: Ex Ante Evidence," *Academy of Management Journal* 35 (1992): 398–412.

23. M. A. Hitt, R. E. Hoskisson, and J. S. Harrison, "Strategic Competitiveness in the 1990s: Challenges and Opportunities for U.S. Executives," *Academy of Management Executive* (May 1991): 7–21. R. E. Hoskisson and M. A. Hitt, *Downscoping: How to Tame the Diversified Firm* (New York: Oxford University Press, 1994), 3.

24. R. E. Hoskisson and R. A. Johnson, "Corporate Restructuring and Strategic Change: The Effect on Diversification and R & D Intensity," *Strategic Management Journal* 13 (1992): 625–634. Hoskisson and Hitt, *Downscoping*.

25. J. Cole, "Chrysler Agrees to Sell to Raytheon Co. Bulk of Its Aerospace, Defense Holdings," *The Wall Street Journal* April 8, 1996, A3; *The Wall Street Journal*, "Business and Finance," June 10, 1996, A1.

26. W. Bounds, "Corning Will Spin Off Its Lab-Testing Division," *The Wall Street Journal,* May 15, 1996, B4; *The Wall Street Journal* "Business and Finance," April 2, 1996, A1.

27. J. Weber, "A Big Company that Works," *Business Week* (May 4, 1992): 125.

28. D. Hunter, "Grace Sharpens Its Focus," *Chemical Week* (April 1, 1992): 15.

29. Hitt, Hoskisson, and Harrison, "Strategic Competitiveness in the 1990s: Challenges and Opportunities for U.S. Executives."

30. R. L. Daft, *Organization Theory and Design*, 4th ed. (St. Paul: West Publishing Company, 1992), 94.

31. B. O'Brian, "Tired of Airline Losses, AMR Pushes Its Bid to Diversify Businesses," *The Wall Street Journal,* February 18, 1993, A1.

32. Adapted from C. Solomon, "Amoco to Cut 8,500 Workers, or 16% of Force," *The Wall Street Journal,* July 9, 1992, A3.

33. M. Murray, "Amid Record Profits, Companies Continue to Lay Off Employees," *The Wall Street Journal,* May 4, 1995, A1, A6.

34. W. McKinley, C. M. Sanchez, and A. G. Schick, "Organizational Downsizing: Constraining, Cloning, Learning," *Academy of Management Executive* (August 1995): 32.

35. K. S. Cameron, S. J. Freeman, and A. K. Mishra, "Best Practices in White-Collar Downsizing: Managing Contradictions," *Academy of Management Executive* (August 1991): 57–73.

36. J. Brockner, S. Grover, T. Reed, R. DeWitt, and M. O'Malley, "Survivors' Reactions to Layoffs: We Get by with a Little Help from Our Friends," *Administrative Science Quarterly* 32 (1987): 526–541.

37. D. L. Worrell, W. N. Davidson III, and V. M. Sharma, "Layoff Announcements and Stockholder Wealth," *Academy of Management Journal* 34 (1991): 662–678.

38. D. M. Flynn and M. Farid, "The Intentional Use of Chapter XI: Lingering versus Immediate Filing," *Strategic Management Journal* 12 (1991): 63–64.

39. W. N. Moulton, "Bankruptcy as a Deliberate Strategy: Theoretical Considerations and Empirical Evidence," *Strategic Management Journal* 14 (1993): 130.

40. K. M. Davidson, "Another Look at LBOs," *Journal of Business Strategies* (January/February 1988): 44–47.

41. A good review of these studies, of which there are seven, is found in S. A. Zahra and M. Fescina, "Will Leveraged Buyouts Kill U.S. Corporate Research and Development," *Academy of Management Executive* (November 1991): 7–21.

42/ M. F. Wiersema and J. P. Liebeskind, "The Effects of Leveraged Buyouts on Corporate Growth and Diversification in Large Firms," *Strategic Management Journal* 16 (1995): 447–460.

43. Davidson, "Another Look at LBOs."

44. M. Schwarz and E. A. Weinstein, "So You Want to Do a Leveraged Buyout," *Journal of Business Strategies* (January/February 1989): 10–15.

45. J. J. Keller, "Defying Merger Trend, AT&T Plans to Split into Three Companies," *The Wall Street Journal;* September 21, 1995, A1, A14.

46. R. Bonte-Friedheim and J. Guyon, "Hanson to Divide Into Four Businesses," *The Wall Street Journal*, January 31, 1996, A3, A16.

47. R. Calori and B. Dufour, "Management European Style," *Academy of Management Executive* (August 1995): 67.

48. S. L. Hwang, "Philip Morris to Reorganize Food Operation," *The Wall Street Journal*, January 4, 1995, A3, A4.

8

Strategic Challenges
for the Twenty-First Century

Mitsubishi Corporation

D oes the world's biggest company have a future? Some seasoned analysts see Mitsubishi Corporation of Tokyo as a "lumbering, prehistoric beast that has outlived its epoch" and "should roll over and die." Although harsh, these doomsday analysts have a point. The core business that built the trading company— hauling raw materials into Japan and speeding finished goods out into the world—has been declining for more than a decade.

Mitsubishi's annual revenues of $176 billion are indeed gigantic. Mitsubishi's revenues are bigger than those of AT&T, Du Pont, Citicorp, and Procter & Gamble combined. In serving its 45,000 customers, Mitsubishi moves as many as 100,000 products, from kernels of corn to huge power generators, around the world. Among the dozens of properties it owns outright are all or parts of cattle feedlots and coal mines in Australia, pulp mills and iron ore mines in Canada, copper mines in Chile, a resort in Hawaii, and the liquefied natural gas fields off the coast of Brunei that have made the sultan of that tiny state one of the world's richest men. The sultan may be thriving, but Mitsubishi is scraping by on meager earnings of $219 million. That translates into a pint-size profit margin of just .12%.

Minoru Makihara, chief executive since 1992, is keenly aware of Mitsubishi's difficult plight. His challenge is to persuade subordinates, who may have become too comfortable, that the need for transformation is urgent. "We have to change the contents of our business," says Makihara. "But in order to change the business, I have to create a sense of crisis. If you are running IBM, you can create a sense of crisis by firing people. Tradition won't allow me to do that here." Makihara believes he must impress on his troops how vital it is to become truly global, to invest in far-away businesses that have no ties to Japan. He also believes the company should have a major place in the multimedia business.[1]

This example is illustrative of the time in which we live. First, notice that the largest company in the world is not European or American, but Japanese. Second, the largest company in the world is facing major challenges that include a meager profit margin and rapidly changing markets. These changes require a major restructuring, which may include entering the multimedia business; however, Minoru Makihara is constrained by social norms that will not allow him to do what he needs to do. Finally, Makihara, although his main concentration is in Japan, is obviously aware of what global companies like IBM are doing.

Global expansion and awareness are rapidly increasing in all industrialized countries and, as noted in the last chapter, restructuring due to competitiveness problems has become commonplace.[2] Although examples of strategy involving international companies have been integrated throughout the entire text, this chapter focuses specifically on international expansion strategies and global business strategies, followed by a brief evaluation of several global markets. The chapter ends with a brief analysis of what the future may hold in store for businesses.

INTERNATIONAL EXPANSION

Organizations seem to evolve through four stages of international development.[3] In the first stage, the **domestic** stage, organizations focus their efforts on domestic operations but begin to export their products and services, sometimes through an export department or a foreign joint venture. Toys 'R' Us, a fairly recent entrant into foreign markets, is currently in this stage. In the **international** stage, exports become an important part of organizational strategy. The organization typically forms international divisions to handle sales, service, and warehousing in foreign markets. Marketing programs are custom-tailored to suit the needs of each country. Hasbro, the toy maker, is in this stage.[4]

In the third stage, **multinational**, the organization has marketing and production facilities throughout the world. More than one-third of the firm's sales originate overseas, and the organization has worldwide access to capital markets. Nike, the shoe distributor, recently entered the multinational stage, passing the point at which one-third of revenues come from non-U.S. sales.[5] Finally, in the **global** stage, the organization is no longer associated primarily with any one country. Global firms, such as Phillips N.V., Unilever, and Matsushita Electric, operate in as many as forty countries or more.

Unfortunately, not all U.S. companies that attempt international expansion are really prepared for it. According to Sheth and Eshghi, experts on international strategy have made this observation:

Many companies become multinational reluctantly. They start off as export houses, and as international business grows and becomes a significant part of corporate revenues, they become more involved in foreign operations. However, the corporate culture still remains domestic, and the international division is treated as a stepchild. The situation becomes one of them vs. us . . .what is lacking is a true worldwide orientation in product design, manufacturing, and marketing functions.[6]

Structural inertia within U.S. companies has been a major impediment to their transformation into true global competitors. Historically, North American companies have been able to prosper by selling goods to the largest and richest market in the world. In the past, some managers considered overseas operations nuisances or simply organizational appendages that generated a few extra dollars in sales revenue.[7] Now, the world has changed. Because global competitors have invaded U.S. markets, U.S. companies must also learn to compete overseas.

International activities should be accompanied by a new mind-set for all members of an organization, from top managers to the lowest level employees. Where will this new global mind-set come from? It has to start at the top of the organization. CEOs who want to create global organizations can start by expanding their organizational visions to include overseas operations. However, they should also assign specific individuals to monitor global stakeholder groups, economic trends, and markets and integrate this information into ongoing strategic management processes through the business intelligence system.

CEOs can create a sense of urgency in the organization by constantly discussing global customers, operations, strategies, and successes and failures with subordinates, the board of directors, employees, and the media. They will also want to visit global operations as a part of their regular routines. Finally, CEOs can communicate the value of employees from countries that are outside of the home country by making sure that they are both hired and promoted as often as Americans.

Organizations are also sending some of their managers to special training programs to help increase their global awareness and vision. The University of Michigan recently provided an intensive, in-depth five-week program for twenty-one executives from Japan, the United States, Brazil, Great Britain, and India to help them become global thinkers. The program organizers first made the participants more aware of the differences that existed between them. Then they helped the participants to work out these differences. The training program was so successful that organizers are planning to make it an annual event.[8]

Global Strategies

Throughout this book, we have provided many examples of non-U.S. based firms in an effort to demonstrate that strategic management principles apply to all firms, regardless of origin. Nevertheless, significant differences exist between the United States and other markets. This section will help demonstrate how firms can take advantage of the differences that become evident when participating in global markets and industries.

Global Product/Market Approach. One of the key issues facing top managers as their organizations pursue international development is selection of a product/market approach. A **multidomestic** strategy entails handling product design, assembly, and marketing on a country-by-country basis by custom tailoring products and services around individual market needs. In contrast, organizations pursuing a **global** strategy produce one product design and market it in the same fashion throughout the world.[9]

Bausch & Lomb successfully adopted a multidomestic strategy to significantly increase its global market share.

The key to global success for Bausch & Lomb is to "Think globally, act locally," letting local managers make their own decisions. This strategy was applied in Bausch & Lomb's Ray Ban division. More than half of Ray Ban's new sunglasses are developed specifically for international sale. In Europe, Ray Bans tend to be flashier, more avant-garde, and costlier than in the U.S. In Asia the company redesigned them to better suit the Asian face—with its flatter bridge and higher cheekbones—and sales took off. Ray Ban commands an awesome 40%

of the world market for premium-priced ($40 to $250) sunglasses. Operating margins have jumped from the low teens in 1984 to just under 25%.[10]

Multidomestic strategies are intuitively appealing from a stakeholder point of view, because they emphasize the satisfaction of segmented customer needs. However, customization may add more costs to the products or services than can be successfully recaptured through higher prices. A well-known marketing scholar, Theodore Levitt asserts that

well managed companies have moved from emphasis on customizing items to offering globally standardized products that are advanced, functional, reliable—and low priced. Multinational companies that concentrated on idiosyncratic consumer preferences have become befuddled and unable to take in the forest because of the trees. Only global companies will achieve long-term success by concentrating on what everyone wants rather than worrying about the details of what everyone thinks they might like.[11]

As a counter argument, some researchers explain that a global product/market strategy is only appropriate if (1) a global market segment exists for a product or service; (2) there are economic efficiencies associated with a global strategy; (3) no external constraints exist, such as government regulations that will prevent a global strategy from being implemented; and (4) no absolute internal constraints exist either.[12]

Some organizations are now pursuing a hybrid **transnational** product/market strategy. An international counterpart to the best-cost strategy discussed previously, a transnational strategy entails seeking both global efficiency and local responsiveness. This difficult task is accomplished through establishing an integrated network that fosters shared vision and resources while allowing individual decisions to be made to adapt to local needs.[13]

Global Expansion Tactics. Firms can apply a variety of expansion tactics as they pursue global opportunities. Among the most common are the following:

1. *Licensing.* Selling the right to produce or sell a brand name product in a foreign market.
2. *Franchising.* The services counterpart to a licensing strategy. A foreign firm buys the legal right to use the name and operating methods of a U.S. firm in its home country.
3. *Exporting.* Transferring goods to other countries for sale through wholesalers or a foreign company.
4. *Joint venture.* Cooperative agreement among two or more companies to pursue common business objectives.
5. *Greenfield venture.* Creation of a wholly owned foreign subsidiary.[14]

Some organizations combine these tactics in interesting ways. For example, Molson Breweries, a joint venture between Toronto's Molson Companies and Australia's Foster's Brewing Group, brews Miller Genuine Draft under license from Miller Brewing Company.[15] If that isn't confusing enough, Miller Brewing Company is actually a subsidiary of Philip Morris.

Among the most important criteria when deciding on an option for international growth are cost, financial risk, profit potential, and control. In general, moving down the list of alternatives from 1 to 5 entails greater cost and greater financial risk but also greater profit potential and greater control. Consequently, these alternatives represent a trade-off between cost and financial risk on the one hand, and profit and control on the other. Of course, this is a gross generalization. Some of the options, such as joint venture, are hard to judge on the basis of these four criteria because the exact nature of the agreement can vary so widely from venture to venture.

Enhancing Global Business-Level Strategies. Organizations that are involved in multiple global markets have advantages available to them in pursuing their business-level strategies. Examples of the many options available for improving competitive position vis-à-vis cost leadership through a global strategy include the following:

1. *Cost reductions through foreign assembly or manufacturing.* Many firms are currently shipping components to foreign countries for assembly by low-cost laborers. Some companies also have some of their manufacturing done in foreign countries.
2. *Branding of finished products that are subcontracted to low-cost foreign manufacturers.* Nike designs shoes but does not manufacture them. They are manufactured in third-world countries according to Nike specifications.
3. *Global sourcing (the purchase of low-cost foreign components or raw materials).* Many U.S. firms buy Japanese semiconductors or Japanese steel for use in their products.
4. *Expanding markets leading to economies of scale.* Some companies could not grow large enough to enjoy the lowest possible production costs on the basis of domestic demand alone. However, expansion into foreign markets can lead to significant increases in demand.
5. *Transfer of technological know-how through joint venture (learning from competitors).* Some foreign firms are more efficient than U.S. firms in producing similar products. Joint ventures with these firms may provide opportunities to learn new technologies that can lead to significant cost reductions.[16]

Global strategies can also lead to competitive advantages through differentiation. Some strategies for doing this include the following:

1. *Distribution of foreign products in the United States.* American firms can purchase elite products from foreign manufacturers for sale in the United States. This strategy is easy to imitate unless the companies sign a contract that provides the American firm exclusive rights to market the product in the United States.
2. *Sale of U.S. products in foreign countries.* In some countries, American products command a premium price because of the image they convey. For example, Coca Cola Company enjoys higher operating profits in Japan than in the United States.
3. *Superior quality through joint venture.* Just as U.S. companies can learn cost-saving technologies through joint ventures, they can also learn how to better differentiate their products through higher quality or some other unique feature.
4. *Licensing of product technology from abroad.* Joint venture is not the only way to learn new technologies. U.S. firms sometimes have the option of licensing product technologies to differentiate their present products.[17]

Many risks are also associated with global expansion. Organizations face the risk that citizens in some countries may not be receptive to some foreign products because of prejudices they hold against the countries in which they were produced. The same risk applies to service firms. Other risks are associated with managing international joint ventures and currency translations, as we discussed previously. These are only a few of many potential risks. The wise selection of countries in which to pursue opportunities can reduce costs and risks associated with global expansion. We now discuss how to select a country for investment.

Foreign Business Environments

Significant changes in the global environment have created great opportunities for organizations that are willing to take a risk and wait patiently for returns. For example, the old Soviet Union may have up to a quarter of the world's undiscovered oil, about equal to what's left in the Middle East. It also possesses more natural gas than any other country. Dozens of companies are rushing to help bring this oil to market; however, as in the Chevron case, instability in the region makes investment recovery difficult and risky. Furthermore, the Organization of Petroleum-Exporting Countries, fearing that a new force in oil will reduce its own power, is considering offering seats in its cartel to Russia, Kazakhstan, and Azerbaijan.[18] Oil is not the only risky business in Russia. Although Russia's many regions are working to attract funds from foreign investors, investments often bring unexpected problems. For example, a British steelmaker that bought Kazakstan's largest steel plant had to negotiate for two months to get more than a dozen old KGB agents to leave their electronically sophisticated corner office in the factory.[19] Furthermore, communist ideals are still popular and some Russian officials are working to reverse business privatization.[20]

The problems associated with business ventures in Russia are similar to those found in most developing countries: an unstable government, inadequately trained workers, low levels of supporting technology, shortages of supplies, a weak transportation system, and an unstable currency. Firms also have to struggle with managing stakeholders that are typically very different—in terms of values, beliefs, ethics, and in many other ways—from stakeholders found in the home country. However, firms that are "first movers" into developing countries may be able to develop stakeholder-based advantages, such as long-term productive contractual and informal relationships with host-country governments and organizations that followers will not have the opportunity to develop. For example, Spanish firms took huge risks by making major investments in Latin America during a wave of privatizations; however, they are now firmly entrenched in one of the world's fastest growing regions. According to one large Spanish bank executive with significant investments in Latin America, "It's not a new frontier for Spanish companies because we discovered America in 1492. But it's a growth frontier. It's a financial rediscovery of the Americas."[21]

Another region with a lot of potential is Asia. The "Pacific Century" refers to a forecast that the world's growth center for the twenty-first century will shift across the Pacific Ocean to Asia. Asia is already the world's biggest consumer of steel and the second fastest growing market for automobiles. China alone has more than 1 billion potential consumers, and television sets and beer are increasingly popular.."[22] In response to the huge market potential, Motorola is doubling its stake in China. Also, Atlantic Richfield, referred to as "the lucky company" by the Chinese, just completed a $1.13 billion gas pipeline project off the southeast coast of China with very few problems. Nevertheless, many companies are not so lucky. Rampant corruption and a culture that often condones counterfeiting can make business dealings difficult. Furthermore, Chinese/American relations are often strained due to China's poor human rights record and its unwillingness to conform to American policies on issues such as copyright protection and arms sales to politically unstable countries.[23] To make matters worse, anti-U.S. sentiment is surging in China:

According to a recent survey of youths, 90% said they feel the U.S. behaves "hegemonistically," with expansionist aims, towards China. When the romantic movie *Bridges of Madison County* played here, film authorities were inundated with phone calls complaining about "unhealthy capitalist lifestyles" of the lead characters, who engage in adultery. Even fast-food restaurants like McDonald's have come under attack for undermining children's health.[24]

Reforms in China are currently progressing slowly, and it is hard for Westerners to forget the blood that was spilled in Tiananmen Square as prodemocracy student protesters faced off against hard-line government forces.[25] However, according to many experts, China is headed toward capitalism, and it is already too late to turn back.[26] Already, money and management from Hong Kong, Taiwan, and Singapore are transforming South China.[27]

In addition to China, other Asian countries hold great potential. The newly industrialized economies (NIEs) of South Korea, Taiwan, Hong Kong, and Singapore have been experiencing growth in real gross domestic product at a level that is nearly twice that of the EC, Japan, and the United States.[28]

Finally, changes in Europe have made it increasingly important for U.S. companies to be involved there. The demise of some trade barriers among European countries has created a more open market of 340 million consumers.[29] Reduction in trade barriers means that companies involved in Europe can better take advantage of regional variations in wage rates and the cost of raw materials, which can lead to lower costs. Also, differentiation is easier to achieve because organizations can draw freely from the technological strengths of each nation. Organizations that have businesses in Europe already enjoy the advantages of a typically well-educated workforce, a well-developed infrastructure, a sophisticated level of technology, and high consumer demand, all factors that are associated with the so-called first world countries. The recent changes in Europe make the EC even more attractive for investment.

Evaluating Foreign Investments. Many characteristics must be evaluated when considering a foreign country for investment. Many of them fall within the general areas of the broad environment, including the social environment, the economy, the political/legal environment, and the state of technology. Other characteristics relate to specific industries and markets. Questions concerning each of these factors are listed in Table 8.1, which is a useful tool for evaluating a potential country.

The wrong answers to any of the questions in Table 8.1 can make a country less attractive. The following examples demonstrate this point: (1) an unstable government can greatly increase the risk of a total loss of investment; (2) an inefficient transportation system can increase total product costs to prohibitively high levels; (3) inadequate school systems can result in poorly skilled workers, which may not have the ability to manufacture technical products; (4) a slowly growing GNP could mean that consumer demand will be sluggish; (5) high foreign tax rates can virtually eliminate profits; and (6) if the local currency is not translatable into U.S. dollars the organization will have a tough time removing profits from the country.

Answers to the questions should also be judged based on the type of activity the organization is considering. For example, a high per capita income is favorable

Social Forces
What currently are the hot topics of debate? How well organized are special interest groups with regard to the environment, labor, and management issues? Are current policies or behaviors of the organization likely to be offensive in the new host country? What is the attitude of potential consumers toward foreign products and services? Will there be significant cultural barriers to overcome? How difficult is the language? How old is the population? What other differences could cause difficulty for the organization?

The Economy
What is the inflation rate? How large is the gross national product (GNP)? How fast is it growing? What is the income per capita? How much impact does the global economy have on the domestic economy? How high is the unemployment rate? What actions does the government take to fuel economic growth? What is the trade balance with the United States? Can the currency be exchanged for the home currency? How high are interest rates? Is the financial sector well organized? How expensive are the factors of production?

Political/Legal Environment
What is the form of government? How much influence does the government have over business? Is the government stable? What is the government's attitude toward private enterprise and U.S. firms? What is the home government's attitude toward the foreign government? How high are tax rates compared with rates in the home country? How are taxes assessed and collected? How high are import and export taxes? What is the nature of the court system? Is legal protection available through incorporation or a similar form?

Technology
Is the country technologically advanced? Do schools and universities supply qualified workers? Are the required skills available in sufficient quantity? Are suitable information systems available? Is the infrastructure sound (e.g., roads, transportation systems)? Is an appropriate site available?

Industry Specific
How large is the industry? How fast is it growing? Is it segmentable? How many competitors are there? How strong are they? What is the relative position of industry participants in relation to suppliers and customers? Are substitute products available? What is the primary basis for competition? Is it possibile to reach the market through a joint venture?

Table 8.1 *Examples of Questions to Ask about a Potential Foreign Market*

if the organization is only going to sell U.S. products in the foreign market (export). On the other hand, low per capita income could mean that wages are very low, which is positive if the organization is only considering foreign manufacturing or assembly.

Competitive Advantages of Nations. Michael Porter, whose name should now be familiar to you, expanded his analyses of competitive environments to include the global economy. In his book *The Competitive Advantage of Nations*, he developed arguments concerning why some nations produce so many stellar companies in particular industries.[30] For example, Germany is the home base for several top luxury car manufacturers and Switzerland has many leading companies in pharmaceuticals and chocolate. He explains that four characteristics of countries actually create an environment that is conducive to creating globally competitive firms in certain business areas (see Figure 8.1). The four characteristics follow:

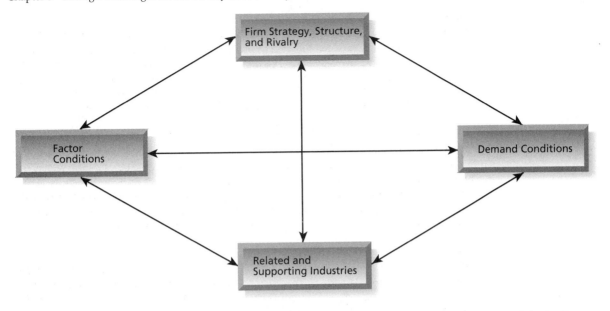

Source: Michael E. Porter, *The Competitive Advantage of Nations* (New York: The Free Press, 1990), 72. Adapted with permission of The Free Press, a division of Simon & Schuster. Copyright © 1990 by Michael E. Porter.

Figure 8.1 *Conditions That Create Advantages for Firms in Certain Countries and Industries*

1. *Factor conditions.* Is the nation endowed with any special factors of production, such as uncommon raw materials or laborers with specific skills, that can lead to an advantage in a particular industry? Does the nation have superior factor-producing mechanisms such as excellent schools or universities?
2. *Demand conditions.* Are the nation's buyers of a particular product or service the most discriminating and demanding in the world? Does the nation's market typically foreshadow global trends?
3. *Related and supporting industries.* Are the suppliers to an industry the very best in the world? Are there firms in related industries that are also global leaders?
4. *Firm strategy, structure and rivalry.* Are the management techniques that are customary in the nation's businesses conducive to success in a particular industry? Does the industry attract the most talented managers in the nation? Are competitors in the same industry strong?

Positive answers to most of these questions concerning a particular industry or industry niche indicate the potential for developing a nucleus of companies that are globally competitive.

Basically, the reason companies can develop a highly competitive nucleus is that tough market environments can create world-class competitors only if the competitors are also endowed with the resources they need to compete. If home markets are uncompetitive, firms will not be sufficiently motivated to produce a superior product. On the other hand, if home markets are highly competitive but the factors of production, support industries, and human talent are not available, firms will likewise be incapable of producing globally competitive products. When these two conditions are met, however, an environment is created that both motivates and rewards excellence.

The logical conclusion from Porter's analysis would seem to be to locate subsidiaries in the nations with the strongest home bases in particular industries. However, he argues that this rarely happens. First, it is difficult in some cases for an "outsider," a foreign firm, to become an "insider." Second, Porter suggests that it is unlikely that the foreign subsidiary in the nation with the natural advantages will be able to influence the parent company "long distance."

Porter does, however, suggest that firms should take advantage of their own nation's natural advantages. He also recommends that some of the principles that apply to the competitive advantages of nations can be applied in any company that wants to become more competitive in the world economy. Specifically, organizations can seek out the toughest, most discriminating buyers, choose from the best suppliers in the world, seek to excel against the most outstanding global competitors, form alliances with outstanding foreign competitors, and stay abreast of all research findings and innovations that are relevant to their core businesses.

THE CHALLENGE OF THE FUTURE

Without question, the greatest managerial challenges lie ahead. It is hard to predict with precision the kind of business environment the next generation of managers will face; however, judging from the recent past, it will probably be associated with increasing global complexity and interconnectedness. Table 8.2 contains a few of the characteristics we expect to find in the business environment of the early twenty-first century.

What kind of leaders will be needed to navigate through the business environment of the future? In a *Fortune* article titled "Leaders of Corporate Change," four CEOs of Fortune 500 companies—Stanley Gault of Goodyear Tire and Rubber, Linda Wachner of Warnaco, Mike Walsh of Tenneco, and David Johnson of Campbell's Soup—discussed their responsibilities in restructuring and reorienting an organization during difficult times.[31] In addition to providing a direction or strategy, each executive mentioned the importance of instilling commitment to the new strategy, setting new and challenging expectations, getting people to rethink what they do and improve upon it, and creating a high-performance culture. In each case, the executive was describing transformational leadership: creating a new vision, instilling commitment to the new vision and way of doing business, and mobilizing change through new structure and systems.[32] Every year, thousands of organizations face severe threats to their survival and need the help of transformational leaders who can provide a new approach.

Increasing levels of global trade and global awareness
Global and domestic social turbulence
Increased sensitivity to ethical issues and environmental concerns
Rapidly advancing technology, especially in communications
Continued erosion of buying power
Continued development of third-world economies
Increases in U.S. and global strategic alliances
Revolution in the U.S. health industry

Table 8.2 *Strategic Management for the Twenty-First Century*

In other firms where business is more usual, leaders perform the same activities but not on as sweeping a scale. They communicate the vision of the organization to internal and external stakeholders, modify organizational structures to better align with internal and external environments, negotiate external alliances, make executive staffing decisions, and sustain the organizational culture.

The tools, theories and techniques found in this book can help you become an effective leader for the next century. We encourage you to apply what you have learned to current and future business situations in which you and your organizations are found.

KEY POINTS SUMMARY

Some of the key points found in the chapter are as follows:

1. Global expansion and awareness are rapidly increasing in all industrialized countries.
2. Organizations evolve through four stages of international development: the domestic stage, the international stage, the multinational stage, and the global stage.
3. With regard to an international product/market approach, a multidomestic strategy entails custom tailoring products and services around individual market needs, whereas a global strategy means production and marketing of one product design throughout the world.
4. Among the most common global expansion tactics are licensing, franchising, exporting, joint venture, and greenfield venture. In general, moving down the list of alternatives entails greater cost and greater financial risk but also greater profit potential and greater control.
5. Organizations that are involved in multiple global markets have many advantages available to them in pursuing their business-level strategies. However, international business also entails higher risk.
6. Significant changes in the global environment have created great opportunities for organizations that are willing to take a risk and wait patiently for returns. Currently, great opportunities exist in the countries from the old Soviet Union, Latin America, and all over Asia. Changes in Europe such as falling trade barriers have made it increasingly important for companies to be involved there also.
7. Many characteristics must be evaluated when considering a foreign country for investment. Many of them fall within the general areas of broad environment, including the social environment, the economy, the political/legal environment, and the state of technology. Other characteristics relate to specific industries and markets.
8. Some nations seem to produce many highly successful companies in particular industries. Four variables that seem to explain this phenomenon are factor conditions, demand conditions; related and supporting industries; and firm strategy, structure, and rivalry.
9. The greatest managerial challenges lie ahead. The tools, theories, and techniques found in this book can help you be an effective leader in the twenty-first century.

REFERENCES

1. Adapted from L. Smith, "Does the World's Biggest Company Have a Future?" *Fortune* (August 7, 1995): 124. © 1995 Time Inc. All rights reserved.

2. R. E. Hoskisson and R. A. Johnson, "Corporate Restructuring and Strategic Change: The Effect on Diversification Strategy and R&D Intensity," *Strategic Management Journal* 13 (1992): 625–634.

3. N. J. Adler, *International Dimensions of Organizational Behavior*, 2nd ed. (Boston: PWS-Kent, 1991); R. L. Daft, *Organization Theory and Design*, 4th ed. (St. Paul: West Publishing, 1992): 228–229; T. T. Herbert, "Strategy and Multinational Organizational Structure: An Interorganizational Relationships Perspective," *Academy of Management Review* 9 (1984): 259–271.

4. D. W. Grigsby, "Hasbro, Inc." In M. J. Stahl, and D. W. Grigsby, *Strategic Management for Decision Making* (Boston: PWS-Kent Publishing, 1992): 725–738.

5. "Nike Net Surged 21% in Quarter to Record; Stock Rises by $6.375," *The Wall Street Journal*, July 9, 1992, B4.

6. J. Sheth and G. Eshghi, *Global Strategic Management Perspectives* (Cincinnati:South-Western Publishing, 1989), 13.

7. C. A. Bartlett and S. Ghoshal, "Global Strategic Management: Impact on the New Frontiers of Strategy Research," *Strategic Management Journal* 12 (1991): 5–16.

8. S. Tully, "The Hunt for the Global Manager," *Fortune* (May 21, 1990): 140-144; J. Main, "How 21 Men Got Global in 35 Days," *Fortune* (November 6, 1989): 71.

9. K. Ohmae, "Managing in a Borderless World," *Harvard Business Review* (May/June 1989): 152–161.

10. Adapted from R. Jacob, "Trust the Locals, Win Worldwide," *Fortune* (May 4, 1992) 76. Used with permission.

11. T. Levitt, "The Globalization of Markets," *Harvard Business Review* (May/June 1983): 92.

12. S. P. Douglas and Y. Wind, "The Myth of Globalization," *Columbia Journal of World Business* (Winter 1987): 19–29.

13. M. A. Hitt, R. D. Ireland, and R. E. Hoskisson, *Strategic Management: Competitiveness and Globalization* (Minneapolis: West Publishing Company, 1995).

14. This discussion of tactics for global expansion was based, in part, on C. W. L. Hill, P. Hwang, and W. C. Kim, "An Eclectic Theory of the Choice of International Entry Mode," *Strategic Management Journal* 11 (1990): 117–128; C. W. L. Hill and G. R. Jones, *Strategic Management: An Integrated Approach* (Boston: Houghton Mifflin, 1992): 254–259.

15. "Court Dismisses Rivals' Bid to Stop Sale of Beer Brand," *The Wall Street Journal*, July 14, 1992, B9.

16. Some of the options contained in this list were based on information found in M. L. Fagan, "A Guide to Global Sourcing," *Journal of Business Strategy* (March/April 1991): 21–25; Sheth and Eshghi, *Global Strategic Management Perspectives*; and Stahl and Grigsby, *Strategic Management for Decision Making*, 205–206.

17. Some of the options contained in this list were based on information found in Sheth and Eshghi, *Global Strategic Management Perspectives*; and Stahl and Grigsby, *Strategic Management for Decision Making*, 205-206.

18. P. Nulty, "The Black Gold Rush in Russia," *Fortune* (June 15, 1992): 126.

19. K. Pope, "A Steelmaker Built Up by Buying Cheap Mills Finally Meets Its Match," *The Wall Street Journal*, May 2, 1996, A1, A10.

20. N. Banerjee, "Russia's Many Regions Work to Attract Funds from Foreign Investors," *The Wall Street Journal*, April 30, 1996, A1, A13; S. Liesman, "Some Russian Officials Are Moving to Reverse Business Privatization," *The Wall Street Journal*, March 20, 1996, A1, A6; C. Rosett, "Communists Mount Comeback in Russia, and Mean Business," *The Wall Street Journal*, March 27, 1996, A1, A4.

21. T. Kamm and J. Friedland, "Spanish Firms Discover Latin America Business As New World of Profit," *The Wall Street Journal*, May 23, 1996, A1, A9.

22. L. Kraar, "Asia 2000," *Fortune* (October 5, 1992): 111.

23. J. Barnathan, "A Pirate under Every Rock," *Business Week* (June 17, 1996): 50–51; L. Kraar, "The Risks are Rising in China," *Fortune* (March 6, 1995): 179–180; K. Schoenberger, "Motorola Bets Big on China," *Fortune* (May 27, 1996): 116–124; K. Schoenberger, "Arco's Surprisingly Good Fortune in China," *Fortune* (February 5, 1996): 32.

24. K. Chen, "Anti-U.S. Sentiment Surges in China, Putting a Further Strain on Relations," *The Wall Street Journal* March 15, 1996, A11.

25. P. Steidlmeier, "China's Most-Favored-Nation Status: Attempts to Reform China and the Prospects for U.S. Business," *Business and the Contemporary World* 4 (1992): 68–80.

26. B. Schlender, "China Really Is on the Move," *Fortune* (October 5, 1992): 114–122.

27. L. Kraar, "A New China without Borders," *Fortune* (October 5, 1992): 124–128.

28. J. Labate, "The World Economy in Charts," *Fortune* (July 27, 1992) 62.

29. S. Tully, "Europe 1992: More Unity Than You Think," *Fortune* (August 24, 1992): 136–142.

30. M. E. Porter, *The Competitive Advantage of Nations* (New York: The Free Press, 1990).

31. J. M. Graves, "Leaders of Corporate Change," *Fortune*, (December 14, 1992): 104–114.

32. Richard L. Daft, *Organization Theory and Design*, 3rd ed. (New York: West Publishing 1989).

Preparing a Strategic Analysis

PREPARING A STRATEGIC ANALYSIS

Strategic management is an iterative, ongoing process designed to position a firm for competitive advantage in its ever-changing environment. To manage an organization strategically, a manager must understand and appreciate the desires of key organizational stakeholders, the industry environment, and the firm's position relative to its stakeholders and industry. This knowledge allows a manager to set goals and direct the organization's resources in a way that corrects weaknesses, overcomes threats, takes advantage of strengths and opportunities and, ultimately, satisfies stakeholders. This book contains a foundation for understanding these strategic management processes.

With case analysis, you can practice some of the techniques of strategic management. Case analysis, to some extent, mirrors the processes managers use to make real strategic decisions. The main advantages managers have over students who analyze cases are that they have more information and more experience. For example, managers have ongoing relationships with internal and external stakeholders from whom information can be gathered. They may also have a business intelligence system and staff to help them make decisions. In addition, managers usually have substantial experience in the industry and company. Nevertheless, managers must still make decisions without full information. Like students, they never have all of the facts or the time and resources to gather them. In case analysis, you must sort accurate, relevant information from that which is inaccurate or irrelevant.

The authors of cases attempt to capture as much information as possible. They typically have conducted extensive interviews with managers and employees and gathered information from public sources such as annual reports and business magazines. Many cases include detailed descriptions of the industry and competitors as well as an extensive profile of one organization. You can supplement this information with your own library research if your instructor thinks this is appropriate.

Case analysis typically begins with a brief introduction of the company. The introduction, which sets the stage for the rest of the case, should include a brief description of the defining characteristics of the firm, including some of its outstanding qualities, past successes, past failures, and products or services. The industries in which the firm is involved are also identified.

The next section of a case analysis can be either an environmental analysis or an internal analysis. Opportunities are defined as conditions in the broad and task environments that allow a firm to take advantage of organizational strengths, overcome organizational weaknesses or neutralize environmental threats. Consequently, both environmental and organizational analyses are required before all of the organization's opportunities can be identified. We have chosen to treat environmental analysis first because it establishes the context in which a firm's strategies and resources can be understood. However, reversing the order of analysis would not be incorrect and is even preferred by some strategic management scholars.

Environmental analysis is an examination of the external environment, including external stakeholders, the competition, and the broad environment. Systematic external analysis will help you draw conclusions about the potential for growth and profit in the industry and determine keys to survival and success in the industry.

An organizational analysis, which follows the external analysis, is designed to evaluate the organization's strategic direction, business- and corporate-level strategies, resources, capabilities, and relationships with internal and external stakeholders, and then determine the strengths, weaknesses, vulnerabilities, and sources of competitive advantage exhibited by the firm. These determinations must be made against a background of knowledge about the external environment so that the full range of opportunities and threats can also be identified.

STRUCTURING AN ENVIRONMENTAL ANALYSIS

An analysis of the external environment includes an industry analysis and an examination of key external stakeholders and the broad environment. Findings are then summarized, with an emphasis on identifying industry growth and profit potential and the keys to survival and success in the industry. Some organizations are involved in more than one industry. Consequently, a separate industry analysis is done for each of the industries in which a firm is involved.

Industry Analysis

Environmental analysis should begin with an industry analysis. The first step in industry analysis is to provide a basic description of the industry and the competitive forces that dominate it. Porter's Five Forces are evaluated, along with other relevant issues.

1. What is the product or service? What function does it serve? What are the channels of distribution?
2. What is the industry size in units and dollars? How fast is it growing? Are products differentiated? Do high exit barriers exist? Are there high fixed costs? These are some of the forces that determine the strength of competition among existing competitors.

3. Who are the major competitors? What are their market shares? In other words, is the industry consolidated or fragmented?
4. Who are the major customers of the industry? Are they powerful? What gives them power?
5. Who are the major suppliers to the industry? Are they powerful? What gives them power?
6. Do significant entry barriers exist? What are they? Are they effective in protecting existing competitors, thus enhancing profits?
7. Do any close substitutes for industry products and services exist? Do they provide pressure on prices charged in this industry?
8. What are the basic strategies of competitors? How successful are they?
9. To what extent is the industry global? Are there any apparent advantages to being involved in more than one nation?
10. Is the industry regulated? What influence do regulations have on industry competitiveness?

External Stakeholders and the Broad Environment

A complete environmental analysis also includes an assessment of external stakeholders and the broad environment. The identity and power of competitors, suppliers, and customers was already established during the industry analysis. At this stage of the analysis, other important stakeholders should also be identified and their influence on the industry determined (see Chapter 2). Any of the external stakeholders who pose a threat or an opportunity also should be identified. One of the outcomes of this part of the analysis should be the establishment of priorities for each external stakeholder group. High-priority stakeholders will receive greater attention during the development of the strategic plan.

The broad environment should also be evaluated. Four of the most important factors are current social forces, global economic forces, global political forces, and technological innovations. Remember that each of these forces is evaluated only as it relates to the industry in question. Forces in the broad environment may also pose threats or provide opportunities.

After describing the industry as it exists now, it is important to capture the underlying dynamics that will create industry change and require new strategic approaches. One useful way to evaluate these dynamics is to group factors that influence the industry into two categories: those that create and influence industry demand and those that create and influence industry cost structures and profit potential. The findings from this part of the analysis will help you decide whether the industry is attractive (growing and profitable) and worthy of further investment (i.e., time, money, and resources). It will also help you identify areas in which the firm may be able to excel in an effort to create a competitive advantage.

Factors That Influence Demand. Many industry factors and stakeholder actions create and influence the demand for products and services. Some of the factors are part of the firm's broad environment, such as the state of the economy. Other factors are part of the task environment, most of which are related to the actions of two key stakeholder groups: customers and competitors. If the underlying factors that create demand are changing, then it is likely that demand patterns will change. For example, demand for washing machines is a function of household formations and replacements. To predict future demand, you would study the numbers of people in the household-forming age bracket, the durability of washers, and economic conditions.

Some of the industry factors and stakeholder actions that create and influence demand and growth prospects in an industry include the following:

1. The function(s) served by the product.
2. The stage of the product life cycle (i.e., the degree of market penetration already experienced).
3. Economic trends, including income levels and economic cycles (e.g., recession, boom)
4. Demographic trends (part of social trend analysis) such as population and age.
5. Other societal or cultural trends, including fads and commonly held values and beliefs.
6. Political trends, which may include protectionist legislation such as trade barriers.
7. Technological trends, including new applications, new markets, and cost savings that make prices more competitive.
8. Programs developed by firms in the industry, such as new product introductions, new marketing programs, new distribution channels, and new functions served.
9. Strong brand recognition, domestically or worldwide.
10. Pricing actions, which stimulate demand.

After analyzing the factors that create and influence demand, you should be able to draw some conclusions about industry growth prospects for the industry and firm. Because you can never be certain about the timetable and ultimate outcome of a trend which, by definition, is changing over time, one technique that may be useful is to develop alternative demand scenarios. For example, if the health of the economy is a major driver of a product's demand, you could consider the upside and downside of an economic recovery using the following type of format: "If the economy recovers within six months, then industry demand for the product could be the highest in five years. If the recovery does not materialize, then demand might linger at last year's levels."

Factors That Influence Cost Structures. After determining growth prospects for the industry, you will want to determine its cost structure and profit potential. As with demand, various factors and stakeholder actions create and influence cost and profit structures in an industry. Among these factors are the following:

1. *Stage of the product life cycle.* In the early stages of the life cycle, firms have large investments in product development, distribution channel development, new plant and equipment, and workforce training. In the latter stages, investments are more incremental.
2. *Capital intensity.* Large investments in fixed costs such as plants and equipment make firms very sensitive to fluctuations in demand—high levels of capacity utilization are needed to cover or spread fixed costs. Industries that have a lower relative fixed cost investment but higher variable costs are able to control their costs more readily in turbulent demand periods.
3. *Economies of scale.* Larger facilities can achieve lower costs per unit than smaller facilities in some instances because of lower per-foot construction costs, more efficient use of equipment, and more efficient use of indirect labor and management. If a facility is so large that additional equipment and management are needed, economies of scale may be lost.

4. *The effects of learning and experience.* With repetition and an environment that encourages and rewards learning, employees can become more productive over time.

5. *The power of customers, suppliers, competitive rivalry, substitutes, and entry barriers.* Powerful customers, suppliers, competitive rivalry, substitutes, or low entry barriers can erode profit potential. The forces, which are part of Porter's Five Forces Model, were discussed in detail in Chapter 2.

6. *The influence of other stakeholders.* These may include powerful foreign governments, joint venture partners, powerful unions, and strong creditors.

7. *Technological changes that provide opportunities to reduce costs.* Technological innovations can allow a firm to invest in new equipment, new products, and new processes or to alter the balance of investments between fixed and variable costs.

After systematically profiling the factors and stakeholder actions that influence cost structures and profits, you should be able to draw conclusions about an industry's profit potential. After the basic environmental analysis is complete, the next step is to perform a more detailed examination of the major strategic issues facing the industry.

Strategic Issues Facing the Industry

A thorough environmental analysis provides the information needed to identify factors and forces that are important to the industry in which your organization is involved and, therefore, your organization. These factors and forces may be categorized as follows:

1. *Driving forces in the industry.* These are trends that are so significant that they are creating fundamental industry change, such as the opening up of Eastern Europe or networked computer communications. Of course, each industry will have its own unique set of driving forces.

2. *Threats.* These are defined as noteworthy trends or changes that threaten growth prospects, profit potential, and traditional ways of doing business.

3. *Opportunities.* These are important trends, changes, or ideas that provide new opportunities for growth or profits.

4. *Requirements for survival.* These are identified as resources and capabilities that all firms must possess to survive in the industry. An example in the pharmaceutical industry is "product purity." These factors do not command a premium price. They are necessary, but not sufficient to be successful.

5. *Key success factors.* These are the factors firms typically should possess if they desire to be successful in the industry. An example in the pharmaceutical industry is the ability to create products with new therapeutic qualities. This ability may lead to high performance.

Having completed an analysis of the external environment, you are ready to conduct a more specific analysis of the internal organization.

STRUCTURING AN ORGANIZATIONAL ANALYSIS

Understanding industry trends, growth prospects, profit potential, and key strategic issues can help you critique an organization's strategies and evaluate its strengths and weaknesses. For example, what might qualify as a strength in one industry may be an ordinary characteristic or a weakness in another industry. A good organizational analysis should begin with a general evaluation of the internal organization.

Evaluation of the Internal Environment

The following questions are useful in assessing the internal organization:

1. What is the company's strategic direction, including its vision, business definition, enterprise strategy (i.e., which stakeholder groups does it appear to give priority), long-term goals, and attitude toward global expansion? If some of these factors are contained in a formal mission statement, share it.
2. How has the strategic direction changed over time? In what way? Has the evolution been consistent with the organization's capabilities and planned strategies?
3. Who are the principal internal stakeholders? In particular, who are the key managers and what are their backgrounds? What are their strengths and weaknesses? Are they authoritarian or participative in their management style? Is this style appropriate for the situation? What seems to drive their actions?
4. Who owns the organization? Is it a publicly traded company with a board of directors? If there is a board and you know who is on it, is the composition of the board appropriate? Does one individual or group have a controlling interest? Is there evidence of agency problems? How active are the owners and what do they value?
5. What are the operating characteristics of the company, including its size in sales, assets, and employees, its age, and its geographical locations (including international operations)?
6. Are employees highly trained? If a union is present, how are relations with the union?
7. How would you describe the organization's culture? Is it a high-performing culture? Is it supportive of the firm's strategies?

Most instructors also require a financial analysis to identify financial strengths and weaknesses, evaluate performance, and identify the financial resources available for strategy implementation. A financial analysis should include a comparison of ratios and financial figures with major competitors or the industry in which the organization competes (cross sectional) as well as an analysis of trends in these ratios over several years (longitudinal). Some commonly used financial ratios are specified in Chapter 3.

When analyzed superficially, ratios can be more misleading than informative. For example, in comparing the return-on-assets figures for two firms in the same industry, the one with the higher ratio could have superior earnings or devalued assets from too little investment. Two firms can differ in return-on-equity results because of different debt-equity financing policies rather than from true performance reasons. When accurately interpreted and considered in the larger organizational context, the analysis may also uncover strengths, weaknesses, or symptoms of larger organizational problems.

Identification of Resources and Capabilities

The foregoing analysis of the internal environment provides an excellent starting point for identifying key resources and capabilities. For example, outstanding resources and capabilities may result from (1) superior management, (2) well-trained employees, (3) an excellent board of directors, (4) a high-performance culture, (5) superior financial resources, or (6) the appropriate level and type of international involvement. However, these potential sources of competitive advantage barely scratch the organizational surface.

You should also evaluate the organization's primary value chain activities to identify resources and capabilities. These activities include its (7) inbound logistics, (8) operations, (9) outbound logistics, (10) marketing and sales, and (11) service, as well as the support activities of (12) procurement, (13) technology development, (14) human resource management, and (15) administration. Chapter 3 provided a description of how to use the value chain.

In addition, an organization may have (16) an excellent reputation, (17) a strong brand name, (18) patents and secrets, (19) excellent locations, or (20) strong or valuable ties (e.g., alliances, joint ventures, contracts, or cooperation) with one or more external stakeholders. All of these potential resources and capabilities (and many others) are discussed in this book. They form a starting point that you can use to help identify the potential sources of competitive advantage. Each company will have its own unique list.

Performance Evaluation

The next step in internal analysis is to describe and critique the organization's past strategies. In critiquing strategies, you will need to describe them in detail, discuss whether they have been successful, and then *evaluate whether they fit with the industry environment and the resources and capabilities of the organization.*

1. What is the company's pattern of past strategies (corporate, business, functional, international)?
2. How successful has the company been in the past with its chosen strategies? How successful is the company now?
3. For each strategy, what explains success or failure? (Use your environmental and organizational analyses to support your answer.)

Many instructors require their students to evaluate the success of an organization on the basis of both qualitative and quantitative (financial) measures. The financial measures were developed during your financial analysis, so you only need to make reference to them here. Some common qualitative measures include product or service quality, productivity, responsiveness to industry change, innovation, reputation, and other measures that indicate the satisfaction of key stakeholders (i.e., employees, customers, managers, regulatory bodies, and society).

Identification of Sources of Competitive Advantage

You are now ready to consolidate your internal and external analyses into lists of strengths and weaknesses, as well as expand and revise your lists of opportunities and threats. In Chapter 1, strengths were defined as firm resources and capabilities that can lead to a competitive advantage. Weaknesses were described as resources and capabilities that the firm does not possess, resulting in a competitive disadvantage. Consequently, each of the resources and capabilities identified during the organizational analysis should be measured against the factors identified in the environmental analysis. The next paragraph describes how to do this.

Resources and capabilities become strengths if they have the potential to lead to a competitive advantage. This happens when (1) they are valuable, which means that they allow the firm to exploit opportunities or neutralize threats arising from the external environment, and (2) they are unique, meaning that only a few firms possess the resource or capability. Use these criteria to assemble a list of strengths. If a strength is also hard to imitate, then it can lead to a *sustainable* competitive advantage; consequently, these types of strengths should be highlighted. Finally, if a resource or capability could have broad application to many business areas, it is a core competence or capability.

Weaknesses also should be listed. These are resources and capabilities the firm does not possess that, according to your environmental analysis, lead to a competitive disadvantage.

Opportunities are conditions in the external environment that allow a firm to take advantage of organizational strengths, overcome organizational weaknesses, or neutralize environmental threats. Consequently, now that the organizational analysis is complete, you should reevaluate your list of opportunities to determine whether they really apply to your organization. You also should evaluate threats to make sure they are applicable to your firm. Threats are conditions in the broad and task environments that may stand in the way of organizational competitiveness or the achievement of stakeholder satisfaction.

At this point, you also may want to add to your list of opportunities some of the potential linkages and alliances that the firm could develop with external stakeholders. For example, if your company is strong in production but weak in foreign marketing, you may see an opportunity to enter a new foreign market through a joint venture with a strong marketing company. Another example may involve neutralizing a threat of new government regulation by forming an alliance with competitors to influence the regulating body.

DEVELOPING A STRATEGIC PLAN

Your environmental and organizational analyses helped you to (1) draw conclusions about the growth prospects and profit potential in the industry and any trends that are critical to the firm; (2) evaluate the past strategies and strategic direction of the firm; and (3) develop a list of strengths, weaknesses, opportunities, and threats. The next step is to make recommendations concerning the strategies the firm may want to pursue in the future. If the firm is not a stellar performer, this should be an easy task. However, even firms that have been highly successful in the past should consider taking advantage of opportunities, and should respond to threats. History has taught us that firms that are unwilling to progress eventually decline.

Strategic Direction and Major Strategies

You should probably begin your strategic recommendations by focusing on the strategic direction and major strategies of the firm. Based on your earlier analyses, you may want to consider adjustments to the firm's mission, including its vision, business definition, or enterprise strategy. Of course, the business definition also helps identify the growth orientation of the business. Are the growth plans taking advantage of industry opportunities? If the industry is becoming mature, should horizontal integration be pursued rather than market penetration alone?

If you determined earlier that the business strategy is not as successful as it should be, what adjustments should be made? Could the company have more success by focusing on one segment of the market? Or if the company is pursuing a focus strategy, would broadening the target market be appropriate? If the company is pursuing cost leadership, would a differentiation strategy work better? If differentiation does not seem to be working very well, would a cost leadership strategy be better? Or would a best-cost strategy be the most appropriate?

Finally, you should examine the corporate strategy (concentration, vertical integration, related or unrelated diversification). Is your corporate strategy still appropriate, given your environmental analysis. Is your dominant industry stagnant? Is it overregulated? Is competition hurting profitability? Should you consider investing in other industries? If so, what are their defining characteristics? What core competencies and capabilities could be applied elsewhere? What opportunities could be explored that relate to the corporate strategy?

It is possible that you may want to leave the strategic direction and major strategies alone, especially if the organization has enjoyed recent success. Regardless of whether you altered the direction and strategies, at this point you have now established what you think they should be. The direction and corporate- and business-level strategies provide guidance for fine-tuning an organization's strategies. Each of the recommendations you make from this point on should be consistent with the strategic direction and major strategies of the organization. At this point, it is time to explore strategic opportunities further.

Evaluation of Opportunities and Recommendations

Using the strategic direction and corporate- and business-level strategies as guides, strategic opportunities should be evaluated further. These alternatives were generated during earlier analyses:

1. *Opportunities that allow a firm to take advantage of organizational strengths.* These opportunities may involve alternatives such as better promoting of current products and services, establishing new products or services, suggesting new applications for existing products and services within existing markets, exploring new domestic or foreign markets, diversifying into areas in which strengths can be applied, and creating joint ventures with companies with complementary strengths. These are only a few examples.
2. *Opportunities for the firm to overcome organizational weaknesses.* Do any of the organizational weaknesses relate to an area that you described in your industry analysis as essential for survival? Do any of the weaknesses relate to key success factors? Firms can overcome their weaknesses through strategies such as learning from joint-venture partners, creating new alliances with organizations that are strong where the organization is weak, or fixing problems internally through R&D, better controls, efficiency programs, information technology, and so on. Again, these are only a few examples.
3. *Opportunities for the firm to neutralize environmental threats.* These often involve creating strategic alliances to offset the influence of a powerful stakeholder such as a government regulator, a strong union, a powerful competitor, or an influential special-interest group. The firm may form an alliance with the powerful stakeholder or with other stakeholders in an effort to balance the power. Firms may also form alliances to help cope with threats emerging from the broad environment.

Evaluation of opportunities means much more than simply accepting them on the basis of earlier environmental and organizational analyses. They also should be evaluated based on factors such as the following:

1. *Cost/benefits analysis.* Do the financial benefits of pursuing the opportunity appear to outweigh the financial costs?
2. *Ethical analysis.* Is pursuit of this strategy consistent with the organization's enterprise strategy? Could it negatively affect the organization's reputation?
3. *Protection of other strengths.* Does pursuit of this opportunity in any way detract from or weaken other strengths? For example, could it damage a brand name? Could it weaken a strong financial position?
4. *Implementation ability.* Will implementation of this strategy be easy or difficult? In other words, does the strategy fit the capabilities, structure, systems, processes, and culture of the organization?
5. *Stakeholder analysis.* How will this strategy affect key stakeholders? Which ones are likely to support it? Are they high priority? Which ones are likely to oppose it? Are they high priority? What are the strategic ramifications of their support or opposition?
6. *Future position.* Will the strategy continue to be viable as the industry and the broad environment undergo their expected changes? Will it provide a foundation for survival or competitive success?

The result of this analysis should be a recommendation or recommendations that the organization should pursue. Many evaluation tools can facilitate the evaluation process, such as a payoff matrix that provides an evaluation of several alternatives based on a standard set of criteria (see Table Case Note 1). However, the tools should never act as substitutes for in-depth analysis of the alternatives themselves. In other words, even if a numeric score-keeping system is used, the numbers should be explained based on a detailed strategic analysis.

Your instructor may not require you to conduct a formal analysis of alternatives based on a standard set of criteria; however, you should still make recommendations concerning changes the organization should make to remain or become competitive and satisfy its stakeholders. Through this entire process, remember that many companies identify areas of strength that are no longer capable of giving the company a competitive edge. What was a key to success yesterday may be a requirement for survival today.

Implementation and Control

Recommendations should always be accompanied by an implementation plan and basic controls. The following are major questions that should be addressed during this section of a case analysis. Items 7 and 8 relate specifically to control.

1. How do the recommendations specifically address concerns that were identified during the analysis?
2. What will be the roles and responsibilities of key internal and external stakeholders in carrying out the recommendations and how are they expected to respond? What actions should be taken to smooth out the transition period or avoid stakeholder discontent?
3. Does the organization have the resources (funds, people, skills) to carry out the recommendations? If not, how should the organization proceed in developing or acquiring those resources?
4. Does the organization have the appropriate systems, structures, and processes to carry out the recommendations? If not, how should the organization proceed in creating the appropriate systems, structures, and processes?

Instructions: Establish which opportunities you are going to evaluate. List them down the right column. Then identify which criteria you will use to evaluate your alternatives. Place these criteria along the top. Evaluate each of your alternatives on the basis of each of your criteria and assign a numerical (e.g., 1 to 5, 1 to 3, –2 to +2) or nonnumerical (e.g., –/+ or pro/con) score based on your analysis. Total your scores to arrive at a recommendation.

Criteria

	Criterion 1	Criterion 2	Criterion 3	Total
Opportunity 1	–2	1	2	1
Opportunity 2	2	1	–1	2
Opportunity 3	1	2	1	4

Note: In this matrix, –2 means that the opportunity is very weak based on the criterion, –1 means weak, 0 means neutral, 1 means strong, and 2 means very strong.

Table Case Note 1 A Payoff Matrix Approach to Evaluating Opportunities

5. What is the appropriate time horizon for implementing recommendations? What should the organization and its managers do immediately, in one month, in six months, in a year and so on?
6. What roadblocks might the organization encounter while implementing the recommendations (e.g., financing or skilled labor shortages)? How can the organization overcome these roadblocks?
7. What desired outcomes or changes should the organization expect once the recommendations have been implemented? How will the organization know if the recommendations have been successful? In other words, what are the objectives associated with your recommendations?
8. What were some of the major assumptions you made with regard to the external environment? Which of these factors, if different from expected, would require an adjustment to your recommendations?

Following the implementation section, you may want to update your audience (your instructor or other students) concerning actions the firm has taken since the case was written. If a case update is required, it should center on actions that pertain to the focus of your case analysis. If you do an update, remember that what the organization did, even if it appears to have been successful, may not have been the optimal solution.

A NOTE TO STUDENTS

If you are reading this appendix early in the course, you will have the rest of the semester or quarter to practice the case analysis process and study the chapter readings. If you are reading this appendix later in the course, we encourage you to go back to earlier chapters and refresh your memory concerning the concepts that were covered. Just as this course integrates material you learned during your years of business study, the case analysis process integrates material from all sections of the strategic management course.

The material in this appendix represents the way we teach case analysis. Because there is no standard method for analyzing cases, your instructor may teach a method of case analysis that differs from our approach. Also, cases can be treated in many different formats, including class discussions (complete with discussion questions to be answered before coming to class), written papers, formal presentations, and class debates. After reading this appendix, check with your instructor for specific instructions and requirements.

INDEX